T0312357

My Family

Also by David Baddiel

My Family

The memoir

———

DAVID BADDIEL

4th ESTATE • London

4th Estate
An imprint of HarperCollins*Publishers*
1 London Bridge Street
London SE1 9GF
www.4thEstate.co.uk

HarperCollins*Publishers*
Macken House,
39/40 Mayor Street Upper,
Dublin 1
DO1 C9W8
Ireland

First published in Great Britain in 2024 by 4th Estate

1

Copyright © David Baddiel 2024
Some of this material appeared in
the show *My Family: Not the Sitcom*

David Baddiel asserts the moral right to be identified as the author of
this work in accordance with the Copyright, Designs and Patents Act 1988

A catalogue record for this book is available from the British Library

HB ISBN 978-0-00-848760-7
TPB ISBN 978-0-00-848761-4

All rights reserved. No part of this publication may be reproduced,
stored in a retrieval system, or transmitted, in any form or by any
means, electronic, mechanical, photocopying, recording or otherwise,
without the prior permission of the publishers.

This book is sold subject to the condition that it shall not, by way of
trade or otherwise, be lent, re-sold, hired out or otherwise circulated
without the publisher's prior consent in any form of binding or cover other
than that in which it is published and without a similar condition including
this condition being imposed on the subsequent purchaser.

St Petersburg synagogue image (eFesenko/Alamy Stock Photo); living room image
(Andreas von Einsiedel/Alamy Stock Photo); Jenni Murray (Justin Williams/Shutterstock)

Typeset in Celeste by Palimpsest Book Production Ltd, Falkirk, Stirlingshire

Printed and Bound in the UK using 100% Renewable Electricity
at CPI Group (UK) Ltd

This book contains FSC™ certified paper and other controlled sources
to ensure responsible forest management.

For more information visit: www.harpercollins.co.uk/green

For Ivor, and Dan

To really take the piss out of something,
you have to love it.

– Julian Barratt

It's, I'd guess, 1977. Which would make me thirteen. I'm in our back garden. Our back garden is a wilderness. It has a large tree in the middle that sheds a lot of leaves which never get raked. Beyond that is an area of mainly bald grass – mainly dried mud would be a better description – bounded by a hedge. In front of the hedge is a shit goal. I don't mean a poor life-ambition. I mean a junior football goal, a toy, basically, with blue posts and orange netting. It has been out there for about four years at this point and is 97 per cent rust. The netting, although obviously originally holey, as netting tends to be, is full of holes.

I'm not playing football, though – despite that being the reason why I usually go into the garden. I'm facing the goal, but I don't have a football. A man I don't know that well is standing very close behind me. He has his arms wrapped tightly around me. He has his hands placed on top of my hands. He is asking me to swing my hips towards him.

It's not abuse. In case you're wondering. Well, maybe it's a type of abuse, but it's a very particular sort, and not the sort that normally crops up in a misery memoir. Which this isn't. He's got his arms wrapped around me and his hands on mine and he's asking me to swing my hips towards him because I'm holding a golf club. By my feet is a golf ball. His name is David White, he is my mother's lover and he's doing his best to teach me how to play golf.

So yeah. It's a type of abuse.

Sarah

My mother's funeral took place at Golders Green Crematorium on 5 January 2015. She died on 20 December 2014, but a combination of grisly factors to do with her having to have an autopsy and Christmas – the juxtaposition of those two things feels wrong, but they were juxtaposed – meant she wasn't actually sent to the flames until just over two weeks after she died.

A lot of people turned up, which is always a good sign at funerals. It suggests my mother had a lot of friends, which she did. I, however, only recognized a few: Norma Glass, Bill and Ruth Mulligan, Naomi and Tony Inwald. You don't know these people and they aren't going to feature much in this book, but I'm listing them because I find their names very evocative of growing up where and when I did – Dollis Hill, in north London, in the 1970s. I find something redolent of that time and place lies within the very sonics of the words *Tony Inwald.*

But most people at my mother's funeral I didn't know. She was someone who, at various stages in her life, had adopted different – and obsessive – personas. Her last, the one she chose for her sixties and seventies, was: Jew. This hadn't *not* been her identity when she was younger, but it wasn't on the front foot. In the early nineties, my parents split up – it's amazing, you might find as you read on, that it took them so long – but they got back together at the turn of the century, and lived in Harrow, where my mum suddenly decided to become a big *macher** at a nearby synagogue, Kol Chai. Kol Chai, in case you have a preconceived notion of what a synagogue looks like, does not look like this:

It looks like this:

---

* Yiddish for Important person. Sorry if you knew that.

Sarah

Like a bit of Brookside Close that even Barry Grant would feel nervous about entering.* Its design does not speak, perhaps, to the deep mysticism and history of the Talmud. But it's a sweet place, and my mum very much decided it was hers, and later in her life was forever organizing events there, trying to get me and my brothers and our kids to come along. She died on the same day that she had arranged, at Kol Chai, a Kaddish – a ceremony remembering the dead – for her own parents: a memorial she never made it to.

While waiting in the grounds of the crematorium, on a particularly pathetic-fallacy-observing funeral morning of grey skies and drizzle, I was approached by a group of older people, most of whom I assumed were members of Kol Chai. Up to this point, generally, when older Jews came up to me, I knew what they were going to say. They were going to say: 'We really loved your *Who Do You Think You Are?*'† This is because older Jews were usually not that keen on the sweary and often not-very-nice-Jewish-boy style of comedy I had spent most of my career practitioning,‡ and so were overjoyed when I did a proper BBC 1 documentary with loads in it about Jewishness.

However, this group of older Jewish people didn't say this. They said, first, 'I wish you long life.' Which is something Jews

---

* I'm aware this is an out-of-date reference that will only connect with a particular demographic. I have already, this early in the book, assumed you, dear reader, are part of that demographic.

† *Who Do You Think You Are?* is a BBC documentary series in which celebrities (yes, I've used that word, which means I'm including myself in that subset – I'm aware this is not a de rigueur thing to acknowledge) trace their genealogical roots. They always like to have a Jew in these series, as a Jew tracing his or her roots means: Nazis, who are of course serious documentary box-office gold. I was the Jew on the first series.

‡ Not a word, I'm aware. But felt right.

say at funerals. Some also said, '*On simcha*', which means 'on a feast day/joyous occasion', i.e. that's what I hope it is the *next* time we meet. Both indicate a very Jewish sense of deferred happiness, of accepting that now is bad but soon things'll be better – and not in the next world, but here, in Golders Green, in Buchenwald. It also indicates something else Jewish, which is that Judaism has only a vague and ambiguous idea of the afterlife. Eternal bliss isn't really a big deal for Jews; odd, given that it's the cherry on the cake for most religions. Jews prefer their rewards and comforts, such as they are, in the here and now – in this life. And so they would wish it, in the face of death, long. They would wish their own death far away.

So they said: 'I wish you long life.' And then they said:

'Your mother was a wonderful person.'

And, 'She was wonderful.'

And, 'Sarah was truly wonderful.'

On and on with the wonderful, already. I get it. It's hard to know what to say at a funeral to mourning family members, and 'she/he was wonderful' is the safest of bets. But that day so many people whom I didn't recognize told me my mother was a wonderful person that after a while it became disorientating.

I need at this point to say something about myself. I have what I consider to be an on-the-spectrum (apologies to anyone medically actually on the spectrum, but I do genuinely think the intensity of it is a little neuro-untypical) need to tell the truth. I know this sounds like boasting. I know it sounds like a thing Alan Partridge might say in a newspaper Q&A: 'What's your biggest failing?' 'Well, if I had to pick one, I'd say I was just *too* honest.' Given all that, I still think it's a real thing. I feel desperately uncomfortable not telling the exact truth, in detail, always. It's one of the reasons why as a stand-up, I'm a very limited performer. I can't do any accents, for example. Obviously, primarily, this is just a lack of talent. But when I try to do them it causes me a strange anxiety, and not only because I'm embarrassed that my attempt at American sounds more like a sixteenth-century scullery maid from the West Country. I feel displaced, discombobulated, by having to move an iota away from myself.

To be clear, I'm not claiming this truth urge as David Baddiel's big moral plus. It has no moral power for me at all. If anything, it seems incontinent, like I cannot contain small, disparate incongruities that most people hardly notice as they move through life. I'm aware: sometimes lying is helpful. Sometimes it spares people difficult emotions.

I used to tell a story onstage, demonstrating my reluctance to lie, through an example of one time I did. This is it:

I was googling something recently and my eight-year-old son was looking over my shoulder and for some reason – I assume because of something one of his friends had told him at school – said, 'Dad, what would happen if we put the words "sexy ladies" into there?' And I said . . . 'I don't know.'

It got a laugh. As a result, I was still doing the same gag a few months later. At which point it went:

I was googling something recently and my eight-year-old son – well, he was eight at the time, but he's nine now – was looking over my shoulder . . .

This information about my son's age doesn't help the joke. It slows it down. It also dates the story. But I could never help myself. I always had to add the truth, to correct the story.

Lying, on the rare occasions I've tried to do it, tends not to work out well for me. In the early noughties, I did a sitcom on Sky called *Baddiel's Syndrome*. It was not a hit and wasn't recommissioned by the network. Sometime later at a restaurant I saw a group of people I knew who worked in TV and went over to their table to say hello. All the ones I knew said hello back. At the end of the table, a woman I didn't recognize got up and said, 'David! How nice to see you again!' and gave me an enormous hug. I felt my usual instinct to tell the truth – to say, 'Sorry, who are you?' – but it would've been very awkward, so for once I swallowed the urge. I said, 'Lovely to see you too!' and returned the hug. She sat down, and the others started talking about recent developments at Sky television.

I said: 'Oh yeah, I was just at Sky a couple of months ago when they cancelled my show. I had a terrible meeting with this fucking awful woman called Kate Barnes.' At which point the woman who'd hugged me looked up and said, 'I'm Kate Barnes.'

It was so embarrassing it was like time stopped. It's hard to describe how I felt in that moment, or exactly what the scene was like – I was about to write 'everyone stared at me' – I think they did, but to be honest, all that's in my memory is the sound of a long, piercing scream. After a couple of seconds, or possibly the entirety of the time-space continuum, I said:

'I'm sorry.'

But I didn't stop there. This is how I tried to make it better. I turned to Kate Barnes and said:

'When I hugged you, I didn't know who you were.'

I reverted, in other words, to my default position of just telling the bald truth. Judging by her expression, it didn't help.

By the way, this woman is not called Kate Barnes. So, I can do it: I can change someone's name to avoid embarrassing them or a libel case. I can, it seems, lie. I just feel bad doing it (particularly in the moment – it's a bit easier in the recollection-in-tranquillity space of writing).

Plus her real name sounds really like Kate Barnes.

This digression is in the service of something, which is that, however polite it might have been for those older Jewish guests at my mother's funeral to tell me she was wonderful, it rubbed up badly against my urge to tell the truth. It felt, to some extent, like a lie. Not least because the thing that bound together all these people telling me she was wonderful was that they didn't really know her. Not in any sort of detail. And truth, of course, is in the detail.

My mother died very suddenly. It felt like an abrupt and profound erasure, a kind of vanishing. Then, the way she was being memorialized, here, at her funeral, felt to me like a second, even more profound erasure. When people die, the memory of who they were becomes sacred. We can only talk about them as having been wonderful people. But if all you can ever say about your dead relative is that he or she was wonderful, you might as well say nothing. To really preserve their memory – to be true to them, as I understand truth – you must call up their weirdness, their madness, their flaws. Because the dead, despite what we might like to think, are not angels.

Or to put it another way. As more and more grave-faced mourners shook my hand and mouthed the same platitudes, I found myself wanting to snap at them, angrily:

'OK, what was her real first name?'

To which I imagine they would have looked confused. Maybe one of them would've said:

'Pardon?'

'If you knew her so well . . . what was her *real* first name?'

Bafflement. Perhaps some embarrassed sideways glancing. Eventually, I imagine, this imaginary conversation:

'Um . . . Sarah?'

'No. It was Frommet.'

Long pause.

'Oh. I didn't know that.'

'Then how do you know she was wonderful?'

Which would've been awkward and rude and fucked up and, at that moment, unnecessary. So instead, I've written this book.

Sarah

When you're trying to capture the essence of someone, you must look away from stereotypes. That may seem obvious, but if you are memorializing, they can be tempting. The priest with little real knowledge of the departed will be drawn to platitudes, to the woolly positives of 'He was someone who cared mainly for others', 'She was a fabulous mother', 'We all remember their wicked sense of humour'. These mantras say nothing; they call no concrete sense of the person to mind.

The way forward is through specifics. People are revealed not in generalizations but in detail, in moments. The rich strangeness of my mother cannot be conveyed in compliments, but in stories, true stories. For example: I mentioned just now my participation in the BBC TV series *Who Do You Think You Are?* The episode I was in ends with two bizarre moments. First, I give my mother some half-broken bricks. This is because while tracing the maternal side of the family, I went to Kaliningrad, now in Russia, but before the war, Königsberg in East Prussia. While there, I found these bricks on an empty stretch of waste ground where once had stood my grandfather's brick factory.

A short, but important sidebar. It's a funny place to have a sidebar, I know, because I've just said 'First . . .' and now you're expecting me to say 'And secondly' but instead there's going to be a few paragraphs containing quite important information before we get there, so it feels like you, the reader, are as it were holding your narrative breath, and that may be uncomfortable. Apologies, but I think this is the right place for it.

Near the beginning of my episode of *Who Do You Think You Are?* my mother, who was born in Nazi Germany, revealed something that no one else in the family was aware of. There are oddities in her birth documentation (beyond the fact that all of it is stamped with swastikas, which remains eternally, deeply odd, obviously). She has two birth certificates, one dated with what we thought of as her birthday, 2 March, while the other has 11 July. No one was ever sure why – there was a possibility that, due to the various extraordinary difficulties involved in being a Jewish family escaping from Germany in late 1939, a certain amount of forging went on. But at the start of the documentary, sitting in my parents' front room, my mum said she had never believed her mother, Otti – the woman who I had always thought of as my grandmother – to be her real mother. She thought rather that her uncle Arno, her mother's younger brother, was her real father.

I had heard of my great-uncle Arno before. As a kid, I once asked Otti, 'Did you have any brothers and sisters?'* and she said, 'I had a brother . . . but you'll have to ask Mr Hitler what happened to him', and I thought: Mr Hitler? The bloke they sing about on *Dad's Army*?†

During the documentary, other facts about him – Arno, not Hitler – emerged. He was eleven years or so younger than my grandmother Otti and something of a playboy. He had just married when my mother was born. This all fits, in fact, with my mum's thinking, which is that Otti, who was thirty-two at the time of my mother's (their only child's) birth – which undeniably would at that time have been thought old to have a baby, especially a Jewish baby in Nazi Germany in 1939 – could not actually have children. But Otti and her husband Ernst were getting out of Germany: and Arno, for whatever reason – well, because most German Jews didn't, would be the reason – was not. In my mum's imagination, at some point in spring 1939, the newly married Arno turned up at their house – almost definitely not a house by then, as all their money had been stolen or had gone in bribes, so their flat, lodgings, whatever – and said: please take our baby to England, and safety, with you.

---

* My truth gene is sounding the alarm, so I'm going to have to state what I actually asked my gran, which was: 'Do you have any other brothers and sisters, apart from Joe?' My great-uncle Joe Radbil was Otti's other brother, who managed to make it out of Germany with her and lived in Wembley for most of his life. Also, if I don't mention this, I will get into trouble with Michael, our one remaining cousin on that side, who will definitely at some point be reading this book. Hello, Michael.

† I should emphasize that my grandmother did actually say *Mr* Hitler here, which made it that much more confusing to a kid brought up on Jimmy Perry and David Croft's masterpiece.

This is a heartbreaking story, and it formed the backbone of my episode of *Who Do You Think You Are?*

I also think it isn't true.

I said this at the time (of course I did). After my mother finished her story about Uncle Arno, I went outside with the camera crew to be interviewed. I said that although the tale she had just related wasn't completely implausible, there was something they should know, which is that my mum was a fantasist. And that for the fantasist part of her, the idea of her father not being the man she'd been told was her father but another man who'd died in the Holocaust, would be exciting and mysterious and – for all its tragedy – glamorous. She would *want* it to be true. But the producers cut this bit. They, like my mother, wanted to believe what she had said was true. Because, like her, they thought it was exciting and mysterious and, for all its tragedy, glamorous. And also because, without it, the dramatic arc of their episode would be fucked.

When I gave my mum the bricks from the remains of her father's factory, she looked somewhat baffled. I had hoped they would feel to her like – I'm stretching the metaphor here – the missing building blocks of who she was. Instead, she reacted more like someone who had been randomly handed two bits of rubble. Which is fair enough, as whatever symbolic power they might have contained, they were undoubtedly also two bits of rubble.

More significant, perhaps, was her reaction when I later told her I hadn't, in my extensive genealogical searching, found any evidence that Arno Radbil was her father. I read out a letter the researchers had discovered and translated, which Arno wrote to Otti, five days after my mother was born, congratulating his sister and saying how excited and honoured he was to be an uncle 'after such a long time'.

On hearing this, my mum shook her head and said – and this is an exact quote: 'So it's cleared it up, from that point of view, and yet there's still a doubt in my mind.' I do like, when I watch this again, the words 'from that point of view'. She was always peppering her conversation with phrases that, like this, tread the water of speech.* These don't tend to survive close reading. From what/whose point of view? Arno's? Mine? The BBC's? Truth's? Really, it's none of them: it's just a holding platitude, meant to suggest thoughtfulness. But it's very indicative of who she was, and so when I watch it now, I feel the strange mix of affection and irritation that my mother always inspired.

Point is: a bit like a conspiracy theorist when presented with the facts, she won't change her mind. A bit like a conspiracy theorist, she *likes* her conspiracy theory. A bit like a conspiracy theorist – sorry, I'm repeating this too much now, but it really is very similar – she likes the mystery and the excitement of her (not-true) version of the truth, and will face down all the cognitive dissonance she needs to hold on to it.

Secondly – at fucking *last* – breathe, reader – there's what she does on my fortieth birthday. It was perhaps odd to include my birthday in *Who Do You Think You Are?* It didn't have anything to do with tracing my family history, although tracing your family history does carry with it a strong reminder of mortality – all these lives, connected, extraordinary, and gone – and so a mid-life birthday makes some sort of sense. But actually, I think the producers kept this in just because it made for good TV – because my mother did something completely batshit.

She had a birthday cake prepared for me. That isn't the crazy

---

* She was also a big fan of the expressions 'dovetail' and 'touch base'.

bit, obviously. It was an expensive cake, from a posh cake shop, and so had almost definitely been bought by the production.

Anyway. The cake. My fortieth. My mum was filmed lighting the candles. 'Happy birthday' was sung. My daughter Dolly, then three, said, happily, 'It's your birthday!' And then all the smoke alarms in the room went off and Dolly started screaming. I said, 'Oh my God it's on fire', and had to grab the cake off my mother and rush out to the garden and get a hose on it, because she'd put *forty* candles on my fortieth birthday cake. Possibly as some kind of sub-conscious revenge on the Nazis, my mother had made me a recreation of the bombing of Dresden on a cake.

I'm aware there is a certain logic at work here. But it's not a logic anyone follows. Clearly no one ever told her that after a particular birthday – what? fourteenth? – people don't have their literal age represented in candles on a cake. Because it's a fucking fire hazard. It's the same reason why on their birthdays, we don't give pensioners the bumps.

Point is, the cake-on-fire fortieth birthday moment was weird, eccentric, barmy, not-very-informed-of-the-normal-ways-of-the-world, reckless, showy, more about her than me, touching, not a little dangerous and comically disastrous. And as such, says more about who my mother really was than a thousand eulogies describing her as wonderful.

My Family

Some background.

Erica Jong said: 'Fame means millions of people have the wrong idea of who you are.' In the UK, I have been moderately famous, with up and down waves to that fame, for about thirty-five years. One of the things people perhaps get wrong about me is my upbringing. I think they assume, because I wear glasses and went to Cambridge University and am Jewish, that my childhood was spent in whatever most British people conceive of as haute-Jewish-north-London-bourgeois splendour. The way I imagine (and probably – because I am subject to Erica Jong's mantra too – wrongly) the Corens (my generation, Giles and Victoria, not Alan) or the Freuds (similarly, Esther, Matthew and Bella, not Lucian or Sigmund) grew up.

I didn't grow up like that. I didn't grow up in poverty either. I grew up in solid lower-middle-class mundanity. OK, that isn't entirely true. I grew up in a very strange world, but it is correct in terms of the mise-en-scène: the location, the fixtures and fittings, the feel of it all. I was born, in 1964, in Troy, which is near Albany, in upstate New York. We left America to come back to the UK when I was three months old. My dad, Colin Baddiel, a scientist, had gone to the US as part of the 1960s brain drain and had been teaching chemistry at a place called Rensselaer Polytechnic Institute. While in America, my mum gave birth to my older brother Ivor and me in the space of two years. Once back in London, we lived in a flat in Maida Vale.

My memories really begin in 1970 when we moved to Dollis Hill. Dollis Hill is in north London, but again, the words *north London* conjure up, I think, something bohemian and mews-cobbled and arts-and-crafts-fronted. But that's Hampstead, or Highgate. It's not Dollis Hill. Dollis Hill is in between Neasden and Willesden Green, and looks like this:

That's the iron bridge across the railway line in Gladstone Park. It overlooks Kendal Road, which our house was on. I used to walk over that bridge a lot between the ages of eleven and thirteen, mainly to go to piano lessons with an odd piano teacher who lived on the other side of the park, and who I now think was a closet paedophile. Again, this isn't a memoir of real abuse so I should stress nothing awful happened. But he did give his lessons wearing a *kimono*: a very skimpy one. He also insisted on placing his hands on my body in various ways while I was on the piano stool, ostensibly to 'perfect my playing position'. Plus he would sometimes – this may not be related to his suppressed desire for me – forgo teaching to talk for ages about how much he supported apartheid and to decry the downfall of what he saw as the social order in the Dollis Hill area, particularly evinced for him by the fact that there had been a lot of break-ins near his house in recent years which apparently always involved burglars who shat in the sugar.

Meanwhile, I agree. They *hate* salt and vinegar.

Point is, the interior of my house didn't look like this:

It looked like this:

Or at least it did on the night of my brother Ivor's bar mitzvah. Usually it looked like that, minus the clearly delicious catering.

It was a house in which every room had a different, violently unmatching carpet, although all patterns were swirly.* It was a home in which no expense had been spared, by which I mean, no expense had been expended, to make anything at all comfortable or luxurious. We had one sofa (in the front room, which was the nearest thing we had to a room that, had we been working class and northern, would've been considered kept 'for best'). It seated two people, as long as the two people were prepared to enjoy feeling conjoined at the thigh. It also had a seat cushion so thin it was like it had been sliced by someone who worked mainly in Parma ham.

In the room we spent most time (the telly room), there were four disparate chairs, only one of which was comfortable. I feel – I can't actually place one right now but surely – that there has been a variety of British observational comedy routines about battling-for-the-comfy-chair in houses like mine, so I won't retread that ground, but by today's standards I'm fairly sure the comfy chair wasn't all that comfortable. Although having said that, it was the only one our cat, Phomphar,† was prepared to sleep on, and cats know their stuff when it comes to comfort.

There was, however, one similarity to the posh living room I showed you a page ago, which is that we did have a lot of books. And stuff.

---

* Apart from the room Ivor is standing in – called the breakfast room – which had lino.

† There's a later chapter that explains why she was called this. In a whole chapter about cats. I know that sounds attractive but I would advise not jumping right to it now.

The reason we had a lot of stuff is because my parents were collectors. My dad collected toys – Dinky Toys, mainly cars, and trains – and my mum, originally, before a swerve in her collecting interest which we shall come to, children's books. They were hoarders. Both, I think, were emotionally damaged people who found it perhaps easier to relate to things than to people. Although, in my mother's case, it was possibly more to do with having most of her things taken away from her when she was very young.

Which brings us to the Jewish thing. In terms of Erica Jong's rule about fame, people are also perhaps confused about this, assuming as I go on about it a lot – I mean, I do, endlessly; like, shut up about it, already – that my background was very Jewish. And the answer to that is: it was. In fact, I think it's possible that until I went to secondary school, I never really met a non-Jew. It's often occurred to me that one reason why I've never felt any Jewish shame – which lots of Jews do – is because going to a Jewish school, and, as I did, a Jewish youth group, and all my parents' friends being Jewish, meant I was wrapped in a bubble.

For some, that might be the wellspring of their Jewish shame – the shock of realizing, as a young teenager, that the whole world *isn't* Jewish, or indeed not even mainly Jewish, making them withdraw. But I think for me the damage was already done. Meaning: I just assumed early on – incorrectly – that Jew was the norm and non-Jew the abnormal, and that's stuck with me.*

But the Jewish thing, as the Jewish thing tends not to, didn't operate in a straightforward way. Like many Jewish households, our Jewishness was full of contradictions. On my mum's side we have, you'll remember, Ernst and Otti Fabian. They'd been very rich in Germany before 1933, and then lost everything, including most of their family. They were responsible for anything in our house that might approximate formal Jewishness. Ernst was a Reform Jew; that means, not Orthodox, no big black hats, nor synagogue services that are all in Hebrew and go on for seventeen hours, plus women don't have to dunk themselves in asses' milk when they're on a period or whatever the bejewsus proper frummers have to do.

Throughout the 1970s, Ernst and Otti would come down to London from Cambridge where they lived and lead our Seders, or Chanukahs, or Rosh Hashanas. These were exciting

---

* I'm not sure how you feel about footnotes. As a reader, I'm never sure about them myself. But as a writer, stuff occurs to me a lot while I'm writing, and I often want to add or contextualize or qualify, and it's sometimes better not to do that in the main text, as it breaks up the flow, which frankly I'm doing enough already. But I'm very wedded to the idea that the truth is always complex, which means overarching theories, like the one I just put forward about why I don't have Jewish shame, are let down by a factual discrepancy. In this case that in amongst the list of my parents' friends present at my mum's funeral were Bill and Ruth Mulligan, who were not Jewish. Ruth in particular. In her childhood she had been an active member of the Hitler Youth.

when I was a kid. An upbringing as mundane as mine was very enlivened by evenings when me and my brothers got presents and, by our standards, reasonably nice food. The high holidays were an event, and worth putting up with having to wear yarmulkes and recite a lot of Hebrew about plagues and Pharaohs.

But it was more complicated than just having to put up with the prayers to get the presents. Most of the schools in the vicinity of Kendal Road in those days were not especially salubrious. Or even safe, certainly not for a Jewish kid. So my parents sent me – and my brothers Ivor and Dan – to the North West London Jewish Day School, in Willesden Green, which was the one where we were least likely to get knifed. Here's a picture of me there:

It was a proper faith school. We (all the boys who went there, that is: not the girls) had to wear not just yarmulkes, but tzitzit. These are tzitzit opposite – fifteen quid on Amazon, who knew? – a kind of Mormon-style undervest with tassels, but stringy ones, not like ones Burlesque dancers wear on their nipples.

The tassels must be seen protruding from your shirt, over your trousers, and if, at my school, yours didn't, or you just weren't wearing them, because frankly they're a bugger to launder, you'd get into trouble. At the school, we were taught – as well as all the usual stuff – Hebrew: Old Hebrew, Biblical Hebrew, not the more useful modern Ivrit they speak in Israel, plus classes in understanding the Torah. The food was totally kosher, which means, even by 1970s school dinner standards, inedible. Kosher laws mean you can't consume milk after meat – an oblique and I've always thought wrong Talmudic interpretation of the biblical verse 'Thou shalt not bathe a kid in its mother's milk' – to me it's an admonishment that should be taken literally, just to avoid mess – so at NWLJDS pudding was frequently a plate of custard made with water. To make this more appealing to us children, the cooks often dyed it blue.*

⬆ **White Polycotton Wool Tzitzit, 36 x**
Brand: Talitnia
5.0 ★★★★★ ˅   3 rating:

£15²⁰

About this item
- Polycotton Talit Katan Tzitzi
- Features wool Tzitzit, each r strings.
- Made in Israel by Talitnia, es
- Tzitzit are certified Kosher u
- Width: 36cm, Length: 90cm

⊟ Report an issue with this p

I could perhaps sum up how Jewish the school was by telling you that I was only ever awarded one line in a school play. Which was:

'Well, Rabbi . . . You certainly do drive a hard bargain.'

Yes, you thought it was just going to be the word 'Rabbi', but on the way was 'bargain'. Which is a joke I can make despite

---

* Many years later, I told my then eight-year-old daughter about this while on the school run. I remember her saying, 'Poor Daddy had to have the blue custard', and felt that in some ways this summed up a section of my life.

everything I've written elsewhere about Jewish stereotyping, because I am Jewish.

So. School was very Orthodox. At home, meanwhile, it was Reform, at least when my maternal grandparents were around. But there's more complexity: my dad. Colin Baddiel's family background didn't involve fleeing from Nazis in Germany, but fleeing from Cossacks in Latvia. His great-grandparent, Barnett Baddiel – almost definitely some other central European name, but 'Baddiel' seems to have been the Victorian immigration official's best guess – arrived in this country in the latter half of the nineteenth century, having smuggled himself onto a boat. I was always told he was headed for New York, but since he couldn't speak English, got off at the first stop: Swansea. Which always made me wonder how many years Barnett spent wandering around the Mumbles before garnering enough of the language to ask: 'Sorry, where exactly *is* the Statue of Liberty?'

Meanwhile, in the way of Orthodox Jews, Barnett had about seven hundred children, most of whom became even more Orthodox. One, Dovid Baddiel, helped to set up one of the most celebrated yeshivas – that's a school for Orthodox Jews where all they do, all day, is study the Torah and the Talmud – in Europe, in Gateshead. Given that all the various Jewish Orthodox children then gave birth to loads of other Orthodox Jews, I have an awful lot of very Jewish Orthodox cousins, few of whom I've ever met. Unable to contact any of them by the end of filming *Who Do You Think You Are?*, because it was Passover, I just went and walked around Golders Green: where I bumped into my cousin, David Baddiel, who I'd never met before. People assumed this was set up. It wasn't.

They are *extremely* Jewish, these relatives. Here is one who for many years taught at the Orthodox Jewish secondary school, Hasmonean. His name was Oshor Baddiel.

He was a very distinguished scholar and member of the Orthodox community. So distinguished he was once commemorated on a stamp.

I apologize. I *apologize*, already.

Anyway, one of Barnett Baddiel's sons, Ben, rejected Orthodoxy, which led to a family schism, and the line I therefore appear on – via my grandpa Henry – is not bothered at all about religion. By the time we get to my dad, we have a stone-cold atheist. Colin Baddiel would show up to the family Pesachs and Chanukahs and Rosh Hashanas, but not take them in any way seriously, joining in the singing only ironically and calling all forms of prayer 'ollywollybolly'. In fact, there was always some tension between him and my mother's parents, because of his tendency not just to call the prayers that, but to say, halfway through them, 'Can we finish the fucking ollywollybolly and eat now?' He was also a fan of full English breakfasts, which meant I often used to eat big plates of bacon and pork sausages before setting off to the North West London Jewish Day School in my yarmulke and tzitzit.

It's a wonder I'm not more damaged. But really, this is just the tip of the David Baddiel Ages 6–16 Emotional and Psychological Confusion Home Life Iceberg.

Sarah

Sarah Baddiel was not a straightforward Jewish mum. Nonetheless, I used to do a joke about her – very early on in my stand-up career – that suggested she was. The joke was:

> My mother is a very Jewish mother. She's the sort of woman who if I fell into a river would shout 'Help! Help! My son, who went to Cambridge University, is drowning!

The Jewish mother stereotype is not an untruth about my mother. Here, for example, is an email she wrote to my older brother and me that would seem to fit the characterization:

> **Do either of you know of an available young lady between 25 to 35. The son of friends of mine is quite lost where to**

begin again after finishing a seven year relationship with his girlfriend. He is tall, blond, slim and fun. He is into aeronautical engineering and runs his own company from Meldreth, just outside Cambridge. He has his own house. Just a thought. He is Jewish but it is not important to him. The right person is what counts. Any thoughts??? I walked back from shul with him and he unburdened himself to me. He has two extremely good looking sisters who are also unmarried but we will not go down that road unless you also know of any available guys. Paul is 30 and the girls are 33 and 35. One never knows.

She was certainly very Jewish. But just in case she ever forgot, she could always check out her birth certificate, which had a big 'J' stamped on it by the Nazis. Her original first name, as I've explained, was not Sarah but Frommet. This was because after 1938 German Jewish parents with newborns were forced to choose their names from a list, and all the names on that list were shit. Here are the options for girls:

Abigail, Baschewa, Beile, Bela, Bescha, Bihri, Bilba, Breine, Briewe, Brocha, Chana, Chawa, Cheiche, Cheile, Chinke, Deiche, Dewaara, Driesel, Egele, Faugel, Feigle, Feile, Fradchen, Fradel, Frommet, Geilchen, Gelea, Ginendel, Gittel, Gole, Hadasse, Hale, Hannache, Hitzel, Jachel, Jachewad, Jedidja, Jente, Jezabel, Judis, Jyske, Jyttel, Keile, Kreindel, Lane, Leie, Libsche, Libe, Liwie, Machel, Mathel, Milkele, Mindel, Nacha, Nachme, Peirche, Pesschen, Pesse, Pessel, Pirle, Rachel, Rause, Rebekka, Rechel, Reha, Reichel, Reisel, Reitzge, Reitzsche, Riwki, Sara, Schame, Scheindel, Scheme, Schewa, Schlaemche, Semche, Simche, Slowe, Sprintze, Tana, Telze, Tirze, Treibel, Zerel, Zilla, Zimle, Zine, Zipora, Zirel, Zorthel.

You may spot Frommet there, next to Geilchen: which means slut. These lists, like a lot of Nazi anti-Jewish restrictions, demonstrate one of the main contradictions of the Third Reich's paranoid and – this adjective feels like it's underplaying it, but it's still, I think, the *mot juste* – weird antisemitism. Jews, as far as Nazi iconography was concerned, were uniformly, recognizably grotesque: they are all fat, they all have huge noses, they are all swarthy, and their hands are always adorned with strings as they puppetmaster their evil way around the governments of the world. All that should make them fairly easy to spot. And yet here you see one of the numerous ways in which the Nazis let slip that they at the same time fret that Jews are almost *impossible* to spot, because they must be checklisted and filed, and given special Jew-y/biblical names as another type of insignia beyond the yellow star to make sure they aren't hiding under the radar. In the psychosis of the racist, the Jew is at once immediately recognizable and invisible.

She was born in March – or July – 1939, in Königsberg. At that point in time, her father, Ernst, would've either still been in, or just let out of, Dachau. This may confuse some readers, as the notion of getting out of a concentration camp doesn't accord with most people's idea of them, but although many people did die there, these were not killing fields: they were not, yet, extermination camps. My grandfather, like many male Jews between the ages of sixteen and sixty, had been arrested after Kristallnacht, made to clean up the rubble of his synagogue, and sent to Dachau. My grandmother then used all their remaining assets that had not been stolen, to bribe officials, to get him out. When, after six months, he was released, the family were given a matter of weeks to leave the country, or he would be re-arrested and sent back, to certain death.

In 1939 it wasn't easy for Jews to emigrate to the UK. It wasn't easy for German Jews to emigrate anywhere, partly because Nazi laws were clamping down on letting them out and partly because other countries placed enormous restrictions on letting them in.

In among all the bureaucracy, and while Ernst was in a concentration camp, my grandparents had to somehow marshal £1,000 – needless to say, a lot of money in 1939 – and show evidence of it in a British bank account. By now they were selling their furniture to live, and had no money. They were forced to beg friends and relatives who had already got out to transfer that money into a British account in order to help them secure entry to the UK.

The process of granting asylum was managed in London at the time by an organization called the German Jewish Aid Committee. I have read all their correspondence to my grandparents, but the letter that raises the goose pimples on my flesh most (and brings home to me just how desperately anxious the waiting for such letters must have been) is this one overleaf, about the addition of my just-born mother to their entry card to the UK.

The part that makes my blood run just that little bit colder is the date: 21 July 1939. With possession of this card, they may apply for their visas in Berlin in 'ten days time'. Which means their actual exit from Nazi Germany would not have happened until the start of August. War broke out on 1 September. I am really only here, writing this, by the skin of my teeth.

They arrived in Britain in late August. They stayed in a hostel

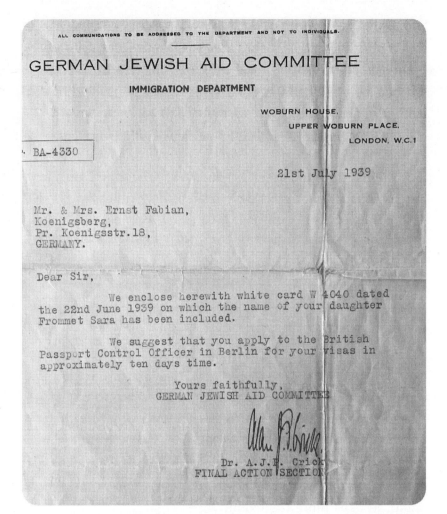

ALL COMMUNICATIONS TO BE ADDRESSED TO THE DEPARTMENT AND NOT TO INDIVIDUALS.

GERMAN JEWISH AID COMMITTEE

IMMIGRATION DEPARTMENT

WOBURN HOUSE,
UPPER WOBURN PLACE.
LONDON, W.C.1

BA-4330

21st July 1939

Mr. & Mrs. Ernst Fabian,
Koenigsberg,
Pr. Koenigsstr.18,
GERMANY.

Dear Sir,

We enclose herewith white card W 4040 dated the 22nd June 1939 on which the name of your daughter Frommet Sara has been included.

We suggest that you apply to the British Passport Control Officer in Berlin for your visas in approximately ten days time.

Yours faithfully,
GERMAN JEWISH AID COMMITTEE

Dr. A.J.F. Crick
FINAL ACTION SECTION

in Whitechapel for a month, before getting a bedsit in Cambridge, where they lived for most of the war. One day in 1941, while Ernst was walking my mum in a pram in a park, he was arrested and, along with most other Jewish German refugees in the UK at the time, interned on the Isle of Man.

Time contracts as you get older. When in the 1970s, I was asking my grandmother about having any other brothers or sisters, her enigmatic reply about Mr Hitler gestured to what seemed a very distant past. Because I was eleven. I was born nineteen years after the war. At that age, nineteen years would have felt like an eternity. But at this age, now – fifty-nine – I remember nineteen years ago. It seems like yesterday. I was doing *Baddiel and Skinner Unplanned* on ITV, FFS. So now I realize that the trauma of my mother's upbringing didn't happen in another space-time universe, and it brings home to me how overshadowed by damage her early life was. Her childhood involved fleeing, then living in one room with her parents – who must've seemed to all the local people around them, not least linguistically, to belong to the enemy nation – and then, when all she needed was some emotional stability, her dad was unjustly imprisoned for two years.

Many books have been written about intergenerational trauma. Most trace the terrible impact it can have on mental health through the generations. And certainly, some of that was passed down in my family. After the war, my grandfather would be in and out of Fulbourn Mental Hospital with clinical depression for the rest of his life. But sometimes, and certainly in my mother's case, the impact is more surreal, the line not so simple – and perhaps more tragicomic than tragic.

One of the things that has become clear to me since I published my book *Jews Don't Count* is how in the closet many Jews are. I received so many heartbreaking letters and tweets about Jewish shame, a need to play down one's ethnicity and blend in, provoked by fear, by history.

My mother, however, wasn't in the closet about anything. But most definitely not her Jewishness. She was never one to hide the fact that she was Jewish; you might *just* be able to spot a clue to that in this picture:

That feels to me a more benign version of the yellow star her parents were forced to wear: the tasty version.

So, coming back to the Jewish mother thing – yes, she was Jewish and, perhaps unusually for one whose life had been directly scarred by the Holocaust, out and proud about it. She was also a mum. I mean, in the classical 1970s sense. She lived in dull suburbia with three children in a marriage that had clearly become disappointing to both parties. She often wore bright green flared Lurex slacks. She would occasionally say things like 'I tell you who I *do* like: that Paul Daniels.' She had terrible taste in curtains. She had a tendency, at meal-times, to tease the possibility to her children that there was quite a special treat tonight for pudding, and when the time came it would invariably be some tinned sliced pears in syrup. Or worse, a fucking tangerine.

She also used, at least in her written correspondence, some very mum-ish grammar. Here is an email she sent in 2014:

Begin forwarded message:

Date: 27 November 2014 21:32:27 GMT
From: Sarah Fabian Baddiel
Reply-To: Sarah Fabian Baddiel
To: David Baddiel

Ivor, Sophie, time for tomorrow please?

I have plenty of easy back up food that Colin can manage himself if necessary.
Thanksgiving today. Hope you are all celebrating with all the "trimmings" including Pumpkin Pie!!!!!

There's a few very my mum things about this. First off, we never did Thanksgiving. Although Ivor and I were born in America, we're not at all American, and the Baddiels were nothing like the family from *Parenthood* (a film I've never seen but I assume includes a big homely Thanksgiving scene with an enormous turducken). We never even *discussed* Thanksgiving. I think this, sent a month before her death, might be the first ever mention of Thanksgiving in our family. But my mum was a woman who would suddenly fasten onto random things in an obsessive way and make them the basis of her personality. I assume at this moment she was going through a Thanksgiving – or possibly, which she did periodically, an all-things American – phase.

Another very my mum element of this email is the somewhat dismissive reference to my dad – well into dementia by this point – being able to 'manage himself if necessary'. Films about dementia, such as *Away from Her*, or *Iris*, or *Supernova*, have conditioned us to the idea that the spouse of the person with the disease, if themselves not afflicted, will instantly adopt a persona of deep, stoic, self-effacing love. Not my mum. The opposite. She was just fucking *annoyed* with my dad's dementia. To be fair, it was fucking annoying.

But to return to the grammar. Notice the five exclamation marks after 'Pumpkin Pie'. My mother loved exclamation marks, but without it ever being clear in what context she was using them. Most people use exclamation marks to indicate that something is a joke. I am violently opposed to *any* kind of indication that *anything* is a joke – I am violently opposed, for example, to the use of winking, laughing, crying or other guides-to-how-I-want-this-to-be-taken emojis on social media or text messages – since signalling that a joke is a joke is the death of joke-ness. In my young stand-up days, when my patter was perhaps more callow and aggressive than in my latter preten-tious Olivier-nominated years, I did a bit premised on the notion that anyone who uses an exclamation mark to indicate that they are making a joke is a cunt. I elaborated on this idea by saying, 'For example, anyone who writes a postcard which says "Nice weather – if you're a duck!!" may as well just write underneath it, "Love, Cunt."' Apologies, obviously, for the language. I was young, as perhaps can be deduced from the word 'postcard'.

But, however much I may disapprove of them, exclamation marks to indicate joke-ness are nonetheless, clearly, a thing, and like many things that are a thing, my mother did not understand how those things worked. Thus, even though we never did Thanksgiving, and none of us would be eating

Pumpkin Pie, these five exclamation marks are not a joke. I don't really know what they are. To some extent they are just . . . exclamatory, which would not be a bad description of her default state.

More significant still are the inverted commas around 'trimmings'. My mum always misused inverted commas. Inverted commas normally enact a transformational quality on the word contained within, which takes two forms: ironic or innuendo. When trolls wish to slag me off on Twitter, for example, they often do so by putting inverted commas around the word 'comedian' – another 'gag' from this so-called 'comedian', they say, implying cleverly that I am not, in fact, one of those. This would be the ironic usage. However, in the 1970s, when Sid James might have said of Barbara Windsor coming back from a beachside ice cream van, 'Blimey, *she's* got a huge pair of "Mivvis!"', the inverted commas that we can assume existed in the script of this imaginary film – I'm thinking *Carry On Clacton!* – denote that Sid is actually referring to Barbara's breasts, rather than her ice lollies. That would be the innuendo usage.

I'm overstating this point to make clear that my mother, in *her* use of inverted commas, was doing neither. When she writes 'trimmings', the side dishes she's imagining *are* trimmings – potatoes and carrots or, I dunno, grits or whatever. Nor are they wink-wink, know-what-I-mean, let's-not-put-too-fine-a-point-on-it-Deidre 'trimmings'. They're fucking trimmings. This still makes me irritated even though she's dead.

Point is, my mother was very much a mum, and without doubt Jewish. But despite all this not, in the final analysis, a stereotypical Jewish mother.

Because what are the characteristics of the stereotype? Notably: obsession with their children. Particularly, in the Philip Roth mould, an obsession with a son. Everything is subsumed in the pride for that son.

In 2010, a film I wrote called *The Infidel*, about a Muslim who discovers he was adopted and is biologically Jewish, came out in the UK. Here I am at the premiere with the film's star, the hilarious British-Iranian comedian Omid Djalili:

It was a big premiere for a small indie film, at the Hammersmith Apollo; we had dancers dressed in Muslim and Jewish costume, and you can see all the photographers there. Well. Not *all* the photographers.

So, OK, you might think – well, that *is* quite Jewish mother-y – there's a strong sense in that picture of, 'Oh these silly men won't get a good shot of my son, I'd better do it.' But that isn't really what's going on here. Because Jewish mums are supposed to have *nachus** in their children, to *qvell*† about their children, to subjugate everything, in other words, to their pride in their children. But what my mum is doing in this photo isn't about trying to get a good pic of *me* – it's about getting *herself* into the picture. I can prove this: because the photo of *The Infidel* premiere that she had up, framed in her house, forever afterwards, is not the one she's *taking* of me and Omid on the red carpet. Which would look something like this:

---

* Reflected pride/glory.

† Hysterically go on about their children's achievements in order to generate reflected pride/glory.

No. It's *this* one:

The one, in other words, with *her* in it.

My mother liked to be in the picture: in the spotlight. To be fair, she actually *is* in *The Infidel*, as an extra, in a scene with a lot of guests attending a bar mitzvah. She wore the same clothes in the film as to the premiere – that dress, that tiara. I imagine when she came to the premiere she thought someone would recognize her from her scene. Which is possible as she does stand out in it. If you watch *The Infidel*, there is a long tracking shot at the bar mitzvah, as Omid's character walks past all the guests, who are meant to be looking straight ahead and bored.

One of them isn't. They are looking to the side and talking animatedly. It's my mother. Not because the director told her to do that. She just didn't listen to him.

My mum also once came to the previously mentioned *Baddiel and Skinner Unplanned,* which was an ITV comedy show in which me and Frank Skinner sat on a sofa and just talked to each other, and to an audience, about whatever came up. As part of the show, we would pick someone out of the audience to be The Secretary, who would write down the subjects discussed that week on a whiteboard.

When she came to the show, it was clear to me from the sofa – I could sort of feel her, across the cameras, and the other audience members, straining at the bit – that my mum *really* wanted to be The Secretary. I put this to Frank: and Frank, who knew my mother well, was not keen. I'm now going to put on record her reaction to our subsequent discussion about whether or not she should get the role, which I think does perhaps qualify the idea of Sarah Baddiel as a purely-proud-of-everything-her-son-does Jewish mother.

> FRANK: Look at the spot you've put me in now. Because
> if I say no, I've robbed an old lady of her dearest
> wish. If I say yes, the show'll be shit.
> SARAH (IN THE AUDIENCE): IT ALWAYS IS!!!

Just to say, those exclamation marks are not meant to imply anything else but that she was shouting this, very loudly, over audience laughter. She got a round of applause and was then chosen as The Secretary.

Later in the same show, she said something else not normally found within the standard Venn diagram of Jewish Mother. At one point, Frank and I begin discussing Kinga. I very much doubt anyone reading this will remember Kinga, but she became famous, very briefly, in 2005, for masturbating with a wine bottle in the *Big Brother* garden. You might imagine this would be a challenging topic to talk about live on national television, with your mother right there. But not as challenging, it turns out, as my mother's opinion on the subject.

FRANK: What do you think about it, Sarah?
SARAH: And why not, it's nice to do such things outside in the open.

Again, she gets a round of applause for this. And clearly loves it. But she is not, in so doing, conforming to the Jewish mother norm. Or perhaps any kind of norm. I then explain to her that, although I never thought I'd have to say this to my mother, there is an 'r' in 'masturbate'. Which, to give her credit, she immediately corrects.

Fame

Speaking of my mother appearing at premieres and on TV, it is perhaps worth considering for a moment my parents' relationship to what I'm going to call, vulgarly, my fame. It's vulgar because of an omerta in our celebrity-obsessed culture, which is that however famous you are, you're never supposed to say the words *I am famous*. Everyone knows fame has its downsides, leading people into all sorts of terrible humiliations, making them go mad, in some cases die, so you would have thought it would be fine to claim it, as it's hardly a straightforward boast. But nonetheless, saying 'I am famous' *feels* like a boast. It feels vulgar. However, I'm saying it, to write this bit.

There has been an awakening recently, in popular culture, to a phenomenon called nepo babies: famous people, who have famous parents, who perhaps would not have succeeded on their chosen path had it not been for these parents. If my children go into the performing arts and are at all successful, they will be accused of it. However, I can't be. Fame, when I was growing up, was a completely different planet. I didn't know anyone famous or had ever met anyone famous. I hadn't even seen anyone famous from afar. With the money I got from my bar mitzvah, I bought an electric guitar, a Columbus Fender Stratocaster copy. It cost about £40, from a shop in Hendon Central. I loved it and was proud of it, but when I told a schoolfriend of mine I owned it, he didn't believe me.

He didn't believe me because an electric guitar was something you saw strung round the neck of Mick Ronson or Noddy Holder on *Top of the Pops,* and wherever the place was where that happened was not reachable from Dollis Hill, not even when the Bakerloo Line became the more glamorous-sounding Jubilee one. It was an object from a parallel universe, one people like me and my friend could never gain entry to.

Here's a photo that I think makes clear just how unglamorous my upbringing was. This is me and my brothers in fancy dress at our primary school, the already mentioned North West London Jewish Day School:

My older brother Ivor here is the ace of clubs, Dan my younger brother is a detective, and me – I'm Miss World. Although to be fair, this is what most Miss Worlds looked like in 1973.

Point being, the mise-en-scène of my childhood was not very like, as I imagine it, Jade Jagger's. The TV was in our living room, but it was not, as it can seem now, a portal, something young people feel they could step into.* Not least because ours was tiny, and black and white, until about 1971 when we got a larger colour one. This was a very exciting moment in our family. It wasn't just the sudden impact on the eyes of saturated technicolour. It also had channel-change buttons that weren't great lumpy sticks, but inset, smooth, lit-up ones so sensitive they worked at the slightest touch. So sensitive, in fact, they once changed the channel from BBC to ITV after Dan did a particularly big sneeze.†

Today, however, I think children believe fame to be nearby. This may be because *everything* since I was a child has become more glamorous. When I went to my daughter's leaving assembly at her primary school, despite it being just a local state school, the whole affair was very showbiz. Beautiful, but showbiz. There were speeches; there were songs – not 'The Wheels on the Bus' but 'What Have You Done Today to Make You Feel Proud?'. There were prizes; every child seemed to be awarded some sort of prize. It was two hours long, and by the end everyone in the room was crying. So it's not ridiculous to say that Dolly's leaving assembly was a bit like the Oscars. On *my* last day of primary school meanwhile, our form teacher Mr Cohen told us we should know that wherever we went in the world there would always be someone who didn't like Jews. That was his inspirational message for us youngsters to take into adulthood. He didn't sing it, to the tune of an uplifting M People anthem: 'There'll always be someone . . . who doesn't like Jews!' No. He just said it, kind of breezily. A terrible thing

---

* Obviously, the screen portal most young people in 2024 feel they can step into, correctly, because they can, is the computer screen.

† Arguably should've been a footnote. But I love that story.

to tell eleven-year-old children; and, of course, he was absolutely right.

I don't think fame has changed me very much. I have watched people around me change because of fame. But I think I had too much of an already-fixed personality before I became famous. I am not good, as I have said, at being not-me. Also, I think my early life was so idiosyncratic and odd that even the bizarre world that fame presents has little on it. This may explain why I've often blundered around in that world. I have made many VIP faux pas. Behind the velvet rope, I have found myself endlessly in embarrassing situations.

Let me give you a couple of examples. In my teens, I was a big fan of the prog rock band Genesis (and still am: let me not renounce them now). In its own way, this too highlights how uncool my life was. In 1977, the thing to like was punk. I *did* like punk, but I didn't really know *how* to like it. The pure mechanics of it, I mean. I didn't know how, for example, to backcomb my hair to make it spiky. I didn't know you had to hold up the strands and then comb them down. I just borrowed my mother's Silvikrin and sprayed a bucket of it on my head, which made my hair look like a dark tangled pool, like something children were warned to stay away from in the woods in public information films of the time. I also didn't know where *SEX* (Vivienne Westwood's punk boutique) was on King's Road, and even if I had, wouldn't have been able to afford any of the clothes hanging up inside it. Instead, I cut holes in a pink T-shirt and fastened them with safety pins, but it just looked fucked, rather than a fashion item.

I was in a punk band at my secondary school. We weren't great. The drummer didn't have a drum kit. He played dustbins instead (which at least exemplified some sort of punk aesthetic). We did have a good name, though: the Salivation Army. Here I am at a Sally Army gig at my school:

I can't remember why we're covered in foam. I assume someone let off a fire extinguisher. It's possible the dustbin drum kit included a fire extinguisher, which might explain it. Anyway, that's not me singing – that's a boy called Phil Griffiths, who absolutely knew how to dress like a punk and backcomb his hair – I'm the one in the cut-off denim shorts. Which perhaps, in terms of illustrating my not understanding how to be a punk, is job done.

Anyway. I went on to be in another, slightly more serious, band and a friend of mine from that outfit called David Gavurin (who would go on to be the guitarist in a brilliant band: the Sundays) introduced me to *Wind and Wuthering* by Genesis. *Wind and Wuthering* is the second album the band released after Peter Gabriel left, so it doesn't even have the cachet that pre-Phil Collins led Genesis has, of being vaguely art-house cool. But that didn't matter. Because I thought it was entirely beautiful. Which meant that in 1977, when it was arguably the least fashionable artistic choice anyone has ever made, I became a Genesis fan.

To me, Peter Gabriel was a God. He was a more divine figure in my musical imagination than almost anyone, except perhaps David Bowie. So when, many years later, I met Peter, it was a bigger deal for me than meeting, say, John Lennon would have been, notwithstanding the fact that Lennon would've been rising from the dead. But because I am not properly attuned to fame, every time I have met Peter Gabriel, it's gone wrong. The first time, I was seated opposite him at a big event and was very excited, but I couldn't hear him. Peter is softly spoken – there was a fair amount of noise in the background and I just said 'Pardon?' a lot. The only exchange I can remember from this meeting was when I said I wasn't a big fan of world music, which is a properly stupid thing to say to the founder of Womad. I can still see the moment of disappointment in his eyes.

This is my archetypal showbiz experience. People say never meet your heroes because you're bound to be disappointed. I say: I should never meet my heroes as *they're* bound to be disappointed by me. On another occasion, in the noughties, I was – don't worry, I shall immediately after relating this anecdote be going to check my privilege – on a skiing holiday with Peter Gabriel. Not just me and him, I should stress, but it did involve extended periods of close contact with him, and so the opportunity, obviously, to make up for the awkward moment we'd had earlier. At one point, we were alone together on a ski lift. As we rose above the white slopes, Peter, a man who is interested in other people, asked about my then partner, now wife, Morwenna Banks,* and what she was doing. I said, 'Oh, she's in the new Harry Enfield show, *Harry and Paul'* – which was recording but hadn't yet come out. Because he had been off the scene for a bit, Peter said, 'Oh, Harry Enfield, what happened to him?' And I replied, thinking out loud, 'Oh, he took some time off . . . he did a show for Sky . . . oh, and later he did a sitcom for the BBC called *Celeb',* and then I said: 'which was about a faded rock star *in fact.'* And then – too late – I thought, Why did I say *in fact*? I meant to say, simply, this is a show about a world you might know. But it doesn't come across like that, that sentence, does it? Because of the words 'in fact', it comes across as 'You'll be interested in this show about a faded rock star, won't you, *being one*?' 'You'll probably want to watch this show about a clapped-out old twat of a music dinosaur, I imagine, because that's what you're like, that's what you are, Peter Silly Gabriel.' And so once again, all I saw in my teenage hero's eyes was hurt and disappointment, on this occasion made worse – you see, payback for that privilege – by having to sit in silence with him on a ski lift as it slowly rumbled its way up a snowy mountain for another six or seven minutes.

Sometime later – and on this occasion, I began to wonder if God, who I don't believe in,† is deliberately making my interaction with famous people ludicrous – I appeared briefly in the Channel 4 teen drama *Skins*. I was coming back on the train from Bristol, where *Skins* was shot, sitting with Harry Enfield (who in the show played Morwenna's husband). And

---

* In a chapter on fame, it's worth mentioning that my wife is, certainly in one respect, much more famous than me, due to being one of the main voices in the most successful pre-school animation of all time, *Peppa Pig*. She is Mummy Pig. Which has always been complicated for a Jewish bloke.
† For further info, see my book *The God Desire*.

– this is true, it's true, how can it be true, but it is – Peter Gabriel got on the train. I called to him, and he came and sat with us. Which was fine. But then I made such an obvious mistake. Peter got off first, and I thought, I must tell Harry about what happened on the ski lift. So I told him the whole story – about mentioning *Celeb*, about saying *in fact* and all that – and he didn't laugh once. Harry just looked pissed off. And I realized, Of course. All he's thinking about is the fact that Peter Gabriel said '*whatever happened to Harry Enfield*', isn't he? Shit. Now I've fucked it with him too.

Sometimes, it's as if my tendency to create embarrassment when meeting famous people is contagious, like I've given it to those close to me. During the mid-nineties I went out with a fabulous woman from Newcastle called Sarah, who did not share all of my pop culture reference points. Once, we were at a party at which the band U2 were present, and the guitarist, The Edge, came over to say hello. Most people there of course knew who he was, and thus he didn't have to introduce himself, but Sarah asked him his name. He said, slightly taken aback, 'The Edge.' She said, 'Pardon?' He went very red, and said, 'Um . . . The Edge?' She said, 'Sorry, what was your name again?' He went even redder – as everyone watching realized with horror that this is exactly the conversation you're never meant to have with this particular person, forcing into the light the truth that his name is not a name, it's an abstract geometrical concept – and said, 'Well, my real name is David Evans, but people call me The Edge.'

Sarah frowned, and nodded. I pulled her away and said, 'Did you really not know who that was?' And she said, 'Well, I could tell he was a rock and roll kind of guy, which is why I thought it was odd he was saying his name was Reg.'

• • •

Earlier, I mentioned Erica Jong's mantra that the more famous you are, the more people will get you wrong. Another way of saying this is that fame is a kind of mistaken identity. With me, sometimes literally. I once met Ronan Keating out of Boyzone and he spent five minutes telling me what a fan he was of mine, which I took as very flattering – until he said 'What I particularly liked was *Blackadder* . . .' When I said, 'No, I'm not Ben Elton', the former Boyzone frontman just looked very cross – like I'd been deliberately trying to trick him with my face.

Andrew Lloyd Webber, for a long time, seemed to think I simply *was* Ben Elton. I heard this showbiz rumour once that when he was writing *The Beautiful Game*, his musical about football, he was looking for a collaborator. He'd seen *Fantasy Football League* and so said to one of his minions, 'Oh, go get me that bearded Jewish bloke off the TV in the glasses', and without really giving this request much more detailed consideration, they contacted Ben Elton. I thought for a long time that this couldn't be true, but then Frank met Andrew, who said to him, 'Oh, I love that show you do on the sofa with Ben.' This was after he'd written *The Beautiful Game*. With Ben Elton.

I don't in fact think I look that much like the various people I am mistaken for. Ben Elton is the ur-mistake, but I am also often expected to answer to the names Ian Broudie (of the Lightning Seeds) and Mark Watson (the comedian). I also once got given a free meal at a restaurant in Swansea because the maître d' thought I was the late lamented DJ Steve Wright. Not all of these people are Jewish, but there is an element, I suppose, of racism here. At least, this recurring mistaken identity would be considered racist if it was happening to a black and/or Asian celebrity. But hey. Jews don't count.

I met Andrew Lloyd Webber once at a showbiz party, and

I said to him, 'Andrew, you know I'm not Ben Elton, right?' And he just looked really frightened, like 'Oh my God what's wrong with *Ben*? Is he having a nervous breakdown?' At which point he moved away, flustered – and as he did, he motioned towards the woman he was with, who wasn't listening, and said, 'This is Sarah.' I had assumed this woman was his wife, but I also knew that 'Sarah' had been the name of his previous wife. So I guessed this woman in front of me now probably wasn't his wife. We began talking, and I said: 'So, what do you do for Andrew?' She looked a bit put out but replied, 'Oh, I look after the estate and the horses.' OK, some form of PA, I thought. We talked for about fifteen minutes and then – because this is fame and it's such a weird world – the presenter Eamonn Holmes, who I don't know at all, came over. I said, 'Hello, Eamonn, this is Sarah.' And she looked absolute daggers at me, and said: '*Is that meant to be some kind of joke?*'

Which was when I realized in a flash what had happened. The woman *was* Andrew Lloyd Webber's wife, his third wife, whose name, I now know, is Madeleine. But earlier, when Lloyd Webber had walked away from me, in a fluster, he'd confused her name with that of his previous wife, Sarah Brightman. I thought: I can't tell her that. I just can't. It's too embarrassing for everyone concerned. So when she said, 'Is that meant to be some kind of joke?', I replied . . . 'Yes.'

And she said: 'Well. It's not a very funny one.' She is of course correct there. Let's stop and just consider that bullet I took for Lord Lloyd Webber. I basically had to let her – and Eamonn Holmes, an important man – think that I, a professional comedian, would find it funny to introduce a man's third wife to someone else by the name of that man's second wife. Presumably this means they now think were I ever to meet

Paul McCartney's present wife, I would find it funny to introduce her as Heather. Or, fuck it, Linda.

After an intensely awkward pause, I went to seek out Andrew
Lloyd Webber. I found him in another corner of the party and
tapped him on the shoulder. I said:

'Andrew, a word to the wise. When you left me a while ago,
you told me your wife's name was Sarah. So I introduced her
to someone else as Sarah, but her name isn't Sarah, is it? It
was really embarrassing. It was awful. Please never do that to
anyone else again.'

And he said: 'I'm really sorry about that, Ben.'

And I still don't know if that was a joke.

I'm telling you these stories about embarrassing myself in front
of the great and the good of the arts world to make you laugh,
hopefully, but also to illustrate how being someone who tends
not to have a filter – Morwenna once said to me, 'Have you
ever thought about saying the *second* thing that comes into
your head?' – is indicative of always being a bit of a fish out
of water in the world of fame. This is related, I think, to my
upbringing, to not quite knowing how to behave in these spaces.
You need, in the engine of fame, always to have at hand the
oil of understanding what not to say. And I don't.

There's a fairly clichéd psychological trope, which is the idea
that people want to be famous because of something lacking in
their childhood. Like most clichés, it does have a kernel of truth.
Certainly, the desire to stand on stage and make rooms full of
strangers laugh – a terrifying thing to do, which requires over-
coming, at the start, intense anxiety – does surely have something
to do with seeking approval or, at least, witness. I know many
comedians and comic performers – Alan Davies, Eddie Izzard,

Robert Webb, Aisling Bea, my own wife Morwenna Banks, to name but a few – who suffered the loss of a parent when they were children. This might imply there is a gap in the unconscious where they feel unseen by some primary observer, and an audience can, even if only temporarily, fill that gap.

Neither of my parents died when I was young. But they were not very bothered with parenting. The way in which they were wrapped up in themselves meant a different lack, for me, of witnessing. I think it's probably true, if simplistic, to say that going on stage in the hope of gaining approval in the form of laughter is, for me, a way of saying to my parents, as they lived and continue to live in my unconscious, 'Over here! Look *this* way!'

The thing I am most famous for in the UK is the song 'Three Lions (Football's Coming Home)'. If you want to talk about mass approval . . . well. 'Three Lions', the music for which was written by Ian Broudie, and the lyrics by Frank Skinner and me, was released to coincide with the Euro 96 international football championship, which was being held in England (hence football coming home . . .). It went, on its release, to No. 1. But unbelievable though this achievement might have been for a bloke who in his boyhood couldn't even convince a friend he owned an electric guitar, this is not the mass approval moment I'm talking about. The song fell from what I believe DJs used to call 'the top spot' after a couple of weeks, being replaced by the Fugees. I thought, Well that was nice, but I guess it's over. Meanwhile, in the actual tournament, England had drawn their first game 1-1 with Switzerland, and the country seemed to be settling in for another disappointing showing by the national side.

In the second match, we played Scotland. Once again, in the first half, England were bland and they went in at half-time with the game goalless. In the second half – this is probably not the book for this, but I'm going to say it anyway – things changed, mainly because Terry Venables put on Jamie Redknapp to play a holding role in midfield, which transformed the shape of the game. Alan Shearer scored an opening goal. Then Scotland were awarded a penalty, taken by Gary McAllister. It was saved – brilliantly, and nothing to do with Uri Geller, despite his claim to have moved the ball by telepathy – by David Seaman. The ball was kicked upfield and then Paul Gascoigne scored one of England's greatest goals of all time. Which meant England won 2-0.

As the teams left the pitch, the sun came out. At the same time, and apparently against the wishes of the FA, who had decided the song was too 'partisan' to play at the end of the Scotland game, the Wembley DJ, whose name I do not know, and to whom I will always owe an enormous debt, put on 'Three Lions'.

And the whole crowd joined in: 87,000 – well, OK, there must have been some Scottish fans there, so let's say 75,000 – England fans began to sing. This was before any big screens at Wembley, so there were no lyrics graphically pasted up for people to karaoke with. They just *knew* the words. Frank and I looked at each other, and then . . . joined in. And I know you're supposed to say the best day of your life is when your children were born, but fuck that: this was the best day of my life.

The thing that made 'Three Lions' – which was much reviled by music critics when it came out, and is still not considered very cool, certainly compared to say, 'World in Motion' by New Order – land so well with football fans is that it spoke to their actual experience. For most people, football fandom, and supporting the England team, doesn't involve, as most football songs had suggested up to that point, expectations of triumph. It's about disappointment. More specifically, it involves a form of magical thinking, whereby you know, rationally and through your own history, that your team, that England, are likely to build up expectations and then lose, but you somehow hope this time – to quote the title of another England song – will be different. That hope is often fragile, but it's always there.

In 'Three Lions', it's there. It's in the defiant lines, after two verses about how all the pundits are saying England are going to screw up again,

But I remember
That tackle by Moore
And when Lineker scored
Bobby belting the ball
And Nobby dancing

It's the combination of knowing we'll probably be shit but nonetheless shoring up the fragments of when we weren't shit against the ruins and coming out fighting anyway that raises, I think, the goose bumps when fans hear our song.

I would say that if you want an example of mass approval filling whatever gap is in me due to lack of parental witness, it would be hard to imagine anything more likely to do that than the whole of Wembley Stadium singing lyrics I co-wrote. And, I guess, continuing to sing them for thirty years (and thus confusing the mathematics: how many years of hurt is it now?). Which it probably has.

Here's an unusual not-often-said thing: I think fame probably has been healing for me. The approbation of strangers is, of course, an innutritious soul food, but if you receive it for long enough and on a big enough scale, maybe it can fill you up after all. I probably now, approaching sixty, feel approved enough, even if large sections of that approval come from people I don't know. But as far as this book goes, I need to note that I can't remember either my mum or dad saying anything about 'Three Lions'. Neither during the heady days of Euro 96, nor on any other occasion when it became the alternative national anthem during football tournaments.

That seems at the very least unusual, doesn't it? I mean, as I said, Jewish parents are supposed to *qvell* about their children. They are supposed to go on and on about their achievements. And, as I have also said, my mother was very happy to bask in reflected glory – although I don't think she thought it was reflected; I think she thought the glory was always essentially hers. But I'm not even talking about them showing off to other people about me. I mean I can't remember them ever in private saying to me, 'That response you've got for that football song – that's amazing.' Or 'We've been singing that song you co-wrote in our house before every game, David!' Or anything like it.

Something needs to be disentangled here. It is not true that my parents weren't interested in my fame. I think my *dad* wasn't, as he wasn't interested in very much outside of his immediate needs. Colin Baddiel couldn't be fucked with most things, and the idea of him turning up to a premiere – even of a film I'd written – would just have been utterly unlikely. My mother, however, was very interested in the fame, just not the work. I don't remember her ever saying, 'That show was funny', or 'I liked this joke you did', or 'You see that, David Baddiel? That's you that is.'

Nonetheless, I think my mum was keener on me after I got famous. For example: in her late fifties, she changed her name, by deed poll, to Sarah Fabian-Baddiel. I think this was because she wanted, at that point, to feel separate from my dad and more like the person she had been before she got married. It's therefore odd, isn't it, that she didn't just go back straightforwardly to Sarah Fabian. But then again, I think she also wanted people to know that I was her son.

This may seem narcissistic on my part, but here's a fame-based story that backs it up. When Morwenna was in *The Vagina Monologues* in the West End, my mother went to watch it and went backstage afterwards to see Morwenna and her co-stars, one of whom was the actress Lesley Joseph. Morwenna introduced my mum to Lesley as Sarah, and as her partner's mother, but didn't call her Sarah Baddiel. Or Sarah Fabian-Baddiel. Not for any reason: you are unlikely in these circumstances to introduce someone by their full name. But being a deeply private person, Morwenna hadn't told the other actors that I was her partner, and so my mother wouldn't have registered as 'David Baddiel's mum' in Lesley Joseph's mind.

This clearly bugged my mum. So she sat Lesley Joseph down and showed her some family photographs. This was before camera phones, so she actually got a small album out of her handbag – she always carried these about with her – and casually went through them all, making sure to point out in a number of them, her son David.

Also in the dressing room was Christopher Biggins, who at the time was appearing in *Mother Goose* at the Arts Theatre in Cambridge, where my mum was then living. She asked him if she could have tickets to see the show. Which may seem a bit brazen. But not as brazen as what she actually asked for: six tickets.

I assumed that Christopher Biggins would've smiled politely and forgotten about it, and that would've been the end of the story. But a few weeks later, Morwenna and I received a message on our answerphone from Lesley Joseph, saying that my mum had turned up during the interval of a performance of *Mother Goose*, somehow got backstage, and knocked on Biggins' dressing room door to ask what had happened to her tickets. Lesley Joseph's voice message continued:

'Biggins said that Sarah said, "You must remember me. I met you at *The Vagina Monologues*, with Leslie Phillips."'

I don't remember, by the way, my mother saying anything about the work here either. That is, I don't remember her saying anything to Morwenna about her performance in *The Vagina Monologues*, or indeed about the show at all. Which in this case is unusual. Because my mum was, always, extremely upfront about sex. Somewhat too upfront: she gave new meaning to the expression *no boundaries*. Where did this come from?

Sarah, Otti, Ernst

It partly came, of course, just from the times. Sarah Fabian-Baddiel came of age in the 1960s, but even though that decade might seem to be what I'm talking about, what I really mean is that my mother was very, very 1970s. She married my dad in 1960, when she was twenty-one, and by 1966 had three children. Which meant the sexual revolution as charted by Philip Larkin wasn't happening for her, or at least, not when it was meant to be happening, between the end of the Chatterley ban and the Beatles' first LP. My mum had to come to it late, after the initial child-rearing was over. By the mid-seventies, in other words, she was making up for lost time.

The 1970s were, as far as I can make out, considerably more sexual than the 1960s. This may be because the only sexual revolutionaries, the only people, that is, actually *having* a lot of new

and different sex in the 1960s, were pop stars, models and Charles Manson. Ordinary people may have watched and read and listened to lyrics about doing it in the road, but most were only doing it, as ever, in their houses, with their spouses, in the missionary position, at the weekends.

But by the 1970s, people seemed to want more of the action. Certainly, it's in the seventies that culture catches up, that films become X-rated, that *Plays for Today* on TV are endlessly about people having affairs, and that my mother stops wearing prim buttoned-up outfits, replacing them with glittery jumpsuits in green draylon with very low neck-lines.

But the obsession with sex goes back a bit further with my mother. Here is a picture of my grandma, Otti Fabian.

Just park the sex thing a minute and let me talk about Otti. She was a very lovely, if occasionally stern woman. I was close to her. When I graduated from Cambridge, she was there, prepared to be photographed with me despite my haircut.

Having come to this country in middle age, she remained very German, and very Jewish. Once, I

was at her house in Cambridge for lunch with my then girl-friend, who was called Janine Kaufman, and Otti had made chick-en soup with kneidlach.* For some reason, despite Janine's surname, her ethnicity had not registered with Otti, and thus as she put the dish down in front of Janine, she said, in a polite explanatory whisper: 'You may not like this – it's very *continental*.'

But that didn't stop her wanting to appear English. It's worth thinking about how difficult it must have been for her after my grandfather was interned in 1941. Part of the reason German Jews were interned was that, following the unexpectedly quick fall of Holland and France to the Blitzkrieg in 1940, tabloid-fuelled hysteria in the UK led to the mass assumption that such surrenders required the existence of spies and fifth columnists working undercover in those countries, and that therefore they were probably also operating in Britain. Meanwhile, for a number of reasons, some to do with propa-ganda, others straightforwardly antisemitic, the Ministry of Information in the UK had chosen not to release to the public information it held about mass executions of Jews by the Nazis already happening in Europe. Which meant that most British people would have had very little idea why Jewish refugees had such an urgent need for asylum in their country and would have considered anyone speaking with a German accent an object of extreme suspicion. As I say, my grandfather was interned. My grandma, Otti (they didn't intern women with young children), alone in Cambridge, with a strong German accent, had to somehow find a job to feed and clothe her family and pay the rent. It was hard, and it was lonely, and it involved

---

* Matzo ball dumplings.

writing desperate letters like this one, in a language she had only just learned.

Copy.

Otti Fabian
39, Garden Walk
Cambridge

October 30 th., 1940

Name of Internee: Ernst Fabian
Camp address: Central Promenade Camp, Douglas.
Address before internement: 167, Victoria Road, Cambridge.
Present home address: 39, Garden Walk, Cambridge.
Registration Book: 747.735 Cambridge.
Class: C.

The Undersecretary of State

Home Office

Whitehall W.C.1.

Dear Sir,
           I beg to apply for a medical examination of my husband
    ERNST   FABIAN

at present interned at Central Promenade Camp, Douglas, I.O.M.,
with the view of his release under clause 3 of the White Paper.

        My husband is suffering from grave periodical attacks
of nervous paralysis of the vocal chords, especially during
the winter months. He was in Germany under constant medical
attention, and our doctor there had warned us that, unless my
husband is very careful, this might develop into a chronic
paralysis. I have now learnt that recently he had another severe
attack which necessitated his admission to the Camp Hospital.
I am very worried about the consequences a prolonged internement
might have on the health of my husband.

        May I add that we came to this country in August 1939
with an Affidavit for U.S.A. where we want to emigrate as soon
as we are permitted. We are Jews and were expelled by the Nazis
after my husband had been put in a Concentration Camp. Now he
has been interned again since May the 12 th., and I have to stay
here alone with my 1 year old baby. I trust, Sir, that you will
consider this case favourably.

        Yours faithfully

Which might explain why, despite the accent, and more so than Ernst – who to his dying day spoke a kind of hybrid German-English and insisted Goethe was better than Shakespeare – she became keen, after the war, after everyone knew the terrible truth of why Jews had to seek asylum here, to present as English. She used to tell people her name was Ethel. On the Queen Mother's ninetieth birthday, Otti wrote to her to offer congratulations. I know this because of the reply I found after she died, and the idea of how much joy this letter would've brought her, in its final confirmation of Ethel Fabian's Englishness, is heartbreaking.

CLARENCE HOUSE
S.W.1

23ʳᵈ August 1990

Dear Mrs Fabian

     Queen Elizabeth The Queen Mother bids me say how delighted she has been to receive your good wishes on the occasion of her 90th birthday.

     Her Majesty truly appreciates the warmth of your message, and sends you her sincere thanks.

     Yours sincerely,

     Angela Oswald

Lady-in-Waiting

One section of her craving to be English involved becoming a very big fan of middle England's TV. *The Good Old Days, Face the Music* – these shows won't mean anything to you if you're under fifty but trust me, they were big in the seventies – and *Hinge and Bracket,* a double drag act, in which two parish ladies would sing and play the piano and seemed to live together in a small country house. I remember watching *Hinge and Bracket* with Otti when I was about thirteen, and she was loving it, laughing and clapping and saying, 'Oh, zey are so funny!' I thought this a little odd, given that she was a – as we'll come to see – pretty straight-laced person. I said: 'You know they're men, don't you?' She turned to me frowning and replied: 'Don't be zo silly. Vy would you say that?' I didn't respond. But about five minutes later, the screen cut to Hinge and indeed Bracket outside, and you could see, despite the efforts of their no-doubt-short-staffed-by-the-Winter-of-Discontent make-up department, two distinct five o'clock shadows. Otti frowned again and said, plaintively: 'Oh. Now I look again . . . I zink zat zey *are* men . . .' She stopped laughing and clapping, and watched the rest of her favourite show in silence. I felt terrible and still do that I had busted her drag innocence. An early example, I'm afraid, of the wrecking ball that was to become the David Baddiel Truth-At-All-Costs Urge.

Anyway, to come back to the sex thing: I always thought Otti looked – and indeed sounded – a bit like the German-American sex therapist, Dr Ruth.

She was in all other ways – particularly in terms of talking freely and openly about sex – not at all like Dr Ruth. But an interesting thing happened when I brought the resemblance up on *Who Do You Think You Are?* I was standing with my mother in the house in Cambridge where she grew up. By the time of filming, her parents were both dead. I'm going to accompany this with some stills from the shoot, to give you more of a sense of it.

DAVID: She looked and sounded a bit like Dr Ruth.
SARAH: That's true, and she'd like herself to have
    thought of that.

'She'd like herself to have thought of that' is, I think, another one of my mother's holding patterns of speech. Or it may be that my mum had no idea who I was talking about but heard the word 'doctor' and wanted to sound approving. I continue:

DAVID: (LAUGHING) No, I don't think she was actually *like*
    Dr Ruth. She didn't talk about sex at all.

SARAH: Oh no. That was forbidden. It didn't exist!

DAVID: She physically reminded me—

SARAH: Yes, I have to say . . .

DAVID: —of Dr Ruth. Her voice and face were the same.

SARAH: I have to say, I don't know how I ever got born with a mother like that, who was so anti-sex.

DAVID: Yes.

Sadly, you can't hear the tone of that *yes*. I thought about putting a stage direction with it. I considered: WEARILY. Or possibly: WITH A FAMILIAR SENSE OF EXHAUSTION. But neither really do it. So you'll just have to imagine the deeply resigned 'yes' of a son who knows his mother is about to have no-boundaries about sex. There is forty years of Jewish suffering in that yes. Here is my face while I said it anyway.

She continues:

SARAH: Unlike Opa, who felt rather differently. But I won't say that on tape.

So that's a boundary there, isn't it? She's saying she's *not* going to talk about her dad's sex life. That's good. Phew. One thing you should know, though, is when my mum *was* about to tell you something about sex, something intimate, she would often preface it by saying, in a rather breathy voice, *you know*. Which was wrong, because normally I didn't know and I didn't fucking want to know. Anyway, with that in mind, let's consider how long she stuck to her resolution *not* to talk about her father's sex life on camera.

SARAH: . . . but I won't say that on tape. *You know*, he—

It was two-thirds of a second. I've timed it. Watching it back now, it still astonishes me: if there are world records for the least time a pledge made on camera has been held, it would break all of them. So. Having broken through that powerful boundary, let's see what my mother felt she couldn't *not* tell me – and the world – about my grandfather.

SARAH: When he came to London, I'd say 'What did you do today?' – and I knew exactly, he loved going to Berwick Street and Soho, and all that kind of area . . .

DAVID: Sorry . . . what are you saying?!

SARAH: Oh yes! I'm not saying anything, you're making it up! He said, 'I've had a very nice time, don't ask where I've gone.'

DAVID: Right.

SARAH: (LAUGHING) And I knew exactly where he'd gone but I knew I shouldn't ask too many questions!

DAVID: Right. This is my grandfather you're talking about.

SARAH: Yes! My father. But he was such a different personality. And he enjoyed travelling.

By 'travelling' – there's a word that really deserves its inverted commas – she means of course *fucking prostitutes*. He enjoyed travelling his penis into paid-for vagina. It's unbelievable, I think. Especially that thing of 'I won't say this on camera. Anyway, my dad loved hookers! *Crazy* for whores! Straight out of Dachau – and into Berwick Street!'

They never used this bit on *Who Do You Think You Are?* Possibly because the sadness of my grandfather's Holocaust survival story – and it is indeed, deeply sad – would not have been enhanced by the curve ball of his daughter detailing how much he loved a happy ending.

If you're wondering, by the way, how I am able to reproduce this scene, including pictures, despite its excision from the final cut of my episode of *Who Do You Think You Are?*, it's because my mother contacted Wall to Wall, the production company that makes the show, and insisted on being sent *all* the rushes.

I don't know if anyone reading this is aware of how much filming is involved in making a one-hour documentary. It's about eighty hours. My guess is that in the history of documentary making, no one's mother has ever phoned up the production company and insisted on this before or since. This was 2004, and my parents didn't have a DVD player, so she insisted, as well, that they put them on VHS. It's about four boxes of tapes. I can't imagine she ever watched them. But she wanted them. She was, as I say, a hoarder, and never more so than of her own life.

Golf

My mother's lack of boundaries, and her frantic sexual upfrontness, informs the central part of her story. Which relates to this:

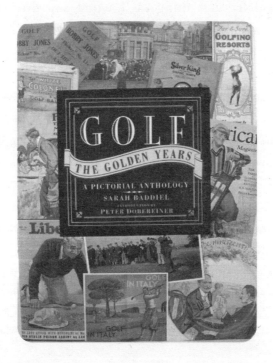

This is *Golf: The Golden Years*, the first – and the most successful – of four books my mother wrote about golf. Here's another:

She's signed this one:

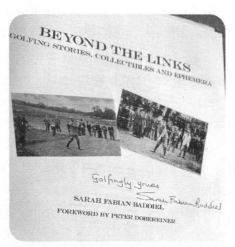

She signed all her books, and much of her correspondence (after the late 1970s), in the same way. In case you're wondering, no, 'golfingly' is not a word.

These aren't exhaustive histories of the sport, and certainly not philosophical musings on the playing of it, à la John Updike's *Golf Dreams.* These are coffee-table books for memorabilia collectors. But my mum's books demonstrate nonetheless a deep commitment to the game. Latterly, when she went into business as a golf memorabilia dealer, she would produce catalogues that always (I'm not sure this is usual for catalogues) carried epigraphs. Here is one:

> What makes the sun shine all the year?
> What makes all cloudlets disappear?
> What binds in friendships, strong, sincere?
> It's golf.

Be honest. Who knew that was the answer?

But my mother never really played golf. In all the time she was obsessed with golf memorabilia, I was aware of her having visited a couple of pitch and putt courses, maybe the odd beachside crazy one, and that's about it. Which, on the surface, is confusing. Golf is a singularly British, clubbable sport. In the latter half of the twentieth century, many clubs still restricted Jews from joining. Golf occupied exactly zero space in our house until the second part of the 1970s. The sport that we liked was football. Not my mum, to be fair, who called it footah. Which is ridiculous. If you're going to call football something annoyingly twee, you call it footie, or 'the footie'. No one calls it *footah.* No one says 'How was the footah?' But she did many things that no one else did.

Her interest up to this point in time lay in children's books. She ran a small business selling them, called Little Folk.

This was not, unlike golf, so apparently random. She liked

books (although never seemed to read any – but liked the idea of them, the trappings of them, the dust covers, the first editions, etc., etc.) and she had three small children. But still, there was strangeness. My mother related to people not in a 360-degree way, but via what they liked. Or rather what she had decided they liked. An obsessional person, she assumed all others had obsessions and that her role was to service these. Sometimes this would involve her deciding what other people liked, in her own mind, and sticking with it, forever. I went through a brief pre-pubescent period when

Sarah Baddiel
Little Folk
JUVENILE AND ILLUSTRATED BOOKS
COMICS   TOYS

43 KENDAL ROAD
LONDON · NW10

I liked Marilyn Monroe and had a photo of her on my bedroom wall. My mother then bought me many more photos of Monroe, which I dutifully put up, even though I didn't like her *that* much, not being from the 1950s. Forty years later, my mum was still giving me first day covers (something else she was very keen on) with Marilyn Monroe stamps on them.

When I was younger, I liked Billy Bunter books. Well, I *may* have liked Billy Bunter books. I liked reading, and the Bunter stories – a series written in the 1920s by Frank Richards, and which were a bit like Harry Potter only with less magic and more fat-shaming – did provide a window into an exciting un-Dollis-Hill-like world of turrets and adventures and buttered crumpets. But to be honest, as with many things back then, I was somewhat gaslit on this by my mother. Since she collected and sold children's books, I would occasionally dip into them, and having expressed a bit of a liking for one Bunter story, I found myself flooded with them – and with

*Magnet*s and *Gem*s (the weekly magazines they were printed in at the time) and *Holiday* annuals (collected stories in yearly copies).

She then enrolled me in a society, called the Old Boys' Book Club, which still exists. I went to many meetings of the Old Boys' Book Club, held at various members' houses around London, in places like Esher and Ongar. My mother diligently drove me to them. She didn't stay, despite her own interest in children's books. She dropped me off and picked me up, about three hours later.

Here's what's peculiar about this. I was eleven. Every other member of the Old Boys' Book Club was about seventy. I should stress nothing untoward went on – this was not a *ring* of any kind – but hey, it was the 1970s, and my mother was typically unbothered by the age difference. What did make the meetings difficult for an eleven-year-old was that they were incredibly boring. Even for an eleven-year-old who has convinced himself, to fit in with a bookish idea of himself approved of by his mother, that he's obsessed with Billy Bunter books. I used to sit there and dream mainly of the tea that would always be provided halfway through. Sometimes there would be jam tarts. But not always.

And then one day, or what feels like one day, she lost all interest in children's books and turned to the Sport of Kings. No, sorry, that's horse-racing. She turned to the Sport of Cunts. I apologize, both for the use of that word, which I know some find offensive – unfortunately I have always been drawn to it, like a linguistic siren call – and to any golfers reading this. I use it partly because it seems to me the *mot juste*, and because of a bit of vocabulary I picked up in Portugal once. During *Baddiel and Skinner Unplanned*, because it was an unscripted show, ITV sometimes sent me and Frank off to do things, random jaunts, to give us topics to talk about during the series. Once, we went for a four-day golfing holiday, with some lessons, in the Algarve. Turns out I'm terrible on the links. It may be that all those club restrictions were doing us a favour and it just isn't a sport for Jews. Either way, by the end of every eighteen holes – eighteen! So many! – I had what felt like golf flu. But however shite I – and indeed Frank – was at golf, to show willing, we wore golf clothes: big beige shorts, collared polo shirts and those weird shoes. And without fail, we would refer to these clothes as 'our cunties'. Frank would knock on my door each morning and say, 'All right, Dave: Have you got your cunties on?'

Why, to return to my mother, did she undergo this Damascene – or whatever the suburban, golf-playing-area equivalent of Damascus is – this Totteridgean conversion? Well. If we dig a little deeper into my mum's obsession with golf, we may discover that it doesn't simply involve a love of . . . oh, now I'm doing this trope again . . . whatever the golf equivalent is of leather on willow . . . polystyrene on wood/iron. It involves a love of something else.

This something else:

This man's name is David White. As you can see, he is the embodiment of 1970s man. The knitwear, the beard, the pipe – you can almost smell the *Hai Karate* on him. He's the kind of man the young Alan Partridge might've wanted to be. And as you can also see, he loved golf. He certainly looks very comfortable in his cunties.

David White first appeared in our lives in the mid-1970s, at which point he suddenly became very, very present. Here's a website called Dating Guide, which happens to have a section called: 'How to Tell If Your Wife is Having an Affair'. And it includes an interesting pointer:

If your partner suddenly has new interests such as golfing, bowling or any other hobby that you have never seen before, beware. This may be a sign that the other person is interested in this hobby so your partner is taking it up.

Given that, let's consider the facts.

Before she met David White, I'm not sure my mother had ever heard the word 'golf'. I'm serious. It's possible that if you asked my mother in 1971 about golf, she would not have known what it was.

That, as I say, was before she met David White. Here she is in our front room some time afterwards:

I'd say that's a bit of a giveaway.

Perhaps we should cut to the chase. When she met David White, my mum fell madly in love with him, and they went on to have a torrid affair that continued for many years. Being my mother, however, this affair involved an obsessive sidebar. In essence, she took Dating Guide's notion that if you're having an affair, you might begin to show some interest in your lover's hobbies and pastimes *not* as something she needed to watch in herself so as not to alert her husband – but more like a very literal *instruction.*

For example, this was David White's car.

This was my mum's car.

David White was a member of the British Golf Collectors Society – so my mum became one too. Here is a photograph she took of something that even by the standards of this story is a little peculiar, which is a wall, or possibly a floor, made up of bricks engraved with the names of the members of the British Golf Collectors Society.

The founding member of the society . . .

. . . is called Bob Kuntz.

Make of that what you will. There is one brick with no name on it, just the phrase 'Golf's Golden Years', which given it is nearly the title of my mum's book *Golf: The Golden Years** makes me suspect she paid for that one, as well as her own. And if you look closely, you'll see that perhaps the real reason my mum cherished this particular photo is that . . .

---

* Maybe there was a cost per letter for this engraving?

. . . David White is on top of her. In fact, David White's member is on top of her.

Most importantly, however, David White didn't just play golf; he ran a golfing memorabilia business.

So did my mother.

Which is one of the strangest parts of this story. My mother's way of showing this bloke that she loved him was to *set up a rival golfing memorabilia business*. With the same *name*. I'm not sure that's even allowed under corporate copyright law.

Golfiana – my mum's version – was a success. She became a well-known figure in golfing memorabilia circles. I've found letters in her extremely well-kept archive thanking her, for sending golf books and/or memorabilia, from figures as glittering as professional golfer Ben Crenshaw, professional golfer's wife Barbara Nicklaus and deputy PM under Margaret Thatcher, Willie Whitelaw.

From: The Rt. Hon. Viscount Whitelaw, C.H., M.C.

HOUSE OF LORDS
LONDON SW1A 0PW

29th November 1989

Dear Ms Baddiel,

Thank you for your letter of the 19th November, and the delightful book "Golf. The Golden years", of which you sent me a complimentary copy.

Here is a whole article about her in *Golf Illustrated*:

GOLF ILLUSTRATED — 27th August 1980

20

SARAH BADDIEL must be one of a handful of individuals in the world who own a silver golf bag and clubs, can turn the clock back and watch some of the game's most precious moments and weigh the swing sequences of "The Great Triumvirate", sing golfing songs that have rarely echoed 19th holes, see Mickey Mouse or Tiny Tots striking a drive and when it rains — can get a fourball together for a day's golf in her living room. And no wonder, Sarah is a collector of "Golfiana" — which to her means anything connected to the game — from James Braid to Fuzzy Zoeller — from ancient clubs to Zebra putters.

LIKE SO MANY before her, Sarah was lured to playing golf by the game's attractions of exercise and fresh air. However, ever since, while in a junk shop she stumbled on an attractive Art Deco of a woman golfer and caddy, those aspects have taken somewhat of a back seat to the exercise of walking down creaky stairs and searching for a "find" amidst the musty air of an old antique shop.

A collector with a grip on golf's past and present

by John Andrisani

Sarah Baddiel in another dimension of the game

History

Since her love for golf began four years ago, she was surprised to find so many golf enthusiasts lacking true appreciation for the royal and ancient pastime. Sarah cites these as "players" while "golfers", she said, "are those who play, yes, but, too, study the game's history, watch the flags blowing in the distance and dream of what it was like playing a long, long time ago". "American professional Ben Crenshaw, a golfing authority, who has such an extensive collection of golf books, and the late Bernard Darwin, are true golfers in my book".

Basics

Nevertheless, Sarah admits, "in most cases it is by no means out of disloyalty for the game that so many lack this serious attitude, but because the majority of golfers fail to realise just how comprehensive is the history of golf or simply do not know where to begin". "Golf collecting is easy, really . . . but you can't get away from the basics . . . it requires patience, determination and luck".

Books, especially first editions, take up much of Sarah's collecting time and her favourites have been penned by Bernard Darwin, who is best remembered for his informative and amusing golf contributions in the *Times*, and he could swing the sticks pretty good too. To name just a few by this author in Sarah's golfing library: *The History of Golf in Great Britain* (1952);

in colour.

"Many golf books are scarce but not expensive and one of my "finds" was a book of poems called *Ridiculous Golf* by H. Boswell Lancaster . . . it looks and insignificant little brown card covered book but is enjoyable to read and I found the gem by accident at a London book fair, amongst a row of fiction — for 50p!," said Sarah.

But Sarah's golf collection stretches further to include china and porcelain, postcards, song sheets, paintings, toys, photographs, ephmera, silver — you name it, chances are, she's got it. "When I discover a cup and saucer depicting a golf scene what I think is, there must be a complete service somewhere . . . and do my best to seek it out," said Sarah. The most prolific designs she tells me have been by

who are known amongst collectors for their cheeky caddie with the head in the shape of a golf ball.

Victorian

Sarah's earliest items are Victorian scraps in full colour of both men and women golfers and a Christmas card which has a three-dimensional image in a pop-up with the verse reading:

Which says:

> LIKE SO MANY before her, Sarah was lured to playing golf by the game's attractions of exercise and fresh air. However,

A truer bit of journalism comes later:

> of Braid or Ballesteros, of old postcards or 19th hole post-mortems — Sarah holds a special interest in the game — for she is a player and true "golfer".

. . . if we assume in this instance the inverted commas are operating in the same way as when my online trolls put them round 'comedian'.

Dealing in golf memorabilia was, for the second half of her working life, my mother's job. She ran Golfiana from home, and also from a stall in an antique market, called Grays, in Bond Street. You might think her interest in golf was something she was just paying lip service to, so as to fit in with David White's world – to gesture to this man that she was very happy to accept, say, Lee Trevino's chances at the 1977 British Open as a subject fit for pillow talk. But it became much more than that. Not, I think, in a planned way. It was more . . . evolutionary. There is a thing in evolutionary theory called species drift, when a trait developed by a species for a specific function, to help them mate and/or survive, gets diverted to a different evolutionary lane. Dinosaurs, for example, evolved feathers, probably as a form of thermal insulation, but for some species, the feathers mutated, developing more and more dynamic properties, eventually leading, as they evolved into birds, to flight. Similarly, when my mum initially professed an interest in golf, it was meant to be a way of demonstrating to David White that she loved him so much she wanted to share his passions. But as time went on, she seemed to lose sight of the fact that her whole interest in golf was for his benefit and ended up becoming a much bigger figure in the golfing memorabilia world than he was. I assume much to his chagrin.

My mother couldn't just pretend to be interested in golf. Golf had to become *who she was*. And because she was our mother, that meant to some extent that golf had to become, in our family, who we all were. I don't mean any of us became interested in the sport. Fuck no. But large sections of the house were turned over to golfing memorabilia. Golf was everywhere we looked. Every ornament, every book, every fixture and fitting.

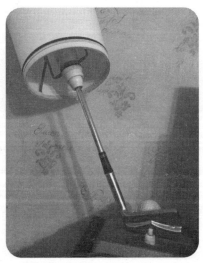

Every painting, every jigsaw.

Every painting that was also a jigsaw.

Every card, every cake.

Even upon my mother's person – she *wore* a lot of golf stuff: club bag brooches, club necklaces, ball-on-tee earrings. These still turn up often, in drawers, at the bottom of boxes, long after her death.

Most pictures of my mother don't just show her in golf-related clothes and jewellery. The frame itself will be golf-y.

Golf was often on the TV and my mother would emote vociferously – screaming with joy and/or agony – on behalf of her favourite player, Severiano Ballesteros, who I think functioned for her as a sort of substitute David White (I'm aware that it should really have been the other way round).

Just to complicate this a bit further: having said that she couldn't pretend, I think at some level my mother *was* pretending. I still find it hard to believe she *actually* liked golf. But I think she didn't know she was pretending, and in her unself-awareness, embraced this pretend identity as if it were entirely real. One thing social media has proved is that, for many people, identity is everything. The flux that is human personality is often too nebulous, too misty, and it's better if who you are is clear and straightforward and, most of all, noticeable. Which, as an identity, *Golf memorabilia nut* was, even if the motivation for it was neither clear nor straightforward.

Sarah

My mother's affair with David White might seem like a complicated thing to write about publicly. Which it is. But one thing should be obvious: my mother was not ashamed of her affair with David White. On the contrary. She was *proud* of her affair with David White. She considered – in a very seventies way – that having an affair was glamorous. Even with Roger Whittaker here.

She was always very keen to let people know about her affair. My brother Ivor tells a story about how, sometime in the early nineties, he took a new girlfriend – her name was Tracey Blezard – down to meet my mother at her stall in Grays.*

---

* My mum's stall was opposite my dad's stall (he sold Dinky Toys: more about that later). Meaning that every day at work, my dad was faced with the name Golfiana, which was also, as we know, the name of David White's business.

Sarah

My mother chatted a little to Tracey Blezard and then started talking to Ivor. At one point, the name 'David White' came up. Without pausing for breath, she turned to Tracey and said, 'My lover of twenty years', before turning back to Ivor to carry on chatting, as if nothing had happened.

A caveat: *my lover of twenty years* is, I think, an exaggeration. It is hard to know exactly how long my mum's affair with David White lasted. It is hard, because, as I say, she was proud of it, and also a fantasist. She was very happy to take what might conventionally be thought of as a negative – whether that be having an uncle who didn't make it out of the Warsaw Ghetto (*but maybe he was my father?*) or a marriage that wasn't working (*but I had a passionate affair*) – and turn it into something self-dramatizing and, in her mind, glamorous. This makes the facts themselves hard to come by. After she died I spoke to various friends about this. One of them was Ruth Mulligan, already mentioned as one of my parents' few non-Jewish friends. Ruth came to see the West End show I did, *My Family: Not the Sitcom*, which covers some of the same ground as this book. She told me backstage afterwards that – and this didn't surprise me – she knew all about the affair: my mother was forever telling her about it. But she believed the truth was that it may in fact not have lasted more than a few years at its height in the late seventies, and perhaps been revived in one-off meetings (at Golf Collector events, which my mum was always going to) through the years. Ruth said she thought it 'fizzled out' after a while.

And yet my mother never gave up on golf. Which may have been a way of demonstrating that she was never going to give up on David White, however much he had given up on her. It may even be the case that her unending dedication to golf and golfing memorabilia constituted a type of revenge. Or, more complicatedly, a type of revenge-cum-plea: revenge mixed in with an element of 'Look, given your particular interests, how much I am someone who you *should* have as a lover.'

I include this information while thinking that the facts, the numbers, of my mother's affair don't really matter. She believed in their love much as she believed in – in some ways, they were inseparable – her love of golf.

I devised and hosted a Radio 4 show once, *Heresy*, and at one point a discussion about the nature of public apology led a woman in the audience to tell a story about how her boyfriend had upset her. She'd asked him to apologize, which he did, but then she'd asked him to post the apology on Facebook. I said, why? She struggled to answer, and I suggested, 'Is it because nothing has any meaning any more unless it's on the internet?' In other words, broadcast. Public. My mother, I think, felt that way about many things, including her affair with David White. At some level, it only had meaning for her if people knew about it, or at least, her version of it.

Whatever the actual longevity of their affair, my mum's obsession with golf lasted the rest of her life. Even when her beloved father died, she had his favourite leather chair re-covered in this fabric:

I mean, I assume she had to have it re-covered in something, as he'd no doubt been fucking prostitutes on it.

Sarah and Colin

My mother's affair had many bizarre elements. It's hard to know which is the most bizarre. Undeniably, it leading to her turning her life, and her house, over to golf is up there. Also, the decision to tell everyone about 'it. But the most amazing thing, probably, about my mother's affair with David White is that despite all this incredible advertising of the fact: *I don't think my dad ever really noticed it.* It's an astounding feat of willed self-ignorance. Not least because David White was always at our house. Here he is round for dinner:*

---

* The woman on his right, facing the camera, is Ruth Mulligan.

Here he is at my fucking bar mitzvah:

Here he is with my mum in our back garden. And frankly it's hard not to read quite a lot into this one.

It's hard, that is, not to assume that in this photo, David White is asking for a particular type of sexual relief, and my mother is offering to upgrade.*

---

* Note two other things here: the pipe. And the single glove. The single glove is not, I think, a Michael Jackson thing. It's a golf thing.

He was a fixture at our house at this time. Since I do not believe that David White's interest in my mother ever matched, or even came close to, my mother's interest in him, I don't think he was ever auditioning to replace my father. But this book began with a memory of him teaching me how to hit a golf ball, which is probably the most vivid one I have of him crossing that particular boundary. As it happens, my memory – which may be faulty as I also have a memory of being very good at football when I was young, which despite my commitment to truth is one I know would be strongly contested by anyone I played with – is that I hit the ball well. My memory is that it soared high in our garden. It may even have gone above the shit football goal. Perhaps David White was an exceptionally good teacher of the golf swing. But there seems something sacrilegious about this. Football was iconic in our house. It was one of the not many things at 43 Kendal Road that bound us three boys to our father. Our dad taking us to Gladstone Park every Sunday after ITV's *The Big Match* was one of the very few things that felt like a family tradition. So the image of the golf ball, pristine, new, an intruder, soaring above the old broken-down but always there football goal – I'm going to call it a deeply transgressive image, redolent of David White's world surpassing Colin Baddiel's, although that might be reaching a bit.

Beyond his continual presence, there were many other ways in which my mother would broadcast her affair, certainly within the house. She would write love letters to David White, hundreds of them. But she would not just write them, and send them, like a normal person. She would copy them on carbon paper and leave the copies around in various places, including, on one occasion, the breakfast table. She would deliberately leave her answerphone on record while talking to David White so their conversations would be preserved. On her desk, she would stack the tiny answerphone cassettes, often labelled 'David W', with the date. You will be thinking, perhaps: Well, she clearly *wanted* her husband to know. I'm not sure. I mean, maybe, but I don't know if that was the primary motivation. Remember, my mother was a hoarder. I think she copied the letters, and kept the conversations, first and foremost because of that. This was a woman who kept virtually everything – old keys, passports, matchboxes, thimbles, ticket stubs to golfing events, lanyards (also to golfing events) – so why wouldn't she keep something intensely important to her, like her lover of twenty years' words, or her words to him?

Here is one of those many, many letters:

Here's talking to you, Boss.   8 pm Saturday

How could we "misbehave" so yet again in a carpark. We are just two crazy teenagers in love. Though I feel angry with myself for not having more restraint to say "No – wait". I know we were both "strung high" and needed to be released and I appreciate the compliment. I came 4,200 miles to be near you and you ignored the sign which read "No touching!" But now I feel even more lonely. I want your arms around me to make love to me slowly, tenderly tasting, touching, licking as only you know how. That special magical chemistry that is all yo own making. I am alone, quite alone in the apar' willing you to telephone me, so that I can organise my travelling plans for next week for any time whilst you will be travelling in the U.S before May 1st. Please try and or

Things to note: the inverted commas again (we will be coming back to those); the lack of guilt or fear of being discovered; the erotic prose, which goes further than perhaps anyone would like (we will be coming back to this, too); and the hint, underneath, of sadness, of this passion not being reciprocated.

I'm guessing that by now a recurring question may be popping up in your mind, that being: Did your dad *really* not know about your mother's affair? When she was *so* blatant about it? When, indeed, the whole golf thing was just the biggest red flag (or maybe a white one, in the middle of a putting green) possible?

My mother was, as is perhaps clear by now, an intensely performative person. I rarely heard her say anything that didn't at some level feel like she was, in some way, projecting a version of herself. But Sarah Baddiel was not a self-conscious self-dramatist – there was no sense of her ever being ready for her close-up, Mr DeMille. She was more method than that. Her part-playing involved a deeper dive. As can be seen from the forty or so years of golf memorabilia.

Just once, in later life, I heard her say something intensely authentic. Something that didn't seem like it reflected back to her a version of herself as she would like to be seen. I remember we were standing in our front garden in Dollis Hill. It must have been the late eighties, as she wouldn't have said this to me if I was younger. But she and my dad had just had a row. They often had rows, but I didn't in all the time they were rowing ever hear them rowing about my mother's infidelity. Most of the time, their rows were about very small things.

I don't remember what this row was about. I remember only that he had been shouting, and had gone in the house and slammed the door. And my mother turned to me and said: 'It's so tiring, living without an emotional life.'

I still can't believe she said this. Not because it isn't an accurate and insightful summing up of what being married to my dad must have been like much of the time. Because it is. But my mum was not given to highly articulate introspection, to chronicling the difficult nuances of her own life. She was given to fully embracing fantasy versions of her own life in order to block out complex realities: the complex realities of the present, like living with a difficult and frequently angry man, and the complex realities of the past, like being from a family torn apart by the Holocaust. It was for me, a strange moment: like my mother had suddenly turned into Anita Brookner.

The accuracy, anyway, is the point. Colin Brian Baddiel was indeed not a man of the emotions. He was a man of science, of football, of, with his children, rough and tumble play, and of shouting 'WHO THE FUCKING HELL IS *THIS* NOW?' whenever the phone rang. Which I think is the key to understanding how he managed not to notice his wife's affair. He shouldn't be thought of as a threatened male, unable-to-cope-with-the-truth, using denial as a shield against breakdown if confronted with reality. It was more that my mother's psycho-dramas were, for him – as almost everything was, for my father – *aggravation*.

And what aggravated him most was my mother and, particularly, my mother's, and I'm afraid I'm going to have to go Yiddish here, *meshugarses*. This is the – probably incorrectly spelled – plural of *meshugarse*, which means, approximately, crazy thing/behaviour. *Meshugarses* is used to denote the various batshitteries that the *meshugenner* – the batshit person

– is forever doing. But it always involves on the part of the speaker, exasperation. It never involves any element of awe or joy or 'I love how crazy you are'-ness. The context is always, 'Oh God, what *meshugarse* is this now?'

At some level, my mother's affair, and the various obvious clues pointing to the fact of it, was just, for my dad, another one of her *meshugarses*. It was just another thing that was suddenly obsessing her and that therefore he wanted to have no truck with. His blinkeredness, his not wanting to have to deal with her infidelity, may have had an element of masculine wounded pride and self-denial about it, but it also had a stronger element, I would say, of 'What the fuck is she up to *now?*'-ness. And when you consider that quite a lot of what the fuck she was up to involved golf, you can see he had a point.

Sarah and David White

My mother's affair with David White was not, meanwhile, without its ups and downs. In the early nineties, as I started to earn some small amount of money as a comedian, I gave my mum an Amstrad. Older readers may remember these computers, the UK's not-very-good answer to the first Apple Macintoshes. They had a memory capacity that would be considered small for a calculator now and used a font that was mainly green.

Amstrads being, essentially, shit, I wasn't that surprised when she called me – they still lived in our old house in Dollis Hill, but I was living about twenty minutes away from them by then, in Kilburn – and said she was having trouble printing something out from the word processor and could I come round? Dutiful son that I – sometimes – was, I went.

When I arrived, there didn't seem much wrong with the technology, and I managed to get the letter printed quickly. But then it became clear that perhaps my mother hadn't dragged me round to fix anything. What she wanted was for me to see the letter she had written to the secretary of Seaford Golf Club. And a very similar one to Mr Martindale of West Sussex Golf Club. Here is that one:

Dear Mr. Martindale,

I believe that Mr. David White is a member of your Golf Club. He was a committee member of the British Golf Collectors Society and Editor of their Journal for three years. In March of this year, he was forced to resign as he had sold eight sets of Hassall's prints to collectors as originals printed in 1909, when in effect he had laser copied them in 1989, putting them in old looking frames!

I would like your committee to seriously consider whether you wish to have this person as a member of your esteemed club, with a record for fraud. You may confirm the information with the BGCS, "Fircroft" Oakwood Close, Chislehurst, Kent, BR7 7JS.

I said: 'What are these?'
And she explained.

My mother was very proud that she had been elected – I don't know exactly when, but presumably a few years before the writing of this letter – a member of the British Golf Collectors Society. In my imagination, David White was no doubt annoyed about this further intrusion into his world, but as I have already detailed, by then my mother's golf obsession had taken on a separateness from him, even though he and his golfiness were still at the centre of all her psychodramas. You must keep that doublethink in mind while considering her actions.

In 1991, she was suddenly ejected from the BGCS. Here is the letter containing the terrible news:

Dear Sarah,

At a meeting held on the 6th March 1991, the BGCS committee considered the situation regarding your personal involvement in the sale of the modern Hassall prints.

It was felt that this episode has brought the BGCS into disrepute and under the rules of the Society the committee feel that they have no option but to invite you to tender your resignation.

May we have this by return please.

Yours sincerely,

Tony

A.L.R. Hawkins
Captain

I can feel A.L.R. Hawkins' pain in having to write this sad letter. *Captain* A.L.R. Hawkins, I should say. Although he does at least provide my mum with the small consolation of calling himself by the familiar 'Tony'. In that there is perhaps a suggestion that one day, once the issue of the Hassall prints has long been forgotten, they could still be friends.

Meanwhile, the Hassall prints. In the world of golf memorabilia, as far as I can make out, being a collector is considered more dignified, more gentlemanly, than being a dealer. My mother was never that bothered about this. She was keen – and succeeded – in making some cash out of golf memorabilia. She had the stall at Grays Antique Market, and a roster of regular clients.

David White, as far as I can make out, was very much not that. He was a gentleman collector, who never sullied himself with anything as mucky as selling any of his golfiana for money. Except it turns out he did: through my mum. She would sell bits and pieces for him and take a commission.

In this case, he had found eight signed prints of paintings of golf scenes by an artist called Hassall, dated 1909, and asked whether any of her clients would be interested. Here is a Hassall print. A real one.

My mum suggested some. One of them was a big American collector who she regularly sold to. She told her client about the Hassall prints and he was indeed very interested, and ended up buying four – for £3,000. I think she got 10 per cent of that. The rest went to David White.

Deal done, you might think. Everyone's happy. Except a year or so later, the big American collector had his collection valued, and it turns out the Hassall prints were, as my mother's letter states, laser photocopies stuck in old frames.

I'm going to write that again. THEY WERE LASER PHOTO-COPIES STUCK IN OLD FRAMES.

I mean, FFS. When Captain A.L.R. Hawkins says this incident brings the British Golf Collectors Society into disrepute, I'd say it brings the entire concept of golfing memorabilia and golfing memorabiliasts (not a word) into disrepute. How the fuck could you ever think such a schoolboy grift was going to work? I mean, this is not one of those complex artistic cons that Netflix documentaries get made about, in which some unbelievably detailed forgery using specially aged paint and canvas is created of a missing da Vinci and the whole art world falls for it. THEY WERE LASER PHOTOCOPIES STUCK IN OLD FRAMES. Except it clearly did work, because no one spotted it until a year after they had been sold, and then only an independent valuer.

When it came out, it was a terrible scandal, and both my mum and David White had to resign from the BGCS. So these letters, the ones she wrote on her Amstrad, were her revenge. These are not letters to the BGCS. They are letters to various golf clubs that David White was a member of, spilling the beans, and pointing the finger at him as the mastermind of the whole devilish scam. She is looking to get him, in the modern parlance, cancelled. In this case, from his membership of these, presumably beloved-by-him, golf clubs. I note that she twists the knife particularly in her letter to the Seaford Golf Club, informing the secretary, Mr Hitchisson, that she 'believes you had one hanging in the clubhouse for a while'.

One important detail. My mother wrote these letters anonymously. Well, that isn't quite true. She used a pseudonym. It was:

> I would like your committee to seriously
>
> this person as a member of your esteemed
>
> may confirm the information with the BGCS
>
> Kent, BR7 7JS.
>
> Yours sincerely,
>
>
> William Wallace.

Much like the forty candles on my fortieth birthday cake, I think this is an example of how my mum often acted like there were parts of living in this world no one had ever told her about. In this case that, if you're going to write an anonymous letter using a made-up name, it might be best for that name not to belong to a very well-known person. Someone so famous they have a much-watched biopic made about them. My mother has basically written 'Yours sincerely, Mel Gibson. P.S. I hate Jews.'

To be fair, she did mix it up a bit on the other letter.

Kent, BR7 7JS.

Yours sincerely,

William Wallis.

She told me all this. The whole sorry story of the con gone wrong. And I asked a question, one that sprang from a sense that what she was doing here, with these letters, was taking her revenge – a revenge implying that she, Sarah Fabian-Baddiel, must be the entirely innocent victim here.

I said: 'Right . . . um . . . aren't you a golfing memorabilia expert now? So . . . when he gave you these prints . . . didn't you spot anything? Didn't *you* think they might be fakes?'

And she replied: 'Well. You know how nutty I am about him, David.'

And I thought: No, Mother, you are just nuts. Because if you *knew* this was a con, if you were basically in on it, neither you nor William Wallace can now place the sole blame, in this hilariously cack-handed secret letter way, on David White. You both basically deserved what you got.

I still think this. But I think, now, I understand a bit more about how my mother saw herself as the victim here. Because she *was* nutty about David White. He did have immense power over her. It's possible she didn't have to employ her golfing memorabilia chops to spot that these prints were LASER PHOTOCOPIES PUT IN AN OLD FRAME, but she went along with it anyway because she felt powerless in the face of her

101

love for him – because, maybe, she felt excited to be doing something criminal with him. I assume there's something intimate and secret and exciting about that. Something sexy. Yes, it's not Bonnie and Clyde we're talking about here, but you know what I mean.

Something I like very much that I discovered in my mum's archives while researching this book is her response to Capt. Tony Hawkins' letter demanding her resignation from the BGCS. Here it is:

Dear Tony,

Thank you for your letter. I am giving the matter my greatest consideration and will be writing to you in due course.

Yours sincerely,

Sarah

Sarah Fabian Baddiel.

I love that. Because if I could prevail on you to glance back at Captain Hawkins' letter, even though it is signed Tony, I would not say that what he is offering here is a negotiation. He says that her actions have brought the BGCS into disrepute, and thus the committee 'have no option but to invite you to tender your resignation'. 'Invite' there is doing quite a lot of heavy lifting, isn't it? It's straining at the edge of its meaning, pointedly ignoring the more apparent word available to suit Tony's tone, which is *demand.* That is how almost anyone would read such a letter.

But not my mother. My mother's ability to distort reality to suit her own kicks in, and indeed Tony is only inviting her to resign. An invitation she will consider, and maybe she will, maybe she won't. You, Tony, and the rest of the fuckers on the BGCS committee will have to wait and see.

She did resign. And we know from the William Wallace letters that she was capable of the most terrible revenges. However, she didn't just take her revenge on David White. You know, of course, that my mum wrote several golf books. The last she contributed to was called *The Sourcebook of Golf*, which is different from the others. It's not a coffee table book, with pretty pictures of her collection. It's more a book for the trade, or rather for the budding golfing memorabilia buyer. It provides an invaluable service to such a person because it suggests the prices you should be paying for your memorabilia. It's a price guide, like *Parkers* for cars. Except: my mother told me once, in a voice cold with vengeance, that in *The Sourcebook of Golf* she had deliberately priced all the items too *low*. Yes. She'd gone for scorched earth. Anyone rocking up to a golf memorabilia shop holding a copy of *The Sourcebook* would be looking to buy those statuettes of Arnold Palmer for about a third of what they were actually worth. It was a grenade, thrown into the heart of the world that had so cruelly cast her aside.

Sarah

Despite the seriousness of #HassallPrintsGate, and the extremity of my mother's revenge, she and David White got over that blip. Well, she did, at least, because I know from the many more letters (or copies of letters) she wrote that her fascination with him carried on. Her candle for him, and for their golf-memorabilia-driven love, never went out.

But there was another element to my mum's personality as she got older. In her late forties she went deaf in one ear and it was discovered that she had an acoustic neuroma, which is a tumour on the auricular nerve. Although it was benign, she was advised to have an operation, the fallout from which created a host of medical problems. The scar tissue alone would give her severe headaches for the rest of her life.

I remember going to see her in hospital while she was recovering. The operation had left her with a Bell's palsy. Over the years, this would get better, although it never disappeared, and I guess my eye got used to it. But when I first saw her, I found it deeply shocking. My mother had, I think, a sort of beautiful face. I say sort of there knowing it may sound cruel. What I mean is her beauty needs to be seen through a Jewish lens, and we live in a culture where characteristic-ally Jewish features are not accepted as the lodestar of conventional beauty.

After the publication of my book *Jews Don't Count*, which

has a section about the casting of non-Jews in Jewish roles, several Jewish actresses contacted me to say not only were they often not cast in Jewish roles, they generally weren't cast in leading roles at all, because they were seen, their agents would report back, as looking *too exotic*. If, however, the leading role they were going for was actually a Jewish character, or a biopic of a real Jewish woman, they still wouldn't get that role, as once the character was a hero, someone, in Sarah Silverman's words, 'deserving of love', the casting director's requirement would inevitably be for someone with fairer skin, bluer eyes, un-curly hair . . . you get the picture.

I'm going to resist the antisemitic aesthetic, and insist that my mother was a beautiful Jewish woman. Not least because she was. Don't believe me, believe Julian Cope, singer, alternative lifestyle activist, frontman of the Teardrop Explodes and a collector of Dinky Toys, who used to regularly visit my father in his stall at Grays Antique Market. This is from Cope's second biography, *Repossessed*:

A Welsh doctor called Colin Baddiel was my favourite dealer. He sold me a Corgi Toys Gift Set 15, which obsessively re-created an entire corner of the Silverstone racing circuit, complete with press box, AA and RAC boxes, and a play-mat . . .

Colin Baddiel, or Doctor Bad Deal as he was known, had a gorgeous wife, an exquisite Jewish beauty called Sarah. They always told me about their son David and what great expectations they had for him on the stage.

I like 'exquisite Jewish beauty' as a description for my mother a lot. Not quite as much as I like 'Doctor Bad Deal' for my dad, but nearly.

I think when my mum had her operation, I was still young enough for it to be shocking to me that her face was now not as beautiful as it had been. Or perhaps, forgetting about beauty, just seeing that shift away from what to me she had always looked like. I was shocked to realize that she was mortal.

She dealt with it in a very her way. My mother's way of creating attention around herself took many forms, but latterly it went a bit Munchausen's. She did, from this time on, become someone who was, if not defined by her ailments, certainly very happy to talk about them a lot. She would usually be keen to tell you that various doctors who she was seeing were invariably 'the best man' in this or that specialism, and that they had never seen a case quite like hers. As previously established, she could always find glamour in the negative.

And interestingly, this desire to broadcast her medical issues didn't get in the way of her, um, primary desires. To wit: in 2008 my mother was about to go to New York. She contacted David White – who, perhaps not uncoincidentally, was due to be in New York at the same time – before she left and sent him this email:

------------- Forwarded message -------------

From: **Sarah Fabian Baddiel**
Date: 15 August 2005 at 11:28
Subject: FW: Global village
To: David White <>,

The leukemia (and now also the Crohn's Disease) makes me very tired, but perhaps you can join me to make the "naps" more interesting!!!!

It is perhaps the least enticing come-on line in the history of come-on lines. Note, obviously, the four exclamation marks and the inverted commas around 'naps'. Although I will concede that this is arguably – and unusually for my mother – a correct employment of the saucy usage of said punctuation.

At this point, some of you may be thinking: Hold on – this is a *private* email. Is this legal to reproduce? What about the ethics of all this? How did you even get hold of it?

Well, if you look very closely at the email again, with the bit that was redacted previously removed, you'll see it was . . .

------------- Forwarded message -------------

From: **Sarah Fabian Baddiel**
Date: 15 August 2005 at 11:28
Subject: FW: Global village
To: David White <>,

Cc: David Baddiel <>, Ivor Baddiel

The leukemia (and now also the Crohn's Disease) makes me very tired, but perhaps you can join me to make the "naps" more interesting!!!!

. . . CC'D TO ME. AND MY OLDER BROTHER.

C-FUCKING-C'D. NOT BCC'D. OH NO. Nothing so discreet.

I asked her about this. I phoned her and said: 'Why? Why would you copy me on this email?' And she said: 'Oh, it was a mistake.' A mistake. Right. 'Oh, I've accidentally cc'd my son. Oh, and my other son! Butterfingers!'

No. She *wanted* us to know.

With all this in mind – and really, everything I've told you – it's perhaps worth going back to that episode of *Baddiel and Skinner Unplanned* featuring my mother. At one point in the episode, she feels the need to say:

SARAH: (POINTING AT ME) I am related to that gentleman,
    he's my middle son. He also has an older brother and
    a younger brother.

Sidebar: this is very my mum. I've always considered that her favourite child was Dan, my younger brother. I mean, she liked me, but she had a proper thing for Dan, possibly because of all of us he is least like my father. But whether Dan, or I, or Ivor, was her favourite, the propaganda in our family was always that we were all entirely the same. No brother was to be treated any differently from any other brother: see, as evidence, the many photographs of us in which we are dressed rigorously the same:

Which is why she feels compelled, on *Unplanned*, to make it clear I am only one of three brothers.

Her declaration of equal parental rights for all three sons gets a sympathetic sound of approval from the audience. Which leads on to this dialogue:

DAVID: Why did that get an 'Aaah . . .' from various
     female members of the audience? Because my mum
     has had sex with my dad three times . . . that got an
     'aaah' . . .

This gets a laugh. The camera cuts to my dad, laughing. Then my mum says:

SARAH: Are you quite sure they're all from your
     father?

My Family

Are you quite sure they're all from your father? This elicits a very big response from the audience. Laughter, applause, but also shock. It cuts back to my father. He is still smiling. But less so.

I say: Hang on a sec. Mother. That's not a comeback to me, that's calling yourself a slag.

I regret saying this now. Although it does get a big laugh, and that's the nature of the beast with a show like *Unplanned*, or at least the way I did it: just say whatever is in your head, don't censor, don't filter. I think of my mind on that show like a squash court wall, just bouncing back whatever comes at it. It often meant I said inappropriate things that I now regret. Even if my mother *was* a bit of a slag.

She betters me anyway with what she says back:

SARAH: No, it's not. It's suggesting I had a good life.

It's suggesting I had a good life. The idea that one of her children may not in fact be her husband's progeny is an indication, as far as she is concerned, that her life was lived to the full. This, I think, is one of the most revealing things – and it's a high bar, she was a woman of almost constant self-revelation – my mother ever said. It's an amazing thing to say, in context, on TV. It's at once deeply solipsistic, almost callous, given that my dad is in the audience, but on the other hand, it inspires in me now, as much does as I get older and think about my flawed, damaged parents, a reflex jolt of sympathy.

Not least because it makes me realize I have picked up a key thing from my mother, which is a very acute lack of shame. I don't really have the gene for shame, and with it, the corresponding one for judgement. Particularly not for judgement about how people live their erotic lives, within the obvious consensual parameters. Although there was one person here who wasn't consenting, which was my dad. So, it's complicated.

It shows that in her own way my mum was a child of the sixties, a woman of the sexual revolution. Except without much revolution. Just mainly the sex. Sex was how she proved she was *modern*.

And something else. As we know from another appearance of hers when I was on TV, *Who Do You Think You Are?*, my mother was always chasing a phantom, lost glamour. Her family in Germany had been rich. They had servants. My cousin Michael tells me they had a fucking *Rubens*. If she'd stayed in a Nazi-free Germany, she would probably have led a very glamorous life. She would've had a big society wedding and married a prince, not necessarily a royal one, but an elegant, high-class man of standing. She'd have lived somewhere grand on the Baltic Sea, surrounded by Rubens and amber.

She may of course not have done any of that, but it was, I think, somewhere in the mix of her imagination, the Barbara von Cartland version of her life, in the parallel universe where Hitler never happened. But in the actual, more Nell Dunn version of her life, she didn't have access to anything equivalent. What she had was Dollis Hill, three children and a husband uninterested in the emotional life. In that context, David White, with his smoothness, his pipe, his polo-neck sweaters, and yes, his golf, with all the clubbable middle-classness it brought with it, was the nearest thing she could get to that prince. Her affair made her feel not just that she was living a good life, but that she was living *her* good life: the one that had been stolen from her.

Ivor and David White

Obviously, one thing that will come to mind if your mum goes on national TV and suggests that not all her children may share the DNA of your father is that maybe you or your brothers do not share the DNA of your father. I'm sure, with me, that I do. I'm sure, looking at photos of my dad from when he was young, that I am a version of him. I don't quite know why I said young then, as I am old, so really if I wanted to make this point, I should be looking at a photo of my dad when he was in his late fifties. However, I think one carries in one's mind an idea of your basic self, your basic look, which hovers around twenty-two, and to my eyes, at that age, he looks like a version of me. Although clearly, the truth is the other way round.

But nonetheless, it preys on the mind. It obviously hasn't escaped my attention that my name is David. But then again, I'm not aware of my mother meeting David White until the 1970s, and I was born in 1964. Then *again*, I'm not positive they didn't cross paths earlier.

There is no concrete evidence that any of us were fathered by David White (or anyone else, apart from Colin Baddiel). There is, however, some comical evidence. When my mum died, because she died very suddenly, my brothers and I had to go through all her stuff. We found many things that told of her not-very-secret passions, some of which I will come to. But we also found endless hoarding of photographs and letters and cards and pictures from our childhood. It was like she had never thrown a single thing from those years away.

In among them, I found a series of drawings by Ivor.

'Here is a Man', that drawing is titled. To the young Ivor's mind, I would suggest, it's an archetypal drawing of a man, a male, a grown-up, a father figure. And he . . . is smoking a pipe.

But my father did not smoke a pipe. I think we know who did.

The pipe's in every single drawing.

Here – in 'This is a Football Team' – not all the men have pipes, but I'm going to suggest that the one who does is the father figure, the *manager*.

Looking at all these pictures, it became harder not to associate the man with the pipe . . .

. . . with the man with the pipe.

The archetypal maleness of the drawings continues hand in hand with the pipe-ness. This one is called 'Here is a Big Man':

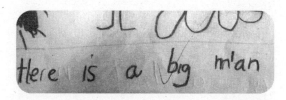

And he's got a *fucking* big pipe.

In fact, if you look closely, you'll see that the pipe is smoking a pipe.

Some might say I'm getting a bit too Freudian, associating the pipe with the young Ivor's subconscious ideas about maleness and patriarchy. I don't think so.

Look at *this* pipe.

Let's look at that a bit more closely.

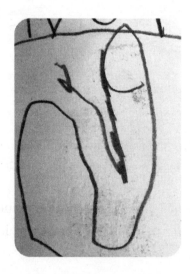

It may not surprise you to know that I've spent a lot of time in therapy.

Obviously, this is all conjecture. And, when you look at Ivor, there's very little resemblance to David White. This, I think, was clear even when you look at photos from when he was a baby.

Ivor

A lot of Freud's assumptions about how personality is shaped from childhood have been discredited, but we still live in a post-Freudian universe in which interpretations of how we came to be who we are rely heavily on who your parents were. This is obviously not the book to suggest that parents have no impact on your early life, but I think what Freud leaves out is that, except obviously in the case of only children, others were involved in your upbringing: siblings. And there is a particular spin on that if your parental landscape was like mine, a combination of craziness and neglect. Your siblings – especially if you are lucky enough to have an older sibling, at least one who cares – operate as a buffer against that craziness and neglect. More: they operate as both a buffer and then a surrogate parent.

Which is quite something, given that Ivor is only eighteen months older than me. But I think it's true. It's true in the practicalities. Both Ivor and I went to secondary schools a fair journey from home. That meant getting up at about 6.30 a.m. in my case to get the Tube from Dollis Hill to Stanmore (on the Jubilee Line) to catch the 8 a.m. coach to school. Generally, Colin and Sarah did not rise from their beds to help with this. Instead, Ivor, who had his own journey to make to a different school, would be up with me and making breakfast for the two of us. When I think about my early life, most of the joy I can remember involves being with my brothers. The madness of our house was much mediated by that. Even in the earliest photos of us, it feels to me like I'm looking to him for guidance, for comfort, for protection.

And later on, when we would have to deal with my father's dementia care, Ivor would be the more responsible one. He did more organizing, more sorting out of the complex bureaucracy of care. He was the parent. Still now: recently he told me someone had asked him what he felt when I first became well known, and he said 'protective'.

I have the weird advantage, because I work on TV, of seeing the effect of this in action. By which I mean, when I see myself on the screen, I'm always struck by – beyond just looking like him – how much my mannerisms, my voice, my way of being, are a version of Ivor's. I am much more like Ivor than I am like either of my parents. This would be true, I think, of a lot of brothers as regards their older brother, but sibling influence is still a lesser-considered aspect of personality.

Anyway, I have much to thank him for, which is why this book is dedicated to him.

Having said that, one time when we were about ten and eight, Ivor and I were playing football in Gladstone Park and some hard kids came up and asked him if they could throw me into some holly bushes. And he said yes. So, in terms of craziness and neglect, maybe he was influenced by my actual parents as well.

The Masters

I've mentioned already the unsurprising information that I have spent a considerable amount of time in therapy. While there, I was always saying to my therapist that it was difficult to find a template for my type of childhood trauma. Within its wide and varied spectrum of psychological modelling, psychoanalysis has never, I think, alighted upon anything quite so specific. Neither Freud nor Jung nor even R.D. Laing seem to have encountered a case study that led any of them to name a series of later neurotic issues as, say, a Nick Faldo Complex.

Or to put it another way: the writing of a story about a boundary-less mother who flaunted her infidelity in front of all and sundry, including her children, might suggest an intense and difficult drama, but frankly, the gravitas of that tone is scuppered the moment you have to include the phrase 'golfing memorabilia'. I think one must accept that whatever damage was caused by all this, it is in the end a comedy.

You can't extract the golf from the story. You can't even extract it from the sex. I don't know if my mother slept with David White at our house in Dollis Hill – I'm fairly sure she did – but one thing I *am* sure is that intimate encounters between them occurred at various golf memorabilia fairs up and down the country, backgrounded by antique tees and postcards of St Andrews and black and white flick books of Bobby Jones' swing.

There would also have been romantic opportunities provided by big golf sporting events, and I do have direct evidence that my mother and David White took that opportunity at least once. In the mid-1990s my father visited me at the flat I was then sharing with Frank Skinner. My mum was away, and my dad had brought over a card that, he said, she'd left on her desk for me. Well. On the envelope it said *David*.

I opened the card. It had a golf scene on it. I thought nothing of that, my mother often wrote me cards and notes on stationery inscribed with golfing images.* Inside was a short message. I read it out, with my father standing in front of me. It said:

> To David,
> In Memory of the Masters,
> when you were my master . . .
> Love
> Sarah xxx

Now, many years later, it's hard to say when exactly in the reading of this card I realized it wasn't for me: that I was not the David to whom it was addressed. When, that is, it became clear to me that what I was reading, out loud in front of my father, was a love note for David White, a back reference to a torrid time he and my mother must have spent together while watching a major golf tournament in the United States. Probably round about the words 'the Masters'. But by then it was too late.

---

* I'm not entirely sure she had any non-golfing cards and stationery.

My father said: 'What does that mean?'

I have talked already in this book about my almost physical commitment to the truth. But even I had to tamp it down in this moment. *In Memory of the Masters, when you were my master.* It's got a very strong suggestion that the adultery in question involved not just golf but BDSM. Perhaps it was both. Perhaps my mother and David White consummated their love in latex plus-fours and Pringle gimp masks. It was just too much to countenance.

So I just said, 'I don't know.' 'I have no idea what it means,' I said. Which is weak, but to be fair even if I *was*, say, Boris Johnson, I have no idea what lie I could've told to make what my mum had written make sense, if it had been written to me.*

One thing to note, again – my father said my mother had left this note on her desk. But she did not have a study. There was a writing desk of sorts, an antique one, in the telly room at 43 Kendal Road, and when I lived there no one used it, but latterly she may have claimed it as her desk. But it would not, my point is, have been behind any actual closed door. My dad

---

* This could only have gone badly. This could only have gone, for example, like:

> DAVID: I think . . . um . . . it's a reference to my time at school . . . when I had some teachers who I called Masters . . .
> COLIN: Right. OK. But why is she calling *you* her master?
> DAVID: Well, when I was at school, I wasn't a Mr, was I? I was young. So I was . . . Master David Baddiel.
> COLIN: Right. But why is she writing you a card in memory of . . . that?
> FRANK: OH, FOR FUCK'S SAKE, COLIN, IT'S NOT THIS DAVID, IT'S TO DAVID WHITE, THE GOLFING MEMORABILIA GUY SHE'S BEEN HAVING AN AFFAIR WITH FOR ABOUT TWENTY YEARS!

I've given that line to Frank because, in my memory, I could tell from his face *he* knew what the line meant. I think my mum had told him all about it.

could've wandered in at any time and seen an envelope, in her handwriting, marked David.

Whether this suggests that my mother, again, subconsciously, or not very subconsciously, wanted everyone, including my dad, to know about her love life, or whether this was genuinely absent-minded, I can't quite call. It's possible the truth is somewhere in-between, that the affair had become such an open secret in her own mind by then that any kind of caution had faded. But I do know something, which is that my dad said, on my reading out that card, what does that mean? Which shows that despite her shouting it from the rooftops, he *didn't* straightforwardly know about my mother's affair.

Colin

The flip-side of what I'm calling (no doubt annoyingly – no doubt it will read to some like those people on *Big Brother* who used to say stuff like 'The thing about me is that I just tell people how it is, take me or leave me') my impulse to always tell the truth is, I think, an acute lack of judgey-ness. It is my belief that all human beings are deeply flawed, and what they present to the world, particularly now that social media has offered them the chance microscopically to curate who they are, tends to airbrush out those flaws. Which is a pity, as it is through flaws that you get to see who the person really is. It's a cliché, but a beautiful and true one from Leonard Cohen: the crack is where the light gets in.

So it should be clear. I don't judge my mother for having an affair. And I don't just mean that I think – which I do – that a combination of trauma in her childhood and emotional arrest on the part of her husband need to be factored into why she did. I mean that in considering anyone's history, the things they did that are 'bad' – at variance with how they ought to behave, that is, as good citizens, parents, mothers, whatever – are a source of fascination, perhaps even of celebration, if what you're interested in is their humanity.

This always felt natural to me, but I notice nonetheless that people who came to see *My Family: Not the Sitcom* were some-times shocked that a son could speak so freely about his mother's unconventional sexual history. Similarly, some people were taken aback by my handling of the topic of my father's dementia. The notion of this being shameful strikes me as being even less easy to comprehend than the idea of my mother's infidelity being so. But I have spoken to people who have told me that, yes, they felt ashamed about a parent having dementia. In one case, a close friend explained that this was because they had, before he got the disease, put their father on a pedestal, and could not bear to see him so reduced. Which made me wonder if my lack of shame about my parents, whether it be related to their sex lives or their decrepitude or anything else, is linked to the fact that I never idealized them to begin with. They always seemed, or at least for as long as I could remember, entirely flawed human beings. Or to put it another way, entirely human human-beings.

Another element of this story some might find problematic would be the notion that I am revealing my father as a cuckold – to use an absurdly medieval word. Again, it would never occur to me to judge him for this. I have been cuckolded – honestly, am I in 'The Miller's Tale' here? – and, even though I suppose men who are themselves medieval will jeer about how much that makes you, in Panto Male World, a loser, indeed, a cuck, like much in human relations, it's not always that straightforward. I am very bad at breaking up with people, so when one of my girlfriends who I'd been with too long had an affair, I was *overjoyed* about it.

But the imaginative associations which spring from cuckold – of a nervous, emasculated, put-upon man – didn't fit my father. Who my father was, in fact, is to some extent best expressed by talking about his dementia. In 2011, he was diagnosed with Pick's disease, a type of frontal lobe dementia. I went with him, and my mother, to University College Hospital, to meet with a geriatric neurologist. After giving the diagnosis, he took me and my mum aside and explained that the symptoms of Pick's disease include, along with short-term memory loss, irritability, sexual disinhibition, rudeness, inappropriate behaviours, swearing and extreme impatience.

I said: 'Sorry – does he have a disease, or have you just *met* him?'

Because Colin Baddiel had always been exactly like that. When he first met Morwenna, it was at my mum's sixtieth birthday party. He opened the door to us and growled: 'You couple of cunts are late.' I pride myself, as you will know, on being always very me but even I am not as me as Colin Baddiel was Colin Baddiel. If Roger Mellie from *Viz* had been Welsh and a bit *more* aggressive – that was my father. This was a man who once, on a family holiday to Devon, farted so badly in an antiques shop, we had to leave the shop. When we returned later in the afternoon, the shop was shut: and the owner had been taken to hospital.

Soon after he was first diagnosed, I remember meeting a woman called Joyce, who'd known my dad since she was a child.* When I told her he had dementia, she said: 'I'm sorry to hear that your father is no longer inside himself.' It's a beautiful thing to say, but not entirely accurate, or at any rate, not in the way I think Joyce meant. What the Pick's disease did is make one side of him – obscenity-loving, eager-to-shock, aggressive-jokey – grow like a malignant lesion, at the expense of other elements of his personality. But it had always been his dominant voice. My father was indeed no longer inside himself: he was *outside* himself. He, his profound he-ness, became unrestricted, exploded, all over the place.

This may be true of mental illness in general. Various members of my family have had what I believe are now called episodes – I sense you're not surprised – and I've noticed that the way these play out does not usually involve the person behaving out of character. Rather it often seems as if they are *extremely* in character, *overmuch* in character. While a breakdown can be a dismantling of personality, it can also be something close to an overdose of personality. Similarly, with my father. The dementia, while diminishing many parts of him, lifted whatever inhibitory mechanism had kept his most basic self at least a bit in check, to create of him a kind of Ur-Colin, a toxic distillation of who he was.

So, the Pick's disease did not, as dementia is thought to do, rob us of who he was, but the opposite. It turned the volume up on who he was. In my mind, he did not have Pick's disease, he had Colin Baddiel's disease.

. . .

---

* She also told me that my father's penis was the first one she ever saw – don't worry – she followed him into the toilet when she was four and he was five.

Even in a house with three boys, with so much testosterone, Colin was always going to be the most male. My sense of my dad when I was young was that he pushed the category of male into something approaching that of animal. He would sometimes sleep on the floor, stretched out in contorted shapes in the middle of a weekend afternoon on the front room carpet. He had so much thick dark hair in his nostrils I found it confusing how he could possibly breathe. And he would sneeze so loudly – never *achoo!* always *A-HOO!* – it would frighten us children every time like a horror film jump scare. Once, he came in from washing the car on a cold day with a line of unnoticed snot hanging from his nostrils so long it reached down, pendulum-like, to his trousers.

His affection – real – for us was never soft: it was conveyed only in football, play-fighting and, latterly, swearing. For my father, calling me or my brothers 'wankers' was a term of affection. Once at a football match, he turned to me and said, of Ivor, who was innocently watching the game, 'He's such a pudding-face goon.' Which, despite my deep love for my brother, really made me laugh. Much, much more than me – his son who, absurdly, would come to be seen as a standard bearer for a mainly bogus phenomenon called Laddism – my father was a superlad. Well before it was a word in common currency, he was all about the bantz.

My dad came from a working-class area of Swansea and ended up with a PhD in biochemistry from Imperial College London. In 1961, before most of the world had even heard of it, he made LSD in his lab and took four times the normal dose. Which is probably why he got dementia.

We three brothers were told this by our parents, I remember, when in our early teens. I think it was designed to ward us off the dangers of drugs. My dad said that when he took LSD he saw his brain appearing in front of him, but giant, and with parts whirring, like an enormous organic grey watermill. He didn't use those exact words but that's the picture he was painting, and I remember just thinking: That sounds *brilliant* – must try drugs asap.

My mother, incidentally, joined in this small meeting of the Dollis Hill branch of Narcotics Not Very Anonymous, telling us she had taken mescaline in her twenties, provided by my dad, from his laboratory. It appears at the time he was a British-Jewish prototype of Walter White – *Breaking Baddiel*, perhaps – but her visions had been all about the Nazis. She said she was able to see her room as it had been in Königsberg when she was a baby. She could see the Gestapo coming in and smashing it up. In a very my mother way, she didn't just consider this a drug-induced hallucination. She told us she'd rung her mother and described the room she saw while under the influence of mescaline and Otti had confirmed that it was exactly as it would've been in 1939.

Which is impossible. It means that when she was about two months old my mum had taken in her surroundings and somehow imprinted them into her subconscious, where they had stayed for about twenty years, before being excavated via the Indiana Jones of mescaline. I know a lot of New Age people do believe we have a form of memory retention from very early on, possibly even in the womb, but those people are – how can I put this? – wrong.

It was very my mother though, again, as with the story about Arno being her real dad, to somehow glamorize her back story like this. The truth of her – of my – family's degradation, disenfranchisement and traumatization in Germany was too impossible for her to process. And so, if her subconscious did anything at all under the influence of mescaline, it would've not revealed any real memory but instead created a new one: it would have made things more bearable. I know this because by that time, in 1939, my grandparents had lost everything and were living hand to mouth and I doubt very much they would have had a separate room for the baby.

By the way, they told all this not just to us, but also to Julian Cope:

I'd known Colin and Sarah since 1984, and we'd sit and talk for hours. They once told me of their experiences as LSD guinea-pigs in 1959. Sarah said she had regressed to her time in '30s Germany and had totally freaked out. Whoa, I was impressed and freaked out myself. I'd recently refused to be interviewed for a BBC documentary about LSD and here were two lucid middle-aged people putting a real perspective on it.

Despite his dabbling with drugs, my father was not a hippy. He was not possessed of much in the way of peace, love and understanding. And he was not a reconstructed man.

Once, when I was about twelve watching TV on the sofa, I put my head on his shoulder. I remember doing this with some trepidation, knowing it wasn't something I normally did. My dad looked at me and said, sarcastically, in a camp voice: 'Oh, I didn't know you cared.' He responded, in other words, to me, his son, putting my head on his shoulder, with the suggestion that that was a bit gay (and that being gay was something to be made fun of).

This, incidentally, in all the things I'm writing about my parents here, is the only time I have felt genuinely damaged by something they did. I mean, I'm sure all the over-broadcast infidelity and the shouting and the lack of niceties and the strange takes on the Nazi past and of course the bloody golf took some sort of toll, but the point of this book, in a way, is to celebrate all that. Because, for better or worse – and as someone who likes to avoid clichés, sorry about this next phrase – it has made me the man I am. And I am absurdly comfortable in my own skin. My own skin may not be of the best – without doubt the skin itself isn't – but the flaws and cracks are intrinsic to my me-ness, and therefore I have no reason to complain of what led to them. I wouldn't even class them as damage, more accidental sculpture. This is what makes this book different from, say, *Spare*.

This moment, though, when I think of it, makes me feel . . . shit. The twelve-year-old me felt – feels – deeply humiliated. Because I remember how much I wanted to show him some affection – partly because I just did, but I think possibly also because I'd understood at that age that sons, somewhere, even in the 1970s, did do things like putting their heads on their fathers' shoulders, even if none of us had ever done it at 43 Kendal Road – and his response was crushing. Even though I am a comedian, and stupidly committed to comedy, it was an early experience of how much a joke at your expense, particularly one made by someone you love, can reduce your soul to ash.

Plus, it did make me anxious about showing physical affection to my father in future. In fact, in perpetuity: for some time after, I was worried that on his deathbed, I might be prevented from holding my dad's hand as he slipped away by the fear he might at any point open his eyes and go, 'Oo, hello sailor!'

· · ·

My dad's PhD, written in his early twenties, is called 'A Study of the Gaseous Reaction Between Chlorine Trifluoride and Paraffin Hydrocarbons'. It's, if you don't know anything about chemistry, unreadable. Here's the abstract:

> This thesis describes a study of the gaseous reaction between chlorine trifluoride and paraffin hydrocarbons (mainly methane) and an attempt has been made to elucidate the mechanism of fluorination of hydrocarbons by this inter-halogen.
>
> The first section of the thesis describes briefly the various ways of introducing fluorine into to an organic molecule. Thus an account is given, in chronological order, of the principal work in the field of direct gaseous fluorination. This includes homogeneous and heterogeneous reactions of both aromatic and aliphatic hydrocarbons and the researches of the main workers in this field have been discussed . . .

Well done if you got through more than a sentence of that. One person who could, however, was my dad. Here he is doing so:

You may think, Well, obviously your dad could read it, but I will add that this photo was taken about a year before he died, when he was deep into dementia. It's one of the curious things about the disease that certain types of high cognitive ability persist long after most of the much smaller everyday ones that get us through the day have gone. Similarly, at a time when he didn't know who I was, he could still beat me at chess. The poignant and sad thing is that I'd often give him his PhD to read, as he always seemed interested and engaged in reading it, but he would also always say, after a few minutes turning the pages, 'Who wrote this?' I once showed him his name on the title page, and he just looked confused and upset. So I never did that again.

My dad's ideas about what was and wasn't important intellectually – which ruled the roost in our house – were pretty inflexible. As far as he was concerned, if you couldn't prove something scientifically, it wasn't worth talking about. He wasn't much given to reading us bedtime stories, or helping us with our primary school Hebrew homework, but he did have a packet of flash cards based on the periodic table, which he encouraged – that is a downplaying of his style: the word *browbeat* may be more accurate – us into memorizing. Each was a different element, and he'd hold the cards and say, 'Right. Lead?', and we would have to say what the chemical symbol was – Pb (it's still in there) – and how many electrons and protons lead has, and its other properties, as far as we could remember. He wouldn't, if we failed to get these facts right, beat us Dickensically (not a word), but would look very irritated, and even though he always looked irritated, it would still be obvious our ineptitude had made him more so.

Chemistry permeated the minutiae of the house. When

asking for the salt at the dinner table, my dad wouldn't say pass the salt, but pass the nackle. There's something very indicative of who he was in that detail: NaCl is the chemical symbol for sodium chloride but it's also a word hovering somewhere between knackered and tackle – even when being scholarly (perhaps *because* of being scholarly, and the sense of effete intellectualism it implies), my dad always needed to include a dash of sweariness, of overt joshing maleness.

It was expected therefore that all three of us would be scientists. Ivor drunk the Colin Kool-Aid completely, and did chemistry, physics and maths A-levels. He will not – well, I've asked him in advance – mind me telling you this didn't work out brilliantly: he got two Ds and an E (and is now a successful comedy writer, obvs). I was going the same way. Parents – if they are as big characters and as primary colours in their thinking as mine – can impose a very intense false consciousness on their children. I was a teenager who regularly got As for English, history and other humanities, and Cs and Ds for chemistry, physics and maths – and yet still, because of the intellectual default imposed by my dad, was going to choose chemistry, physics and maths as my A-level subjects right up until the last minute. I only didn't do that after a teacher, whose name I don't remember – poor, given that this man has been crucial in my life, and in the biopic would be played by Dustin Hoffman – took me aside and pointed out that this pattern of achievement on my school reports maybe revealed which end of the intellectual spectrum my brain was best suited for.

It also demonstrates the disconnect we had at home. We were at least in one respect a very traditional Jewish/immigrant aspirational family: focused on educational achievement, specifically on reports. It was a big deal when we bought ours home, particularly for my mother, who would comb through them for As, nod at Bs, and look pained at every C and below. But not pained enough to say 'Hold on, Dai,* based on my endless scouring of these reports – and frankly, I could be looking at them much less microscopically and still notice this – you seem to be choosing completely the wrong subjects.'

More disconnect – or frankly, just a very good example of how at this point in the 1970s the word *parenting* was not a word, or at least not for my parents – is illustrated by the moment I finally followed Teacher Mr X's advice and told my dad I was going to do arts subjects for A-levels. It took me a while to build up to it. As I have said, our dad never hit us, he was never physically violent. But I feared his temper, none-theless. We were all scared of it. When I say he was irritated all the time, this implies something niggly, tetchy, frustrated. My father's anger was louder, fiercer than that. His irritation always carried with it a sense of genuine rage. In a way my dad, like my mum, may have anticipated social media, in that everything – *everything* – made him go from 0–100 in angry shoutiness.

Certainly, at this age, around fourteen or fifteen, approaching his looming back as he sat at the breakfast room† table to tell

---

* This is what my mum called me most often. It wasn't the Welsh pronun-ciation. I should probably have spelled it Day, but that looks to me like a surname. She called me this, and sometimes the Day of Days. She also sometimes called me the Jam in her sandwich, meaning that I was the middle son of three. Which does somewhat position the other two as the less exciting two bits of bread. I don't know how they ever felt about that.
† We didn't have a room specially given over to breakfast. We had a little kitchen with a room off it which would be for most people I guess called a dining room, but for some reason – I mean we did eat this meal in here as well – the breakfast room.

him my further education plans, I was frightened of that shou-tiness. I screwed my courage as best I could to whatever fragile sticking posts I had and told him my intended A-level subjects. He didn't shout. He stayed sat at the table, looking into the middle distance. And then he said: 'It's a waste of a brain.'

So as I say: not great parenting. Not 'you're my child, follow your dreams, fly, my pretty, fly!' Uh-uh. *It's a waste of a brain.* And I guess I showed him, didn't I? By ending up as a big successful writer/comedian guy. Except: I spend all my time now reading science books, endlessly trying to understand the mysteries of quantum physics. Which is partly because as I get older that's the only route I have as an atheist to feeling like I'm getting close to an actual understanding of the mystery and meaning of life – or the granular reality of it, anyway. But I think also it's a return of the repressed. I think I may as a youth have rebelled against Dr Colin Baddiel, PhD, by taking a different intellectual path, but in truth, I always, and very much now, think and thought of science as where the true cerebral work is done. Colin Baddiel settled that idea in me very young and even though I didn't follow him into the lab (because I couldn't), I basically think that what I've done in my career, including now, writing this book, as far as proper brain labour goes, is namby-pamby winging it.

In fact, science didn't really work out for Colin Baddiel either. He had hopes of doing something amazing in research and may well have had the aptitude for it, but circumstances, including having three children in his twenties, meant he took a middle management job at Unilever, running a laboratory in Isleworth. Which may not sound too much like giving up on your science dreams, except the laboratory's job was to test rival companies' products, using mass spectrometry.* That may still not sound too much like giving up on your science dreams, except that the products concerned were shampoos and deodorants. It did at least mean that in all the time I lived at home, I don't think we ever had to buy any shampoos or deodorants. We just had a series of mysteriously unbranded cans and bottles marked 'Project 54' or similar.

When Colin Baddiel was in his early forties, Unilever closed the Isleworth lab. They offered him another job but in Port Sunlight in Liverpool. At the time – me, Ivor and Dan were all teenagers by then, and all our friends were in London – no one wanted to go. Now, I wonder if it might in fact have been interesting. We didn't have the internet then, so it wasn't possible as it is now to google and discover that Unilever in 1928, in Port Sunlight, had created around its plant a utopian idea of a workers' village.

Instead of going to Liverpool, Colin took voluntary redundancy. I think he assumed he'd get another job in science quickly, given that he had a PhD in chemistry, but he reckoned without him being my dad: without, that is, being someone who would be rude and truculent in interviews and didn't own one reasonably smart suit. Two years later, he was still unemployed. During this period, he – both my parents, but mainly Colin – became completely obsessed with money, in the sense of not spending any. This is not unreasonable, given his

---

* In all the time his lab was doing this, and despite the many times he explained it to me, I still don't really know what that is. As far as I can make out, it basically involves, like, putting a bit of the other product on a piece of . . . I dunno . . . I want to say blotting paper? And then looking at the layers it makes as it separates out really, really closely. Yeah. That's it.

circumstances, but to be honest, that was the default at 43 Kendal Road even when my dad *did* have a salaried job. And indeed before: after he died, his one-time best friend Lionel,* whom I'm named after – David Lionel Baddiel is my full name – told Ivor and me some stories about our father we didn't know, including that our parents had gone to stay at Lionel's house in Thornbury *for their honeymoon*. Perhaps this clarifies what I was saying earlier about how my mother might have felt she'd missed out on her glamorous phantom parallel-universe life in Germany.

But it – Colin's miserliness – went into overdrive when he lost his job. Throughout the early eighties, my father would go apeshit if anyone left a light on anywhere in the house. He wouldn't let us have friends back in case they, and I quote, ate some toast.

Some of this anxiety about money I now see as related to his background. My dad's dad, Henry Baddiel, was a tinker: he sold cloth in Swansea from door to door. He and my grand-mother Sylvia lived in a terraced house with an outside toilet. My dad had a twin brother, George, who died in childhood. Sylvia (a woman, like my mother, of some thwarted ambition: she was a brilliant classical pianist, having spent a year at the Royal Academy of Music before marrying Henry and, I always got a sense somewhat bitterly, departing London for Swansea) once told us the story about how my dad cycled back from school waving the results that meant he'd got into university,

---

* They fell out at some point in the mid-eighties, when Lionel sold him an Austin Princess for three hundred quid which a month later turned out to have a crack in the engine. They had a big fight, Lionel refused to return the money, and my father didn't speak to him for forty years; meanwhile, I'm still stuck with the terrible fucking middle name.

and she cried while telling it, perhaps because she was just sad that time had passed, but also I think because she was remembering the force of that scene, of a moment that meant her son would not be spending his life scraping to exist just above the bread line. As she cried, my dad was doing a lot of raising his eyes to heaven and saying, 'Yes, yes, we've heard it all before', because the story of his own escape from poverty was also aggravation.

But even given that time creates in me a sense of forgiveness I didn't have as a teenager, when frankly I was just pissed off I couldn't have friends back in case they ate some toast, my father was at this point in time properly mental about money. Which is what makes his interaction with Michael Barrymore even more startling.

Dinky Toys

Having given up trying to get employment in science, Colin decided to make his hobby, collecting Dinky Toys, into his job. Dinky Toys – and Corgi toys, and Matchbox toys, and tin-plate toys – preceded golf memorabilia in our house. Before they had to share space on our shelves with ceramics of 1920s lady golfers and the like, the toys were the only ornaments we had.

I was a little bit of a collector myself when I was young. A very exciting element of my childhood involved going to swap meets. Swap meets were events held normally in village halls or aircraft hangars or fields in places like Bishop's Stortford, where toy collectors would come from far and wide to exchange and sell their wares. My dad would set out a trestle table with his toys on it. Here is a photo of us at a swap meet. I remember that I thought the way I was wearing that hat was very cool: hence the very cool face I am making.

Around 1983, after it became clear that no one was going to offer him a new job in science, my dad suddenly decided the career possibilities offered by Dinky Toys were just too inviting to turn down, and that became his business. He opened a stall at Grays. Here's a photo of my dad's stall that he took himself. I assume he was thinking only about getting a good photo of his stall, because I'd say he misses something fairly obvious that was going on in front of it.

Anyway: Michael Barrymore. One day, the at-the-time very

Dinky Toys

popular TV entertainer – who collects Dinky Toys – came to the stall. He bought a few things but said he would come back for more. My dad – who never watched much TV besides *The World at War*, and football – had no idea who he was, but another stall holder, Pete McGasky – who my dad invariably called Pete McGhastly – informed him that this last customer was a very big star. So that night my dad had a watch of the Barrymore-hosted hit ITV game show *Strike It Lucky*. A few weeks later Michael came back, ready to buy some Dinky Toys in bulk. My dad nodded at him, and said:

'Oh hello, I watched your show. It was shit.'

I've never worked in retail, but that seems (particularly coming from a man desperate at that time to keep his income stream flowing) not a great bit of sales technique.

Meanwhile, some people believe this is when it first all started to go wrong for Michael Barrymore.

Sidebar: I told this story to a famous comedian friend of mine on the day before my dad's funeral, and he – himself not a man known for politesse – said: 'Was your dad a fucking arse-hole, then?' Which was quite a thing to say given my father had died two days earlier, but my friend had a point: such direct rudeness is funny in the telling but, being myself someone who has been subject to people who think they can just say 'you're shit' in various ways to your face, it isn't that much fun. But then again, I have bumped into Michael Barrymore a few times at comedy events and he often used to speak fondly about my dad and his Dinky Toy stall at Grays. So either my dad didn't actually say it, or Michael generously forgave him, or, most likely, took the whole thing as a joke.

· · ·

One other story perhaps worth telling about my dad's Dinky Toys – and one that also ended up intersecting with my weird relationship to fame – involves my uselessness. Since I've done many different things, people say many different things when they meet me – primarily 'Is it coming home?', but also 'I'm a Jew that does count!' and sometimes, even, still 'That's you that is', although obviously, these days, shakily – and in among them recently has been a new one: 'Are you actually like you seemed to be on *Taskmaster*?' For those who don't know, *Taskmaster* is Alex Horne's and Greg Davies' very funny show that used to be on Dave and is now on Channel 4, in which comedians compete against each other performing surreal tasks. After my series of *Taskmaster* went out, Morwenna, who'd been nervous about me doing the show, was pleased. She was pleased because at last the world had been given a demonstration of what she has to live with. I think she thinks – perhaps not incorrectly – that because I am thought of (by some) as brainy, that therefore people are surprised to discover I am in fact an idiot. But I am. I am a man of intense – well, the word isn't really impracticality. It's more that in my day to day I go at life at quite an odd angle and end up in a lot of absurd scrapes. This is because I don't stop to think about how to deal with . . . stuff, and it's related to my lack of a filter. I say, when asked something, or when I'm speaking on stage, whatever is in my head. Similarly, in my life, I often do whatever is in my head. I am a first responder. Not in the sense of being helpful at the scene of an accident, but in the sense of responding to stimuli, whatever it might be, with whatever is my first instinct.

Which is why on *Taskmaster*, when, for example, the task was to lasso Alex Horne from some distance, it seemed to me a good idea to tie wooden spoons to the rope. In order – still seems obvious to me, tbh – to firm up the lasso so it became a bit more like a discus. (It didn't work.) Sometimes, I get snagged by the first thought, like when the requirement was to order some ice lollies into a rainbow spectrum while blindfold, and my instinct was that the best way to work out what flavours they were without the sense of sight was to smell them – to the point where Alex Horne had to say, 'Is there maybe another way . . . using *another* sense . . . that you might be able to work out what flavours the ice lollies are?' There were many other examples. At the end of the series, I came resoundingly last. Greg Davies perhaps summed up what I'm trying to say here when he said he felt for me, as, like all the other contestants, I had to do the sometimes-difficult tasks but, in my case, I had the added difficulty of 'being David Baddiel'.

Anyway, this un-useful way of being was in place very early on, as can be seen in the incident of Gavin Pryde's dad's toys. Gavin Pryde was in my year at school. He had found out that my dad collected Dinky Toys and so came up to me one day and said *his* dad had some toys and would my dad value them – maybe, he could even offer for them. I said yes: because I thought that perhaps Mr Pryde's toys *would* be amazingly collectable, and my dad would be grateful to me for finding them. The next day, Gavin handed me the toys, wrapped in a tea towel. He was, I remember, hushed as he did so. He stressed that they meant a lot to his dad and I should be very careful with them. I nodded, excited that this level of reverence might mean my father, someone who in the normal course of events was irritated with me, would be pleased and happy I'd found these amazing toys.

Except I didn't find them. I lost them.

I'm still not entirely sure how this happened. What I remember is that I had a locker at school and I put the toys in there, at lunchtime, to take home that night. When I came back to the locker at home time, the toys had gone. And the terrible thing is, I am sure no one broke into my locker (not least because it was locked) to steal them. I think something . . . just distracted me while I was supposed to be storing the toys, and I put the heavy tea towel bulky with models on top of the lockers and forgot about it. Which meant I left some toys out, in a boys' school, and they were taken, probably by a boy who thought, not unreasonably, they had just been left out for the taking.

I never found out who this was. I asked around, depressed and anxious, but the toys were lost. The next day, I had to tell Gavin. And I can still remember, with a cold stab of awfulness, his face. Not just that he was pissed off and worried what his dad was going to say and all the other obvious reactions. No. I could read in his eyes an assumption. Which was that what had actually happened – because no one, surely, could be enough of an idiot to mislay these precious toys – was that I had gone home with them, and that my dad had said, 'Hey – these are worth a *fortune*! I know! Just tell him you *lost* them and we'll split the proceeds!' Which, of course, was absurd. My dad would never have split the proceeds.

I felt terrible about it. But twenty years later, I did *This Morning with Richard and Judy*.

I went on *This Morning* – which in the nineties was hosted by Richard Madeley and his wife Judy Finnigan – a number of times. The first time I went on this conversation happened:

RICHARD: This New Lad thing that's associated with you
    – that pisses you off, doesn't it?
ME: Richard, I can't believe you've said the word piss.
JUDY: Yes. I think you should apologize.

Dinky Toys

RICHARD: So sorry, David.

JUDY: Not to him, to the viewers!

But Richard and Judy, despite the odd Partridgean moment like this, did their research. Which is why they also asked about my dad collecting and selling Dinky Toys, and next thing you know, I'd told them the Gavin Pryde story. I think I turned to camera and said, 'If you're out there, Gavin, I'm sorry.'

About two years later, I was on *This Morning* again. About halfway through the interview, Judy said: 'We've got a surprise for you.' In the studio, they cut to a live link to Mallorca, and there, sitting on a deckchair in what looked like a lovely villa, was Gavin Pryde. They'd found him. And Gavin, tanned, sunny and happy, said he forgave me.

It is, perhaps, a remarkable example of the ability of fame to heal. Because I very much doubt if I'd got in touch with Gavin Pryde in a more mundane way that he'd have been so forgiving. But having said that, I do remember saying to Gavin, across the oceans: 'I really did lose the toys.' And him clearly, while forgiving me, still not believing it.

Small coda: You may think: how could you have lost those toys? They were right in front of you. Well, I am astonishing at losing things. Literally as I write these words, I am in something of a state because this morning – I feel we know each other well enough now for me to tell you this – I had to collect a sample for a stool test. Let's not go into the details of that. Suffice to say I did it. I placed the sample in the small tube, then in a protective bag. And then mislaid it. Somewhere in my house. At the time of writing, it's still missing. Yes. I have literally lost my shit.

Irene and Stuart

Neither this book nor the stage show *My Family: Not the Sitcom* constitute the first time I have used my family as material. If you were to read my first novel *Time for Bed*, published in 1996, some of the characters may ring a bell:

> Talking about killing your own mother . . .
>
> 'Hi lover! How's things? I'm just glad we're able to touch base. I've been trying to dovetail things together with you and there just hasn't been the time, has there? The thing is what with the H.A.C. meeting and going up to Harrowgate for the aeronautical auction, I've been literally rushed off my feet. Quite literally.'
>
> 'WILL YOU FUCKING SHUT UP YOU STUPID CHATTERING OLD WANKBAG!'

That is a scene set in the house of the parents of the main character, a twenty-something waster – and insomniac – called Gabriel Jacoby. Perhaps you've spotted already that *Time for Bed* is something of a roman à clef. However, obviously, I made some very clever and profoundly obscuring changes to my parents. The mother is called not Sarah but Irene, and she is obsessed not with golf but the Hindenburg. She is president of the Hindenburg Appreciation Society, a group that meets regularly to talk about and eulogize every aspect of the famous German airship, apart from the fact that it crashed.

Irene and Stuart

I think I chose the Hindenburg because it tied into other parts of my world – the German-ness, tin toys – but also because it felt so violently random. Beyond that – let's be honest – I'm not really disguising anything much:

Everything my mother does is in some way Hindenburg-related. Her car number plate is LZ 129; the one band I was never allowed to bring any records of into the house was Led Zeppelin (check out their first album cover); she has a T-shirt – this is true – that says 'I heart The Hindenburg.' Combine all this with a tendency to overuse the phrases 'dovetail' and 'touch base': that's my mum.

Similarly, the way Irene talks about the Hindenburg, and the world of the Hindenburg Appreciation Society, is exactly how my mother used to talk about golf memorabilia. Or rather, how it felt to listen to my mother talking about golf memorabilia:

'I mean, the first thing I ever wrote was just a little piece in *Aviator's Weekly* about the aluminium piano in the starboard side saloon, and, I can promise you, Gabriel, I never thought that would lead to anything. But – it's amazing, really – it was that article that interested Joy, and next thing you know she was on the phone and I was starting work on *Lighter Than Air*. Well, as you know, Peter Blandham didn't like it at first . . .'

No, of course I didn't know. I don't know who the fuck Peter Blandham is. But this never stops Irene Jacoby. She has wrapped herself so warmly in her solipsistic cloak that she assumes everyone is born already intimate with her weird cast of Hindenburgabilia characters. Peter Blandham, Carrie

Rosenfield, Jeremy Elton, Derek – Derek I know so well we're just on first-name terms – Patsy White, Laurence St Hilaire, and the Tinderfields: names that pass on the conveyor belt of my mother's conversation like prizes on *The Generation Game* – you don't know where they've come from, or where they're going to, you just know you're supposed to remember them.

Meanwhile, my father is even more cleverly disguised:

My father shouts at her. That's all he does these days. He shouts at my mother. Alright, be fair: he doesn't just shout at her. He shouts and swears at her. And, to give him credit, he does comes up with some corking swearing. My father is the WBC (*Wanking Bastard Cunt*) Heavyweight Champion of Swearing. The appellation 'wankbag' is just at the beginning of his range. 'Cunthead', 'Tossturner', 'Fuckslob', 'Hairy Great Pudding-Face Arsewank' – thirty-two years with my mother has really stretched his linguistic invention.

It continues:

'Shush, Stuart.'
  'DON'T TELL ME TO FUCKING SHUSH, YOU INFURIATING SHITBASKET!!!'
  My mother laughs. It might seem strange, but I suppose it's the obvious defence, not only against being called a shitbasket, but also against facing up to thirty-two years down the shitbasket.
  'SHE'S LAUGHING! SHE'S BLOODY LAUGHING NOW, THE RIDIKALUS OLD BOLLOCK-WAGON!'

Irene and Stuart

My dad cannot pronounce the soft 'c' in ridiculous, perhaps because the whole idea of softness is alien to him, so it always comes out like this, ridikalus. He stomps off, happy, I think: expressed, fulfilled.

Reading it now, I'm almost taken aback by the detail: by how much Irene and Stuart are Sarah and Colin. My dad indeed pronounced ridiculous as 'ridikalus', and I did indeed always think of this as another example of his lack of softness, although it may also just have been down to his Welsh accent.

I notice something else reading it, which is a lack of empathy. Some of it feels, now, powered by the coldness of youth. And while I do agree with Nora Ephron that everything is copy, I think the sliver of ice in my heart has thawed since I was younger. Or at least: I think, keen as I remain to tell the truth, the whole truth and nothing but the truth about my parents, and certain as I remain that at heart that truth is comic, the laughter I wish to generate is of a different kind now. If you were to buy and read – please, don't let me stop you – *Time for Bed*, as a sort of spin-off to this book, I'm fairly sure you would not find the portrayal of the Sarah and Colin stand-ins entirely heartless – let me not review my own novel, but hey, there's depth and pathos and all sorts later on – but it is written with a remarkable lack of any sense that my parents might at some point read it.

How puzzling that I am more compassionate to them now in this book, which they can't read. Ah well. I am talking here principally about my mother. I don't think my dad would've been bothered by the depiction of him as a swearing machine, and I'm sure not by the portrayal of their marriage. Also, I was pretty sure when I was writing it that he *wasn't* going to read it, as he didn't read novels and was, as ever, deeply incurious about most of my work.

However, my mum did read it. I know this because she told Ivor she thought it was 'shit'. Which at the time upset me, but I now think is fair enough. I now think I should have had it as a blurb on the back of the book, underneath Roddy Doyle's 'Very, very funny'. 'Shit' Sarah Baddiel.

Some people are born with an abundance of empathy – Morwenna was – but lots of us must learn it. I notice from social media that the fundamental issue with trolling, or indeed with people who do not consider themselves trolls but are still happy to scold or 'pile on' to others in the name of a cause, is a lack of empathy. Graham Greene said that hate is 'just a failure of imagination' and he was right: it's the inability to imagine how that hate impacts on the other, that the person being attacked is a human being. I was the same when I started doing stand-up, and indeed when I was first on TV. There was a sketch on *The Mary Whitehouse Experience* in which Rob Newman and I outlined a way of getting round swearing by replacing the c-word with the words 'Henry Kelly', the then presenter of *Going for Gold* and *Game for a Laugh.* That got a laugh and we thought no more about it. Many years later, I saw Henry Kelly in a pub, and felt, despite my genetic aversion to it, ashamed, but the shame isn't the point. I realised the obvious truth that he was a real person with real feelings, and I would not, of course, have gone up to him in that pub and called him a cunt, and therefore should not have done so on TV.

You might have thought the noticing of the humanity of those closest to you would be taken for granted, but conversely, perhaps that's the easiest to slip by. I appeared on the first series of the light entertainment show *Room 101*, presented by Nick Hancock, in which guests put into said room things they couldn't stand. If you want an example of how doing a show like that doesn't occur in a vacuum, I put in the very good Liverpudlian actress Margi Clarke – again, I now think completely unfairly – and soon after, her brother threatened to beat up both me and Nick Hancock. To be fair to me, I also put in this photograph.

Which was taken on the day of my bar mitzvah. There are obviously many things that make this image worthy of a prime placement in my personal Room 101, but the key one is: I know that chair is not garden furniture. Someone – I suspect my mother, as obviously we were not a family who would have  employed a professional photographer for this event – has *brought that chair out of the house for me to stand like that.* The horror, the horror.

But more on point for this book, I also put in golf memorabilia. The way I did it was by talking about how much I disliked golf and the fact that I had a personal reason for this. Nick then showed a clip of someone talking about how they'd spent over £2,000 on a golf ball. A someone who he then revealed to be my mother.

I didn't go into the whole David White thing. I presented the golf obsession as just some random craziness that my mother had one day decided to devote her life to. 'She's just mental,' I believe I said. I don't think I ever checked in advance with her about this. If you actually watch it – it's available on obscure parts of the internet – it is all said with affection, in the tradition of 'I've got a mad mum' comedy. But still. The day after *Room 101* went out, my mother came out of her house in Cambridge to discover her car like this:

Which, obviously, is awful. It's an object lesson, perhaps, in how things you say in public about actual people have consequences.

There are a few other things to note here. My mum didn't just take this lying down. She went to the *Cambridge Evening News* and got them to come round and take a picture, and they did a whole article about it. I think part of her thought it might be good advertising for Golfiana. Also, however horrible it is, it is still funny. It reminds me a little of the moment in *I'm Alan Partridge* where his car gets spray-painted with the words 'Cock Piss Partridge'. I also feel there's something comic about the fact that the light on the side of the bonnet acts as a full stop to the sentence Golf Is Crap.

But that funniness comes up hard against its actual impact. When I was first trying out *My Family: Not the Sitcom*, I included this picture, and it really didn't work. It just got a shocked silence. Because, I think, by the time I was doing that show I had evolved a way of talking about my mother that expanded rather than contracted her humanity. I was still – don't get me wrong – employing it for laughter, but in painting a much fuller picture of her, the audience felt informed, they felt they knew her and even as they were laughing, loved her. Therefore, this will have come across as hard and cruel and sad. Which now, I think it was.

Comedy

My dad may not have known who Michael Barrymore was, but nonetheless funniness was a big deal for him. Some of his bantz came in the form of catchphrases, endlessly, Tourette's-like, repeated. I remain uncertain how many were of his own invention, as opposed to stolen or re-modelled from *The Goons*. Among his favourites were: singing a version of the Victorian parlour ditty 'Just a Song at Twilight' that went 'Just a pong at twilight'; describing his watch as his 'ever wrong never right'; in response to one of us announcing, as we left, 'I'm off', always saying 'You've been off for years.'*

The nature of his catchphrases was often vaudevillian,

---

* Latterly, when he would come to our house, he would always say, as soon as Morwenna or I or one of our kids opened the door, 'Coffee, not instant', but I'm not sure this quite qualifies, as it was more of a request than a catchphrase, although said repeatedly enough to be both.

requiring his children to play the straight men. After a big lunch or dinner, he would sit back in his chair and say, 'I'm feeling almost human.' At which point, one of us would reply, 'Why aren't you *completely* human?' And he would say, 'Because then one of you buggers would be asking me for money.'

My father's sense of humour was . . . I want to say his only saving grace. That isn't quite true. Although graceless in many ways, he did in fact have a few saving graces. He was, by the standards of the time, a present father. He was protective. Once, when I was about eleven, a brick came through our front door (our front door, like many in the 1970s, had a central panel of frosted glass), and within seconds my dad was outside confronting the brick-thrower – not, it turned out, a neo-Nazi or skinhead targeting Jews, but a drunk bloke who'd had a row with his wife and mistaken our house for his own. I can remember my dad running out, shouting, 'What the fuck are you doing?' in a way that felt – well, that *was* – brave.

Also his sense of humour wasn't his saving grace, if by saving grace you mean it somehow redeemed his personality. It didn't, because it was entirely of a piece with the rest of him: old school, relentlessly male, thriving on the put-down, the jab and the comedy of insult. But it was funny. He was funny. Not only that, he put a lot of store by funny, on the value of funny.

We didn't have much music in our house. We had what in those days was called a music centre, which for anyone younger than forty reading this is a record player, but my parents rarely listened to actual records on it.* Rather, our house was soundtracked constantly by the small radio in the kitchen tinnily playing classical music on Radio 3.

The records that did get played, regularly, were comedy ones. Notably a series of sketches by Peter Sellers, called 'Songs for Swinging Sellers', and an EP by the Goons, which included 'The Ying Tong Song' and 'I'm Walking Backwards for Christmas'. These had a big impact on me – I can still recite most of the Sellers sketches and the lyrics of the Goon songs – but these days they give more of a sense of a particular moment in British comic time, of who my dad was.

The currency of funny was established early in our house but my real comic awakening, my baptism of funny, came when I was about thirteen, when Ivor played me a cassette called 'Derek and Clive Live'. This, in case you don't know, was a bootleg recording made by Peter Cook and Dudley Moore while apparently very drunk, in ad lib conversation, where they mainly swear, in obscene and graphic ways. Most of it wouldn't be allowed out of the recording studio now, for fear of intense cancellation.

I had never heard anything like it. It was for me – even though I have said already that I liked the form but in its musical incarnation couldn't really understand how to do it, or to be one – punk. By the time I listened to the tape, they

---

* Having said that, my mum was briefly obsessed – in a somewhat erotic way – references to him turn up in a number of the letters to David White – with Neil Diamond, who is, after all, the Jewish Elvis. And my dad owned two singles, 'Cry of the Wild Goose' by Frankie Laine and 'Ode to Billie Joe' by Bobbie Gentry, which, once in a blue moon, he would play repeatedly. If you flicked through their record collection, you would find some terrifying-looking vinyl with photos of people like Otto Klemperer in artistic agonies conducting the Berlin Philharmonic but these were never actually played.

were already middle-aged men, men from the 1960s, but it didn't matter. What appealed to me, and still does, was the liberation of it: the idea that you could literally say the first thing that comes into your head, not, as Morwenna has sometimes advised me, the second, and that, in itself, would be hilarious. Of course, this assumes the first thing in your head is always something obscene and graphic. But there is a truth to that. Derek and Clive – I thought – were speaking to me from the anarchic truth of the human heart. It is comedy reduced to its essence. It taps into the Tourette's in all of us. And as such, it's intensely, deeply childish.

Much comedy involves the stripping away of the façade of adulthood. Which is why many years later, my most successful sketch, the one that propelled me and Rob Newman onto the stage of Wembley Arena, was called 'History Today', in which two distinguished old professors slag each other off like primary schoolchildren.

It was soon after hearing this cassette that I first became interested in the idea of being a comedian. I had very little idea how to do this in 1978. There were other comedy acts, less underground than Derek and Clive, that I also loved, that I watched on TV – notably Monty Python, Morecambe and Wise, and the Marx Brothers – but I found myself also drawn to something new, which was the beginnings of British alternative stand-up comedy. Alternative comedy was only to come into being as a movement the following year, with the opening of the Comedy Store, but already on the television, I knew that I was really laughing at Jasper Carrott, Billy Connolly and Victoria Wood. Because they were the ones talking about real life, doing what is now known as observational material. It's a bit of a degraded term in 2024, implying generic have-you-ever-noticed-ness about the differences between men and women, or cats and dogs chat-GPT'd out by post-Seinfeld hacks. At that point in time, however, Jasper Carrott talking about things I had actually experienced, like loonies on the bus, as opposed to structured jokes where Englishmen, Scotsmen and Irishmen went into pubs and enacted scenarios that weren't in any way real, felt hilariously revolutionary.

The only vague sense I had of a path into comedy, though, was via the Cambridge Footlights. I knew Python had come out of there, and Peter Cook. I also knew it had been a long time ago. But that was why I decided to try and get into Cambridge, which involved staying on at school for an extra term to do what was called the Oxbridge exam. After primary school, I went to Haberdashers', a private school in Elstree. I feel I need to add – partly because all British people are twitchy about class, but also because you may be confused as to how my parents, already on their uppers, paid for this – that I got in as part of the last year of direct grant entrants, a system which meant the fees your parents paid were means-tested. If your household did not have a lot of income, the state covered most of it. In my case, they covered all of it.

At Haberdashers', the boys who stayed on to do Oxbridge, whose year was called 6S, also put on a school revue at Christmas. It was performed at lunchtime, and ran for a week, and would, invariably, be shit. It consisted mainly of jaunty songs about school life that no one in their right mind would ever laugh at.

When it came to my year, I co-wrote the 6S Revue with various other boys, including a very funny lad called Nick Golson, who would go on to be the first of my many – perhaps too many – double-act partners. Instead of the usual gentle babble, we created a series of sketches that made vicious fun of the teachers. It seems amazing to me now that we were allowed to write this without any staff members checking the script. But perhaps that's just the nature of the pupil-teacher beast. Some years later, *The Mary Whitehouse Experience*, the show that began my career on TV, included a sketch about a parents' evening and a teacher claiming to know his nickname among the students:

MR AVERY: Birdy! That's what they call me. Because my name's Avery, you see!
PARENT: Oh. It must be another teacher who my son calls *Mr Embryo-Head* then.

Which was very in the spirit of the 6S Revue. The teachers left us to our own devices because they thought we would be harmlessly nice. They were wrong.

The main sketches I remember from that show – and I am occasionally still reminded of it, because old men sometimes come up to me and tell me they were in the audience and it is seared into their memories – are: one where the much-despised librarian, a strict Christian, has sex with a blow-up doll on his desk, while shouting his catchphrase 'If you want to talk in the library, you can't!'; another where the head of geography strips off to reveal bondage gear, and mounts a photocopier that he has fallen in love with; and me doing an impression of the head of music, who every so often in assembly would stridently encourage us to sing up our hymns vigorously to Jesus, only I did it wearing an enormous fake nose – he had a big nose – and shouting, 'Fucking sing louder! Fucking to Be a Fucking Pilgrim! Let's fucking hear you!'

It stormed it. I mean, I'm not claiming any of this as up there with *Curb Your Enthusiasm*. But in terms of what I was saying earlier about the new comedy talking directly to the audience about their experience: it landed. It was my first time doing comedy on stage, and the feeling of hearing an audience properly laughing was, I knew then, crack.*

We got into terrible trouble. The show didn't run for the whole week. That was its one and only performance (and indeed, the end of the 6S Revue forever at Haberdashers'). I was hauled up in front of the head teacher, who said he was considering expelling me. But, in a remarkably straightforward bit of cynicism, he then said, 'Hmm . . . you're going to Cambridge, aren't you?' – Habs was very keen on keeping itself high in the Oxbridge league tables – and just let me off.

The show had another effect: for the first and only time at that school, I was cool. I was the boy who had not only made everybody laugh, but also nearly got expelled. Which meant comedy became even more like the crack I'd never heard of.

I went to Cambridge and ended up as vice-president of the Footlights. This was not, it turns out, career in comedy – job done. There may be some readers who assume I am part of an intake into British TV of Cambridge Footlights members who sailed straight from university on to BBC 2. I wish I had been: it really would've been so much easier. But, as we know, truth is in the detail, and the detail is that the conveyor belt – which absolutely did exist for twenty years, between *Beyond the Fringe* in 1961 and *The Cellar Tapes*, Stephen Fry, Hugh Laurie and Emma Thompson's show, in 1981 – was shut down abruptly with the advent of alternative comedy (at which point, btw, it became much more useful, like Ben Elton, Rik Mayall and Ade

---

* Obviously, I had never heard of crack then, and would've been far too frightened to take it if I had.

Edmondson, to have gone to *Manchester* University). This shutting down was sealed with the very funny *University Challenge*
episode of *The Young Ones* that characterized 'Footlights College'
as posh entitled twats. Stephen Fry, Hugh Laurie and Emma
Thompson were very happy in that episode to play up to being
posh entitled twats, somewhat drawing up the ladder on those
of us not-that-posh entitled twats who hadn't got into telly yet.

The comedy I performed in Footlights was not like that of
previous years. By the time I was running the club, I had been
to the Comedy Store and become obsessed with some of the
comics I'd seen there. (I brought the brilliant, sadly no-longer-
with-us Jeremy Hardy, and many others, up to perform at the
Footlights clubroom.) This influenced me in my early days as
a performer. To my knowledge (and I'm happy for any comedy
historian to contradict me), I was the first person in Footlights
history to do stand-up, by which I mean, to come on stage as
myself and just talk, rather than doing a character monologue
or a sketch. In the Footlights Revue of 1986, I did one routine
about being Jewish and another one about masturbation. As
you can see, my work has come a long way since then.

I did do sketches as well. The stand-out sketch, which I
performed with Nick Golson, who had followed me into the
Footlights, involved two very Derek and Clive type men
discussing how modern and high-tech the toilet has become at
their local library. It ended like this:

NICK: And what was really nice is that after I bent over
    and pressed the flush button . . . out the side comes a
    lovely little picture of my turd.
DAVID: (AFTER A SHORT PAUSE) Yeah. No. Um. What
    you've done is . . . you've shat on a photocopier.

My point being that despite the notion prevalent at the time of Footlights *versus* alternative comedy, of the two being binary opposites, the show I wrote and performed in was in fact very influenced by what was happening on the sweary, punk London cabaret circuit. This may also be why Owen Dudley Edwards, theatre reviewer of the eminent newspaper the *Scotsman*, said, of our show in Edinburgh: 'On this evidence, the Cam is an open sewer.' It was the first of many such reviews that were to speckle my career.

Having said all this, there *was* one very posh moment in my time in the Cambridge Footlights, which I feel I should tell you, as it also conforms with my earlier point about always fucking up with famous people. One night, we performed in front of the Queen and Princess Margaret (I told you it was posh). This was because a contemporary of mine at Cambridge was Prince Edward. He had some theatrical ambitions, but frankly wasn't funny enough to get into Footlights. Instead, he was in a sub-Footlights comedy and theatre group called CULES (Cambridge University Light Entertainment Society). I knew he wasn't funny enough to get into Footlights as I'd seen him hosting a CULES revue at a May ball, and none of his jokes were going well. His response wasn't to draw on some deep comic reserve, as you are supposed to in these circumstances – a bad night can happen to any of us – but instead to get what I would call *tetchily regal*. 'Bloody laugh, can't you?' and 'Well, I think some of you might have thought *that* joke was funny at least!' were some of the ways he imperiously failed to turn his compering shtick around.

Anyway, another night, CULES were doing a charity show at a theatre called the ADC, and Footlights were enlisted with the job of supporting them. This was unusual, as Footlights

were by far the senior partner in the Cambridge comedy hier-
archy, but then again, Prince Edward's mum and auntie were
coming up to watch him do his CULES thing. Before the show,
Edward came down to our dressing room and explained that
there was going to be a line-up afterwards where we would
meet the Queen and Princess Margaret. 'If the Queen speaks
to you,' he said, 'you must call her Your Majesty and then after
that, Ma'am. And if Princess Margaret speaks to you, you must
call her Your Highness and then after that, Ma'am.'

I thought – and still do – that this was ridiculous. It is utterly
ridiculous to call another human being Your fucking Majesty.
Nonetheless, I had no intention of breaking protocol, in case I
was executed.

We did the show. I did a routine that was mainly about my
hair. For a lot of the eighties, I had very big, what I liked to
think of as Robert-Smith-Off-Of-The-Cure, but it may have been
more Pat-Sharp-Off-Of-Capital-Radio, hair. One of the interesting things about the only photo I have of this occasion is
all you can see of me is my hair.

Yes, that's me in the lower left-hand corner, looking like a
poodle sitting on a man.

This is relevant because in the line-up proper, where the two big royals shook our hands, there didn't seem to be much in the way of talking. The Queen appeared, and wafted past me and everyone else with just the slightest touch of flesh. I expected the same of Princess Margaret, but in fact, she stopped, grasped my hand and said, in a high royal squeak: 'Oh! I recognize you from your hairdo!'

It's an interesting idea that the performers that night needed some sort of keynote thing about them to keep them in the memory of the royal attendee, given that this was about ten minutes after the curtain went down. It implies perhaps that none of the others had made any impression on the Queen's sister at all. But meanwhile, I wasn't expecting it. And as a result, I completely forgot what I was meant to call her and replied:

'Oh, do you . . . Princess Margaret.'

And honestly – you know how honest I like to be – she frowned, and looked at me like: *Who's that?* Like no one had actually called her that before.

Then there was just a very odd moment when she tapped her foot repeatedly on the wooden floorboards in front of her and said: 'I don't know how anyone can dance on a stage like this!' Before a footman appeared and led her away. I didn't get executed. But it was a close-run thing.*

---

* I had another Prince Edward-involved incident many years later. On *Baddiel and Skinner Unplanned*, which initially went out live, an audience member asked a question that involved a reference to Edward being gay, a rumour at the time. I said – after pointing out that it would be fine if he was – that I knew he wasn't, as I had been friendly with a woman who went out with him at Cambridge. Frank said: who? And I just said her name. This was very stupid, as the woman in question, who lived by then in America, had long-lens photographers squatting outside her house the very next day. I sent her flowers and apologies. It is a pertinent bad example of my squash-wall mind.

After I left Cambridge, I went on the London cabaret circuit (for, it turned out, six years). My first attempts to get gigs taught me a salutary lesson about comedy and the times I was living in. I remember phoning the Comedy Store and a man there asking if I'd had any experience in comedy, and I said, proudly, 'I was vice-president of the Cambridge Footlights' – and he put the phone down. So after that I tended not to mention it as much, and just went back to square one.

The cabaret circuit at the time was undoubtedly rough. Older comedians tend to talk this up a bit, as it makes them – us – seem more like Wild West pioneers. It's not, however, untrue. My early years on the circuit consisted mainly of making my way to places I'd never been before, in or near London, like Darenth or Sydenham, and agreeing to take a door split even though there were more comedians on the bill than people in the audience. I played the infamous Tunnel Club, less a club and more of an outcrop of the Blackwall Tunnel, where the heckling consisted not only of words, but also of ashtrays aimed very precisely at comedians' foreheads.* My first gig at the Comedy Store started at three o' clock in the morning, which is when the open spots were in those days. Before I went on – of the six open spots that night, I was the fourth – a fight broke out in the audience and a number of people were thrown out. I did my five minutes to, as I remember it, complete silence. I didn't die exactly, as I didn't get booed off, but it was like the audience had.

Remarkably, in a way that seems impossible to me now – I have no idea where the drive and conviction you need as an unknown stand-up to overcome playing to what feels like

---

* On one of the nights I played there, the legendary compère Malcolm Hardee introduced another act by saying, 'He's a Welsh poet. Take aim.'

zombies comes from, but these days it is not anywhere to be found in my soul – I kept at it. By about 1988, I was established, regularly playing the Store. I still consider one of the most exciting episodes of my career the moment when Kim Kinnie, who used to book the comedians, and who ran the Comedy Store with a rod of iron, entered the dressing room and said, after I'd just come off following a storming twenty minutes, 'I think we'll move you up to compere next week.' Because in 1988, compering the Comedy Store was the Holy Grail indeed. That was what the godfather of alternative comedy, Alexei Sayle, had done, and that was what I'd seen brilliant comedians like Mark Thomas and Tony Allen and Steve Frost do before me. Here is a photo of me compering, still on the wall at the Store. Which I always really like when I sometimes see it. Btw, that's Malcolm, the compere at the Tunnel, above me.

I still had the occasional bad gig, of course. I remember one night at the Store when, although I didn't get tetchily regal, nothing would turn the audience my way, and I knew it was over when I heard a voice above the general 'get offs' and 'you're shit' shouting from the back, 'THE WALLS ARE CLOSING IN!' Despite my atheism, I took this to be the voice of God, and accepted its implied advice to depart the stage.

I remember leaving that night, trying not to catch the eye of any member of the audience. Frank Skinner once said to me that if you get a bad review, or die onstage, there's nothing you can do to lift the shame. It's like, Frank said, wearing a wet blanket: you just have to wait for it to dry out. This is a brilliant analogy. But as I got to the exit, the comedian Jim Tavaré came in and said, 'How did it go?' 'Terribly,' I said. He looked at me, and despite the myth that all comedians like nothing more than seeing other comedians die, he said: 'You're brilliant. You'll be back tomorrow. And you'll storm it.' Which felt like Jim had applied a blow dryer to a small corner of my sopping poncho.

Obviously, it's not *that* much of a myth. Along with the other acts, I often used to watch the open spots at the Store. Although you might like to think an established comedian would be doing this hoping for the best for the new guys, clearly that's not always the case. Once a comedian came on called Cynical Sid (a novelty name is never good). It was obvious as soon as Sid began that comedy wasn't his destiny. Once again, but thankfully this time not as the target, I heard the 'fuck off!' and 'you're shit!' shouts begin. Sid ploughed on, bravely but mistakenly. Eventually – and again, it was a loud voice at the back, coming out of nowhere, like God's – a man said: 'Everybody hates you. Everybody hates you. *You must know from school.*'

This is, I think, one of the great heckles of all time. There was no coming back from it.

I used to tell this story onstage. Latterly, I noticed other comedians were telling it too. But in their stories, *I* was the act being heckled. This may just have been an overlapping confusion. Or maybe because those comedians assumed – not entirely incorrectly – that I was hated at school.

I'm not going, in the way of showbiz memoirs, to delineate the arc of my career from that time on. This book is about my family – with some digressions – so I need to get back to that. But I do think that given the way my family was, the only possible route forward for me was comedy. There is a thing now, part of the rise of what is annoyingly called cancel culture, where you can get into trouble for jokes. This can be because the joke is deemed offensive, but it can also be because of a notion that the subject matter is somehow off-limits to laughter. This is a category error, as it's never the subject matter that counts in a joke, it's the joke. It's the details, the specifics of the joke. You can do a Holocaust joke that is appalling and cruel and antisemitic, and you can also do ones that humanize the victims.

As far as my family goes, I would say that just as it is more allowable for a member of an ethnic minority to joke about that ethnic minority, I feel more able to joke about my family because I am, after all, a member of my family. But something else. *Laughter is not always mockery.* This is something that in our eager-to-scold present has got completely lost. Laughter is the only thing that truly separates us from the animals. As an atheist, I recognize it as God's greatest gift to humanity. We think too much now in terms of power – we think everything can be understood in terms of power dynamics – and in comedy, that leads to the situation of people who have no sense of humour telling comedians they are *punching down*. But comedy is so much richer and more complex than that moral geography implies: a good joke whirls and twists; it operates, like a sub-atomic particle, in a superposition, neither up nor down, but spinning in all directions at once.

So, one last comedy story. In the first series of *Fantasy Football League*, one of the regular guests was Peter Cook. I was incredibly excited about this, but, in all honesty, he wasn't that great on it. There may have been many reasons for this, including Peter not being that bothered about being great on these annoying whippersnappers' show, but either way, it wasn't the hoped-for summation of working with my comedy idol that the young me would've liked. Worse, I bumped into Peter in the make-up chair of another TV show soon afterwards and he accused us of editing him to make him look less funny than he had been. Which we really hadn't – we'd done our absolute best to make him get as many laughs as possible.

This depressed me. I felt – and for once, not because I'd said something stupid – that I'd fucked up with one of my heroes: my prime hero. Then, one day, I was walking through Hampstead and I bumped into his wife, Lin. She was very nice, and said: 'Oh, come back to our house, Peter would love to see you.' I thought, He wouldn't, but she was very insistent, and eventually I gave in.

And turns out he did. Seem pleased to see me, that is. I don't know if he'd forgotten his gripe about the *Fantasy Football League* edit, but he was very friendly, and we ended up sitting in his living room for hours, watching football. Lin may have regretted asking me, as periodically, she would come in and remind Peter they were going out later and he needed to change. After she'd done this for the fourth time, with increasing irritation, Peter said, 'OK, OK.' I said, 'I'll go', but he said, 'No, hang on.' He then went into his bedroom. About five minutes later, he came back into the living room wearing a pair of enormous checked flared trousers, a sparkly sequinned shirt and a white Panama hat.

'NOT LIKE THAT!' shouted Lin. Peter looked at me and smiled. And I realised that Peter Cook – *Peter Cook* – had done a joke (a big, time-consuming, wife-annoying visual joke at that) just for me.

After that, we became friends, and I used to see him a fair bit. It was obvious, however, that he wasn't a well man. One thing he liked to do was leave extremely long, extremely funny messages on his friends' answerphones. One day I came back to the flat to a message from Peter that was about ten minutes long. It was really funny, but after laughing at it, I clicked delete. A week later, he was dead.

I wish I'd kept that message somehow. Not just because that's what people say in these circumstances, but because of what the message was about. The night before he had watched me on *Room 101*. And the subject of his ten-minute-long funny rant on my answerphone was that I was clearly an idiot for not loving – and he was prepared personally to introduce me to its joys – the game of golf.

Sarah and Colin

Something that often happens with marital infidelity is that it gets set in the context of sexlessness: of, that is, a marriage having failed, with the most acute sign of that failure being that the husband and wife do not have sex any more.

This wasn't the case with my parents. I had insomnia from an early age. There are a variety of possible psychological reasons for this, but one thing that definitely didn't help was the many nights I spent being woken up terrified in my bedroom by the sounds my dad made during sex. As a kid, obviously, I didn't know that's what it was. For years, I assumed there was a wounded walrus in my parents' bedroom. I've watched a lot of pornography – really, a *lot* – and I have never heard a climaxing man make that sound. The only person who I think might make a similar sound to accompany sexual ecstasy is Chewbacca.

Just to give you a clue as to how frightening it was – when I was a teenager, my already-mentioned friend David Gavurin, who I called Dave, stayed over. Key to this story is the information that I wasn't sleeping in my own bedroom but in my younger brother's room. Dan wasn't there, so I was in his room, which contained a reasonably large single bed (whereas mine, even into my late teens, housed a bunk bed, which made sleeping in it with my girlfriend – Janine – bizarre).

I was, at least initially, allowed to bring my girlfriend back to stay the night. My mum was very keen as we grew into teenagers on saying, as evidence of her being a liberated sixties/ seventies mother, 'Don't worry, when you have girlfriends, they should stay the night here. I don't mind what goes on as long as I know you are safe under our roof!' Later, this would go a bit wrong – during the time of no toast, or rather, no one being allowed back in case they ate some, Janine fell under the ban, and I ended up arguing with my mum about this in front of various people and calling her an idiot, and she slapped me in the face and I went and stayed at Janine's for a week. Which brought its own issues, as her dad was very much not a sixties/

seventies suburban sexually liberated type of dad – really, there's a whole other book to be written in the margins of this one.

But at the time of this story about Dave, it was all fine. Janine was allowed to sleep with me in Dan's room. A peculiar sentence, but a true one. One of the other things about Dan's room, apart from it having a bed that it made sense to have sex in, was that although it also adjoined my parents' bedroom, something about the acoustics of our house meant you were not, if you were sleeping in it, liable to be accosted by quite so much sonic detail of my father's sexual shouting.

So. Dave was staying over, as was Janine. Dave in my bedroom, Janine and me in Dan's room. I remember going in to see Dave before he went to bed and saying, 'Listen, they – my parents – might have sex, and you should know my dad makes some very weird noises . . .' He responded in a teenage, bored, *Hey, I'm sixteen, I know what sex sounds like* manner. O . . . K . . . I said, with that ellipsis in my voice, and shrugged – maybe all dads make sounds like that? – and went to Dan's room. At about three o'clock in the morning, a knock on the door woke me up, confused, and I heard Dave whisper, from outside, 'Can I come in?' He opened the door wearing boxer shorts and a T-shirt, and even in the half-light I could see he was ashen, *white* with fear. He said:

'Dave . . . I think your mum's died.'

I stared at him. I pretty much knew already, just from those words, what was happening and how this would play out. But nonetheless, I said:

'What?'

'I know it seems unlikely,' he said, 'but your dad is making the most incredible noises. Screaming and crying . . .'

I said: 'They're having sex. I told you.'

Dave shook his head. 'No. Really. These sounds . . .' He grew intense. 'The only time I've heard someone make a sound like that . . . it was my uncle. At my auntie's funeral. He knelt in her grave and made that . . .' Dave raised a terrified finger towards the adjoining wall, '. . . noise.'

I sighed, said, 'Right . . .' and got out of bed. We tiptoed across the landing back to my room and stood, both of us in our boxer shorts, by the bunk bed. After about fifteen seconds, we heard:

'WRUUGGGHHHAAAGGGKKKKKHHHPPPLLLTTT!'

Or similar.

I said, 'They're having sex', and went back to bed.

These sounds were very disturbing when you didn't know what they were. It is possible – even though I was breezy with my friend about them – that at some deep level I was damaged by the confusion they would've caused at an earlier age. But it wasn't as disturbing as the time when I was about thirteen and I heard my mum in the next room having sex *without* my dad. On her own. Doing that activity that, many years later, on live TV she said was a lovely thing to do outside in the open. She made a lot of disturbing sounds while doing this, but the most disturbing, for me, was the one she made right at the end, which was the sound of her screaming, three times – the word *David*.

I think by then I kind of knew what was going on. Enough at least not to rush in and say, 'I'm here! I'm here! How can I save you?'

When I did this bit onstage, it got the most extreme reaction of any story in that show. Not the biggest laugh – that would be the reveal of my mother cc'ing her ill-but-still-sexy email to David White to me and Ivor – but the most shocked. It got a big laugh

(I'm still enough of a stand-up to need to tell you that) but you could hear in the laugh a sharp intake of breath. Occasionally, it did occur to me – despite my basic lack of filter – to consider whether there were elements of this story I should leave out.

Well, obviously I considered that throughout the process of making the show. Making any comedy show involves leaving many things out – primarily things that in the telling onstage do not get laughs. I tried out *My Family: Not the Sitcom* many times before it became the show that opened at the Menier Chocolate Factory in 2016, and it continued to change throughout the two years I performed it in the West End and all over the world. What people noticed was its honesty. See below:

Comedy

My Family: Not the Sitcom review – David Baddiel is breathtakingly honest

★★★★☆

Michael
Billington
@billicritic
Wed 18 May 2016 12.10
BST

f y ✉ 68

As it happens, I'm not being completely honest here, as I don't really think you need to have that specific visual evidence to corroborate the information that honesty is what people took away from the show. Clearly, I've knowingly included the screenshot of the good review I got from *Guardian* theatre critic Michael Billington, because I want you to see it. Similarly, earlier in this piece, you didn't need to know that *My Family: Not the Sitcom* had a long run in the West End, followed by tours in Australia and Canada. Or that it was nominated for an Olivier award.

As a self-proclaimed honesty addict, let me also tell you about the one bad review this show got, from Quentin Letts in the *Daily Mail*, who considered it a form of 'revenge'. It made him feel sad for my family. Interestingly, because I've been in therapy for a long time, I'm prepared to give this idea the time of day. It is entirely possible my over-honesty about my parents is a form of revenge. I think it's possible some of the anger I may have towards them for their unbounded non-parenting when I was younger has got sublimated into comedy. But the truth is always complex. Because I think in that sublimation, revenge gets mixed with memory and the softening that comes with time.

I did leave some things out of that show. I left out – I see I'm not doing it now – the time my dad burst into tears in our kitchen, apparently triggered by the pressure of having to read out some Hebrew at the synagogue at my younger brother's bar mitzvah, but almost definitely actually triggered by being made redundant at the same time as, however much he was not noticing the details, knowing something was going very wrong with his marriage. I was in the adjoining room (the breakfast room). It was the only time I was ever aware of him crying, and still now, as I think of it, I find it strange and unsettling and upsetting. The noise he made was weirdly similar to the wounded walrus sex noises in his bedroom.

But much less funny. Which is why I left it out of that show.

The only people who could, I think, raise a valid objection to the material in *My Family: Not the Sitcom* were my brothers.

Neither of them to be honest were that keen on the basic premise. After I emailed Dan (who lives in America) a few months following our mum's death, to tell him I was thinking about doing a warts-and-all comedy show about our parents – he wrote back, simply: 'You're not doing it.' Ivor, I spoke to in person. He came round to my house and sat down and said: 'Look, we could talk about this for two hours, and go back and forth on it, but I may as well just ask you upfront: are you going to do this?' And, without hesitation, I said: 'Yes.' Which I guess tells you something about the sliver of ice in the heart of the writer/comedian – or about the Nora Ephron mantra, which means the same thing, that everything is copy – but there is something else. I knew before I had written or performed the show that it would, in its own way, be an act of love. A show that celebrated the warts. Or, more specifically – but I think this is of necessity borne out of love – an act of reclamation. Because, as I've said, my mother died abruptly, the lack of time, the lack of dying time, meant there had been no long goodbye, no mobilization of memory. What I was trying to do with *My Family: Not the Sitcom*, and already had an instinct about before I even started it, was – this sounds creepy, I think, but hey – reincarnate her. To describe her in such detail – and to leave nothing out – that she would truly come alive again on stage. Not truly at all, of course, but in the sense that people use that phrase – to push it as far it could go. And then – obviously I didn't know this in advance – perform it across the world for two years, thus giving me, with a whole load of people who never met her, the chance to properly say goodbye.

Despite his misgivings, Ivor came to the first night. At the end, for an encore, I came back on stage to do a Q&A. When I announced this to the audience, I saw many people in the crowd, theatre critics, other comedians, various great and good, with their hands up, but I said: 'Sorry, I'll answer any questions in a minute but first of all, I need to know what my brother thought. Ivor? What did you think?' I looked out into the room – the light was blinding and I couldn't see him, but I heard his voice, which is much like my own, say: 'I loved it.' And then he added, 'I loved it because it felt like she was in the room.'

Sarah, Colin, Henry, Sylvia

Forty-three Kendal Road, as you may have gathered by now, was an over-sexualized house. My parents both had large stashes of pornography in their bedroom drawers. This was, in a way, yet another form of collecting. My mother's consisted mainly of editions of *Playgirl*, which displayed pictures of naked men, invariably looking into the middle distance, invariably with moustaches. My father's were more exotic, hardcore magazines he'd picked up on travels abroad, principally *Color Climaxes*. I don't know how old I was when I first came across these – hard not to say oo-er following that, but fortunately or unfortunately, I was definitely too young for that innuendo to work. I'd say I was about nine or ten, and though immediately fascinated and drawn into the beginnings of a lifelong addiction, I didn't understand where most of the bodily fluids I was seeing spattered across various bodies came from.

Certain habits are set in you very young. I don't mean the obvious habit here. As I said earlier, Ivor has always been more responsible and organized than me, as befits the older brother. He has complained to me often in later years that I was much more slapdash when it came to returning my father's pornography to whatever order it would've lain in in his bedside drawer after, um, use. Ivor, he has since told me, was religious about this, being, apparently, terrified my parents might cotton on to his illicit viewing of my dad's stash. I wasn't so methodical. Once I took a copy of *Color Climax* out of their room and into the bathroom. Before I'd really got deep into this particular edition, however, I heard someone coming up the stairs, so hid it under the laundry basket (an item I can still see clearly: cylindrical, padded, off-white with roses). Then forgot about it. Sometime later, while in bed, I heard my dad in the bathroom shouting, 'What the fuck is *this* doing here?'

But to be honest, Colin and Sarah weren't so great at keeping their pornography hidden either. Once they left a copy of *Club International* on the breakfast table. In the middle of the table, like it was a condiment. Like, 'What would you like with your Findus Crispy Pancakes, David; some very fulsome pubic bush?' *Club International*, by the way, was a British pornographic magazine. That's the sort of thing they were called in the seventies: *Club International, Penthouse, Mayfair.* I think there was a belief in the 1970s that wanking was aspirational.

My parents were negligent in general with leaving inappropriate material around. Every year for our holidays we went to Swansea. This, while we're on the subject, was part and parcel of the mundanity of my childhood. I apologize to anyone from Swansea reading this, and it's apparent from more recent visits that it is now an extremely vibrant place, but between the years 1970 and 1982 the city was not an exciting destination to holiday for a child/teenager. Don't get me wrong, I *was* excited to go to Swansea. I was particularly excited when we graduated from staying at my grandparents' terraced house in

Glanbrydan Avenue to a BnB in Sketty Road, because it meant the three of us boys stayed in one room. I can still remember Ivor saying in his sleep, 'Can I have some lemonade?', which gives you some sense of the wildness of Baddiel hopes and dreams in those years. More importantly, there were cooked breakfasts every morning.

But still, Swansea wasn't the most upbeat holiday destination. Later, in my early twenties, I went with two friends to the Gower Peninsula, to Three Cliffs Bay, and thought: How ridiculous that my parents never drove us the half an hour out of Swansea to here, where the beauty is extreme. Ridiculous, but typical: my parents weren't very bothered with beauty. Maybe my mum was, or might have been, if more had been available. Meanwhile, days out were mainly at the Mumbles, which is also beautiful in parts, but we spent almost no time in those parts, instead hanging out entirely in the caravan park, where Colin's old friends Martin and Norma Glass had a two-bedroom Stirling with chemical toilet. They did, to be fair, also have a SodaStream, an item that could transform still liquids into fizzy ones, which seemed the most exciting idea in the world (I imagine Ivor may have mentioned this in his sleep as well). Otherwise, we would go by ourselves to Swansea Bay, whatever the weather, where the tide went out so far that trying to get to the sea felt like walking back to England.

And we spent really a lot of time at my grandparents' house, not doing very much: watching TV, playing board games, reading. One summer, when I was about fourteen, my dad was reading *'Rommel?' 'Gunner Who?'* by Spike Mulligan and left it on a table in my grandparents' living room, where me and Dan were sitting with Henry and Sylvia (pictured out for a walk, probably in the Mumbles, here). Which might not seem that

negligent except my dad should've remembered his mother's tendency to pick books up at random and read from them out loud. She picked up and read, in a stentorian voice, this imagined conversation between Evelyn Waugh and Randolph Churchill. She intoned it all carefully, I remember, leaving a pause after WAUGH and RANDOLPH for the dialogue.

WAUGH: Ah! That's better! I'm braver than you, I wear a woolly outer garment. I'm braver than anyone! When a German plane comes over, I never take cover, you know why?

RANDOLPH: Yes, you're a cunt.

There was a long, long beat of silence, before Sylvia looked up and said, slowly, thoughtfully, as if – sorry – tasting the word: *'Cunt.'* The letters seemed to hover in the air in front of her. She continued: 'What's that?'

I chose, after some small consideration, not to answer her. It looked for a while like no one would. I could hear Ivor laughing – he was in the kitchen grating sugar, he tells me, because our grandparents' larder was so cold it had coagulated. Then my grandpa said, 'Oh, that's terrible. I haven't heard language like that since the *trenches.*'

I love that Grandpa Henry said that. It certainly suggests his life had been a little closeted between Armistice Day and this moment in 1978. Then again, it does also suggest he had heard the word a lot back then. Which is a bit worrying in terms of his popularity among his fellow troops. Perhaps on Christmas Day 1914 he was the only British soldier who refused to play football.

Either way, my grandmother sensed something was awry and abruptly shut Spike Milligan's masterpiece. As she did so, she noticed on the back an obviously – to most eyes – fake quote.

She read that out loud too: '"I resign," General Montgomery.'

'I'm not surprised after reading this,' she said, with great disdain, and put the book down.

Neglect

Jerry Seinfeld has a joke about how, for his parents, their children were like racoons. As in 'I think there's one about here somewhere but I've no idea where it is.' Without doubt, parents in the sixties, seventies and eighties did not feel they needed to *be there* for their children like parents do – like I do – now. But even given that, I think Colin and Sarah Baddiel somewhat took the not-being-there biscuit.

It was mainly small things. For example, I was never taught to tie my shoelaces. Actually, that's unfair. I never *learned* to tie my shoelaces. My mum had a big flat cardboard model of a shoe she did briefly use to try and teach all three of us, but I found it difficult – I am a weirdo, at some level – to transfer this knowledge from one dimension to three, and soon gave up, which meant having to ask random adults to tie my laces until I was about fourteen. Thus, when eleven, and playing proudly for the North West London Jewish Day School football team, I had to ask the only adult present to do it: the referee, who also happened to be a rabbi. Despite being a rabbi – 'Better a patient person than a warrior,' says the Old Testament – his tolerance for an eleven-year-old asking him repeatedly to tie their shoelaces was limited (to be fair, I think he did miss the odd offside while doing so), and he couldn't be bothered to do it properly, so they kept coming undone. After the third time of asking, he just ignored me and eventually I had to sit the game out in my socks. This is still why, in my heart of hearts, I believe I never became a professional footballer.

But there were more complicated, darker things that went down in my childhood. And in varying degrees, in those situations, my mum and dad were not what Instagram posters, when they post about their parents, call *my rock*.

When I first went to Haberdashers', I found going to this new school intimidating. It was a big place and it felt – because it was, in Elstree, near Watford – miles away from home. I've mentioned travelling on the Tube to catch the 8 a.m. coach to school. If your parents paid a bit more, you could catch the

8.30 coach. My parents obviously didn't do that, so I had to catch the earlier one and, because I was an insomniac even then and so very tired in the mornings, I often missed it. If you were caught on the 8.30 coach when your parents hadn't paid for it, you would be thrown off and have to walk miles to catch a bus to school. This happened to me many times.

I was so unhappy at the school that in my second year I became ill. Well. Kind of. In my house, you were only considered ill if you had a temperature. I'd put this down to my dad, an empiricist, a scientist, but also maybe to both of them not really wanting to be bothered with ill children if there wasn't something concrete which demonstrated without doubt that they were genuinely ill. One morning when Ivor was nine, he told my mum he felt sick. She took his temperature and because it was normal, off he went to North West. Later that day, after throwing up in class and rolling about on the floor in agony, he was rushed to hospital with appendicitis.

That didn't work out so well for Ivor, but I realized I could use it to my advantage. When taking our temperature, neither of my parents – 90 per cent of the time it would have been my mum, but occasionally it was my dad – would stay in the room. I mean, obviously. My dad would've been too bored, and my mum would've had calls to David White to make. Which allowed me to take the thermometer out and hold it against a radiator or a lamp. Once I figured out I could do this – I must've been pretty skilful at it, as mercury thermometers at the time were hard to read, and I'm not sure how I ever prevented ours from suggesting I was about to spontaneously combust – I did it continually. Or at least, for a whole term. In my second year at Haberdashers' I was off for six weeks. Eventually, they sent me to hospital and put me in an observation ward, where doctors and nurses, would you believe it, stayed with me as I lay in bed with the thermometer in my mouth, and thus I turned out suddenly not to have a temperature. And went home.

I appreciate, by the way, that this is an example of me lying. It may in fact be an example of how I used to be able to lie as a young child, but that changed as time, and things I witnessed at home, went on. Or it may be that it is not exactly an example of lying. Because I was unhappy at the school, and my mental health would've been affected. I didn't feel well, and I needed to demonstrate this to my parents, and knowing that I could only do this through the thermometer, that's what I did. It's an early example, perhaps, of what the internet now would call living my truth.

I found it hard to make friends at Haberdashers' initially. At one of my first classes, our form teacher asked us to say one interesting thing about ourselves. Most boys said something about where they came from or maybe what football team they supported, or whether they collected stamps. Because of my dad's insistence on the importance of science – and because I was a bit of a twat – when it came to me, I expounded on Pythagoras' Theorem. I said, 'The square of the hypotenuse is equal to the sum of the squares on the other two sides.' This led to most of my classmates thinking I was a bit of a twat. It also led to some graffiti to that effect on some school walls, although I believe the word used was Bastard – 'Baddiel Is A Bastard', in chalk.

Interestingly, my closest friend from primary school, Saul Rosenberg, went there too. But rather quickly, Saul found other friends. When I tearfully told my mum that he was having a party and hadn't invited me, she phoned his mum and complained. As we know, this always works. I was invited to the party, but Saul didn't speak to me.

To be fair, that was an example of non-neglect, of my mum parentally responding to some social difficulties I was having and trying to help. But even then, it was at some level more to do with her than me. For my mother, my friendship with Saul operated as an early version of her tendency to think of people, including her children, in terms of what they liked, rather than anything more complex. As far as she was concerned, me liking Saul, and being best friends with him, was very much a building block of *who I was*. She often used to refer to me and Saul as being 'like two peas in a pod', which wasn't really true, given that we ate bacon and eggs for breakfast and Saul's family had three kitchens – two to avoid mixing milk and meat, and one extra reserved just for Passover, when Jews are not allowed to eat any form of bread.

But the incident with Saul leads on to a much more disturbing issue. I have talked about the shock, if you've grown up in a Jewish bubble, of realizing the whole world isn't Jewish. You'd think this would have been mitigated by the demographic of Haberdashers', where about 40 per cent of the boys were Jews. However, this large proportion of Jewish kids wasn't universally appreciated in the school, which meant I was confronted with a force I hadn't been up against before, except in my vague sense of terrible things happening to my family in the (then understood as) distant past: antisemitism. In the 1970s, in my school, and no doubt others, low-level antisemitism was tolerated. In 1979, for example, we had a mock election to go with the real general election taking place that year. I actually stood for it, as an independent socialist candidate. I know what you're thinking: Oh, you *were* a bit of a twat. This would be confirmed by the photo of me (apparently wearing – although I can only pray it was in fact a V-neck – a three-piece suit) in the school magazine that covered the election.*

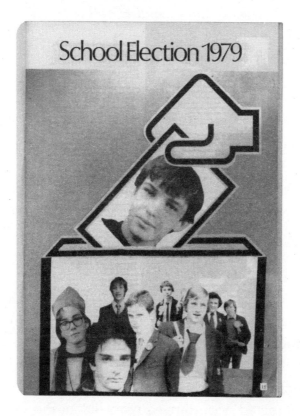

Among the various other boys who announced their candidacy for that election was an older boy, a sixth former, standing for the National Front. The National Front, as many of you will know, was a far-right party committed to racism and the

---

* I got nine votes and remember being dumped, after the election, by some other members of the Salivation Army, with my election leaflets, in a bin. The winner, incidentally, pictured going into the ballot box, was Peter Bradshaw – who would go on to be a close friend of mine, and also the *Guardian*'s cinema critic – standing for the Satanist Party.

repatriation of immigrants. It focused its hate on Black and Brown people, and also on Jews, but that was less trumpeted in its leaflets. However, the boy in question ran mainly on a platform of decreasing the number of Jews at the school. This would not have been a huge imaginative leap, as Haberdashers' had, until very recently, imposed a quota.

Meanwhile, it was well known that certain teachers very much agreed with those sentiments. One RE teacher was known to have begun a lesson, on Yom Kippur, by saying, 'Right, we can have a good session today as at last there's no Yids in.'

My form teacher was a man called Mr W—. I looked up to Mr W—, and indeed across him, as he was extremely wide and muscly, also being the head of rugby.* One day in my third year, I was taking part in a race on the school track. I was coming last. I have never been good at running. I only like sports that include a ball. In my thirties, I tried to run regularly, for my health, but also because various people told me it's good for the mind – that while running, they think of many things that put the soul at ease. I think of only one thing: running, and when it's going to stop.

And so there I was: thirteen years old, in this race, coming around the last corner, keen to get to the end. So keen in fact I fell over, knocking over the boy in front. This was an accident, but I assume from a distance it may have looked like I was trying to cheat, to trip him up so I wouldn't come last. I wouldn't

---

* I arrived at Haberdashers' not realising that, in its attempt to brand itself as a posh school, rather than one mainly for the bourgeoisie, which is what it was, there was no school football team, only rugby and cricket. This really depressed me, as I was remarkably shit at rugby. It is also the other reason, in my heart, why I didn't become a professional footballer.

normally assume this – it wouldn't have occurred to me – were it not for the fact that a friend of mine, Ashley Baron Cohen,* told me he was standing behind Mr W—. Who turned to another teacher, Mr T—, and said, darkly: 'Jew.' And Mr T— replied, 'Of course.'

When Ashley told me this – that my teachers thought that obviously I was a cheat, because I was a Jew – it devastated me. I can still feel the clammy sense of fear, of the safe-world falling away, that this generated in the child-me. I told my parents. And then, in my memory, there is nothing. I mean, I have a sense that they might've been a bit shocked. But unlike the much less problematic incident with Saul Rosenberg's party, they didn't do anything. They didn't ring the school and insist on speaking to the headmaster. They didn't suggest taking me out. They didn't even talk to me that much about it. Faced with a world without CCTV or iPhones on which audio of wrongdoers can be surreptitiously recorded, there may have been little they could do. But my memory is that they just sort of shrugged. Maybe they thought, You see: Mr Cohen was right.†

---

* He is Sacha's cousin. Sacha also, some years after me, went to my school. One of the odd things about Haberdashers' is it was a breeding ground for Jewish British comedians and comic writers. Other alumni include Matt Lucas and Robert Popper, the writer of *Friday Night Dinner*.

† Mr Cohen, in case you've forgotten, is the teacher at my primary school who told us that wherever we went there would be someone who didn't like Jews. Meanwhile, during the writing of the bit about the school revue, I contacted my co-writer Nick Golson, who told me something I never knew, which is that a teacher was led out during the performance, having had a meltdown. I was – even at a distance of forty years – not unpleased by this information, as the teacher in question was Mr T—. Hashtag karma. And all that.

More Neglect

I went on public transport on my own from an early age, not just to go to school. This often led to not-great times. One of my first stand-up jokes was: 'I've been beaten up twice in my life, once for being Jewish, once for being a Pakistani.' It got a laugh because the audience clearly thought, Oh yes, he could be either, but like most of my jokes, it was just true. The Jewish moment happened when I was set upon by a group of Sieg-Heiling skinheads outside Pimlico Tube, and the Pakistani one while waiting for a bus near Wembley Park. The reason I know the motivation for the latter beating is that the large man punching me continually called me the P-word. I did consider saying, no, sorry, I'm Jewish, but I'm not sure that would have helped.

These were both in my early teens. But I was using the bus and Tube on my own from the age of ten. At that age I liked to go to Hamleys, a massive toy shop in Regent Street, which I thought of as Mr Magorium's Wonder Emporium, even though that film would not be made for thirty years. I didn't get given enough pocket money – because that would involve me being given some – to buy anything, but I would go on my own and just look at the toys, sparkling in the windows or occasionally, excitingly, being demonstrated by staff.

I'm aware this is a bit Dickensian, a bit Tiny Tim. But let me crash through the easy sentimentality with something more disturbing. One time coming back from Oxford Circus to Dollis Hill on the (then) Bakerloo Line, on a crowded train, a bald man (in my memory, he was in a grey mackintosh, which given what you're about to hear feels clichéd, but I think it's true) sat down next to me. He smelled, I remember, badly of what we then called BO (also clichéd; also true). But he began smiling at me. I smiled back. He said, quietly: 'Been shopping?'

'I've been to Hamleys,' I said.

'Get anything nice?'

I shook my head.

'With mum and dad?' he said.

'No,' I said.

At this point, his eyes narrowed and his voice lowered. He leaned into me, his acrid smell intensifying.

'Do you have hairs yet? Down there?' he said.

So, I knew what was happening, I think, instantly. Paedophiles were folk devils even then. There were public information films on TV about *stranger danger*. Even my parents had warned their children not to take sweets from strange men.

But now, I think, it would not happen, like this, on a Tube train. Now, I think the ten-year-old boy would start shouting, 'He's a nonce!' or something similar. Then, I just went cold and clammed up.

'Do you think about girls yet?' he continued, whispering close to my ear now. 'Does it come out sometimes when you think about them?'

These are exact quotes, as his words are still burned into my memory. What strikes me as odd now is that they were all questions. He didn't say 'I bet you think about . . .' It was rhetorical. Part of what was abusive about it – and in this memoir, which isn't about abuse, this and the previous story about antisemitic teachers are exceptions – was his staging this pouring of poison into my ear as a conversation, as if I was going to think about these questions, and answer. Part of what was delicious to the abuser was the idea that I would have to turn these scenarios over in my mind.

It would – maybe – be funny to say that I, of course, *did* think about those things. In my general pre-teen life, that would be the case. But in fact, in the moment, I was just wiped out with terror.

There were many people around, but I didn't know how to make what was happening apparent to them. At the following stop, I rushed out and jumped back onto the train in the next carriage. At each of the following stops, I ducked down beneath the seats, convinced he would be getting off and would see me from the platform and rejoin the train.

Eventually, two young men sitting together said, 'What are you doing?'

And then I did say: 'There's a paedo in the next carriage and I'm frightened he's coming to get me . . .'

They looked at each other and said: 'It's OK, we'll protect you.'

Which was nice of them, except they got off two stops later. I saw the man get off one stop further on. He didn't notice me, ducking down under the seats.

I didn't tell my parents straight away, but I remember not going back on the Tube for months. My dad eventually asked why and I gave him some truncated version of what had happened. He asked why I hadn't told them at the time. I shrugged, unable to explain. That was the end of it.

· · ·

More Neglect

Colin and Sarah's parental absences increased as we got older. That might seem normal, but there are still moments when you might have expected them to turn up. But no. For example, some of you may have noticed that this already shown photograph of my graduation . . .

. . . does not include my dad. That's because he wasn't there. I'd just got a double-first from Cambridge University. But for my dad, the drive to Cambridge and the hours of sitting through watching other young people pick up their degrees would've been aggravation.* No doubt watching me pick up mine would too. I had three guest tickets to the event, so one was taken by my grandma and the other, by her friend Thelma. Here she is:

---

* Which, by the way, it is. I went to my daughter Dolly's graduation. Apart from the three-second moment when she, in her gown and mortar board, picked up her scroll, most of the ceremony, from my POV, was very dull. But the idea of me being a no-show at that event is unimaginable.

191

That's a tiny example. Perhaps a bigger one is: in 1984 I got arrested. While back from university for the holidays, I went to a demonstration called Stop the City. Stop the City, a precursor of Occupy and Just Stop Oil and other radical pressure groups of more recent times, was a ragged collective of punks and anarchists and left-wingers brought together by an unfocused sense that making a loud anti-social nuisance of themselves in the City of London would bring down capitalism. It was, like many things in those days, and indeed ours, more a cry of pain from an alienated class of young people than a coherent political movement. Even though I was much more straightforwardly politicized than I am now – back then, I was a regular on CND marches to Molesworth, the Cambridgeshire version of Greenham Common – I went along more because I thought it might be exciting than because of any real engagement with the anarchic ideals of STC.

It turned out to be a bit more exciting than I would have

liked. The Metropolitan Police that day chose – as they some-times still do – an extremely heavy-handed approach. They used horses and riot shields and flares to intimidate the protesters. At one point they kettled a group of about five hundred in a narrow alley behind Threadneedle Street, at the end of which they had set up a barrier.

Pressed against that barrier, right on the edge of that group of protesters, was me. I could feel the weight of the other five hundred moving against me like a huge angry animal. I was terrified. But on the other side, three policemen were shouting at the crowd to stay behind the barrier. Ultimately, I chose defying these shouts over being crushed, and scrambled to the other side.

Whereupon they grabbed hold of me, hard, and told me to get back over the barrier. There were many reasons why I couldn't do this. Number one, I would potentially have died. Number two, it wasn't physically possible: I would have had to crowd surf, to have been lifted like Iggy Pop by the three coppers up in the air, over the barrier and back into the melee. And number three, which perhaps illustrates why David Baddiel, Jewish nerd, should not have been at Stop the City in the first place, my glasses had fallen off.

'FUCKING GET BACK OR WE'LL NICK YOU!' one of them was shouting, over and over.

'My glasses . . .' I remember saying, pointing at my NHS John Lennons, presently in the gutter. Which were about to be crushed and broken, like the old babooshka's in *Battleship Potemkin*, by the heel of one of the policemen as they wheeled me round and carted me across the road to a waiting Black Maria.

They threw me inside the van, where another three or four

policemen proceeded to chuck me about for six or seven minutes, literally just throwing me from side to side, jeering and swearing at me. I was, once more, terrified, although it did later, in my early days as a comedian, lead to this joke:*

> It's very frightening being beaten up by the police. Because at least when you're being beaten up by skinheads, you can think, well, maybe at some point the police are going to turn up. But when you're being beaten up by the police, there's no point in thinking, God, I really hope some skinheads appear . . .

Finally, after a number of other arrests, the van filled up – my experience, by the way, was far from the worst of it: I saw another protester have his wrist broken as he struggled against being thrown in the wagon – and they drove us to a police station, putting us all in a cell. Gradually, over the course of the day, the cell filled up, until there were about thirty of us. It was summer, and extremely hot. In the hours I was in there, the police handed round only one small paper cup of water, which by the time it got to me was mainly spit. The cell had an open toilet in the middle and I was desperate to go – but I'm a man who finds it difficult to activate his bladder in any form of public space, even a row of urinals with dividers between them, so that was impossible.

Towards evening, they started to let people out. Police would come in and shout out some names, and my cell-mates would

---

* There were many, many comedians in the eighties who did jokes about police brutality. I would say that I, the Cambridge graduate, was the only one who had actually experienced it.

get up from the floor and leave. I began to get very worried they'd get mine wrong. I have an unusual name, to Anglo-Saxon ears, and before I was well known (and still now), I used to hear some very baroque, 'Taxi for Mr Bladiblub!' spins on it. I became convinced my name would be read out wrong and indeed at one point a policeman came in and called out, 'OK, Bedadi!'. I put my hand up and they led me out. Only for Mr Bedadi to follow me out, leading to rather a long discussion with the policeman about whether or not I was trying it on like a cunt.

Finally, after another hour or so, he read out the name Baddiel (fairly well, in my memory, but then I had explained the pronunciation issue a number of times by then). And I was freed.

I don't have much recall of my parents' reaction. I think the lack is itself instructive, because although it's a long time ago, I have a strong sense they weren't that bothered. My dad may for once have actually have been quite proud of me, being a man who hated authority and who himself as a young man had spent a night in the cells on a charge of drunk and disorderly in Swansea after throwing up on a policeman's boot. About which he was quite proud.

But that wasn't the end of it. I was charged with obstructing the police in the course of their duty and obstructing the highway. About three months later I was tried, in a court of law.

Now, some privilege, which I referred to checking earlier, and must again. Although at this point in time I wasn't famous or wealthy, I was clever enough to have gone to Cambridge University, where I was close friends with a young woman called Marion, whose stepfather was an eminent lawyer – in the next decade Tony Blair made him lord chancellor – by the name of Derry Irvine. Marion, being radical and left-wing, felt

I should have some legal representation at the trial and so asked her stepfather for help. He kindly instructed one of the junior lawyers at his chambers, Michael Supperstone, to represent me. For nothing.

I do accept this as privilege, by some measure, as most of the people arrested at Stop the City that day were not offered, by the state, anything more than the most basic legal aid, and most of them were processed at their trials quickly – with no questions asked about the police versions of events – and sent down. Most defendants were spending about fifteen minutes in court before being led away for between three to six months inside.

Which was clearly the expectation at my trial. It took place in the forbidding surroundings of the City of London Magistrates' Court. I'd turned up in a suit, last worn possibly at my bar mitzvah. My hair was pinned up at the back of my absurdly big spiky mullet (it occurs to me now how stupidly attached to that look I must have been not to just get it cut) to try and look respectable. Actually, the police lawyer showed to the court a photo of me at the moment of being brought into the cells, I think to demonstrate that whatever respectability I was presently trying to achieve, I normally looked like this:

It should have worked. It was obvious from the word go the judge hated me. Everything about the way he looked at me said, 'I just want to lock you up and go and have lunch in my club.'

However, he hadn't reckoned on Michael Supperstone (now Sir Michael Supperstone – not sure if his work for me led *directly* to the knighthood), who did something that seemingly had not happened previously at any of these trials, which was to cross-examine the police witnesses. There were two of these, and their basic narrative was that I, David Baddiel, using all my north London Jewish golf-memorabilia-and-Dinky-Toys-fuelled rebelliousness, had jumped over their constructed barrier in order to instigate a violent charge of the entire kettled Stop the City mob against the police.

There are a few issues with this version of events, beyond it not being true. There was no way in the world even then, when I was twenty, that I could have leapt over, in one bound, a waist-high barrier, particularly while being constricted by hundreds of bodies around me. The word the police were looking for, which I believe I have used earlier, was 'scrambled'. I'm not sure you can *scramble* to instigate an attack of any sort, unless you're in a Spitfire. Moreover, if I was attempting to corral everyone behind me into this revolutionary surge, it failed spectacularly. I don't remember shouting, 'Come on, Stop the City! Come with me and let's take the Establishment down!', because I didn't, but if I had, the fact that *no one at all* followed me over the barrier meant it was a cartoonishly epic fail.

The other big problem was that when my lawyer dug into the details of their stories – where exactly each of them had been standing when they saw me instigate this charge, what time exactly it had happened, how long I refused to stand down from my storm-the-barricades position etc., etc. – their accounts matched up about as well as my parents' carpets.

It took about two hours, but in the end it was apparent that Supperstone had destroyed the prosecution case. There was a good moment at the close, when the obviously pissed-off judge said to both lawyers, 'Have you anything to add?' The police counsel shook his head. Supperstone, however, seizing his movie moment, rose and began, with some dignified rhetorical emphasis:

'In this country, your honour, the right to demonstrate is—'

'Yeah, all right, case dismissed,' said the judge, waving him away.

There is some comedy here, but to be clear: this was scary. I was very close to being sent to prison, a place where I feel I would not have thrived, however much someone like me likes to think I would have been the joker who would've been spared the beatings and the sodomy by making everybody laugh.

And here's the thing: my parents didn't come to the trial. Not just my dad this time: neither of them.

I don't know if they – or I – had not understood but, had it gone differently, I would not have been coming home from the City of London Magistrates' Court for quite a while, and when I did, it would have been with a criminal record. I get that this too is aggravation, but it is in fact exactly the aggravation that you, I think, sign up for when you decide to become a parent. I know you don't say for better or worse to your kids but one likes to imagine it's implied. Again, the idea, if one of my kids ended up in court, of Morwenna and I not turning up, at least to wave at them as they went down, is not plausible.

I actually had to check this, just now, with my ex-girlfriend, Janine, because at some level it seems incredible. She confirmed it: none of the uncomfortably hard wooden seats in the court-room that day were occupied by Colin and Sarah. Janine could confirm this because she, bless her, *did* come. In fact, she said, heartbreakingly: 'It was me who pinned up your hair.'

Soon after this, Ivor underwent a different type of trial. In the second half of the 1980s, I shared a flat in Kilburn in north London with my brother. One night, he came home saying he'd smoked some 'killa bud'. This was a phrase, common at the time, for high-grade cannabis, probably what would come to be known as skunk. I didn't think anything of it.

Not then anyway. About a week later, after a series of increas-ingly weird behaviours – including Ivor saying he could read minds,* that he was in touch with the cosmic secrets of the universe, walking down Kilburn High Road in a green felt hat with a penny whistle claiming to be the Pied Piper, hearing God through the clanks in the radiator, and going to visit the rabbi who had bar mitzvah'd us asking to be turned back from a man to a boy – I started to think maybe the killa bud had been a bit off. I particularly thought it at two in the morning, when, after he had called all our friends to come to our flat to hear more of his newfound messianic wisdom, I ended up taking Ivor to casualty – mental health services were not very

---

* My favourite episode following this claim was a moment in our kitchen when he insisted a friend of ours think of something and he would know what it was. She refused, saying she was concerned about his mental health and would prefer not to go along with this madness. But Ivor persisted, saying he would prove, if she would do this, that it was not madness. Finally, after about an hour, she gave in. After a moment's pause, and shutting of Ivor's eyes, he said, 'What were you thinking of?' She said, 'Orange.' Ivor said: 'Oh. I thought it was cat bowl.' There was a cat bowl in the kitchen. Come to think of it, I believe there were some oranges too.

developed in those days and I didn't know what else to do – and a doctor diagnosed first strike symptoms of schizophrenia. At which point, I proffered the information about the killa bud and the doctor said: 'Oh, it might be a cannabis psychosis.'

After this, Ivor veered from being still manic and mad to comatose (thanks to being put on anti-psychotic drugs) and, eventually, into depression. I've comedied this up a bit in the telling – and some of it was hilarious – but like much else in this story, it was also painful. It was painful in the straightforward sense, as in, in the arse, as Ivor would often do things like call me at the Comedy Store, which by this time I was regularly compering, and insist I come home between shows (in my time, on Friday and Saturday nights, there was one at eight and one at midnight) because he had urgently to tell me something that he couldn't possibly do on the phone, invariably to discover that, once again, God had revealed to him the secret of the universe. Which might seem like a compelling enough reason to rush home from Soho to Kilburn, except, y'know, He hadn't.

It was also painful in a deeper sense. In that I started to think I had lost my brother forever.

It's hard to tell how much of Ivor's psychiatric state at this point had a psychological component or, to put it another way, a parental component. But the episode does provide a shining example of the neglect-almost-raised-to-the-status-of-an-art-form negligence of my parents towards their children. One day, in a manic state, Ivor decided to walk from our flat in Kilburn to our parents' house in Dollis Hill because he wanted to tell Colin Baddiel the secret of the universe. This walk would've taken him about ninety minutes, during which time he was shouting things at passers-by about how he'd seen the light and that they should dance to the music of the cosmos and so on and so forth.

When he got to 43 Kendal Road, however, our dad's attitude was . . . aggravated. It involved – Ivor tells me – a lot of him saying, 'So what the fuck's going on, Ivor?' and 'What the hell's the matter with you?' Ivor decided in response to say nothing: to just sit there in silence. For about an hour. I had thought for many years that this was because my dad's default response to this, as to any other situation which disturbed his fragile peace – irritability – had shut Ivor down. He says no. He says he saw in that moment that my dad, a man of science, would not be able to handle the truth that he, Ivor, had been given the central facts of existence, and if my brother were to tell my father these facts as they had been revealed to him, it would destroy Colin Baddiel. I remain unconvinced about this: both that it would have destroyed my dad and that it wasn't, at heart, the irritability and anger that shut Ivor down. Because however much Ivor was twenty-five at the time, and possessed in that moment of a consciousness turbocharged by psychosis-generated euphoria, behind it somewhere would've still been the child whose reflex response (I know this because I am that child too) in the face of that irritation and anger was always to shut down.

Anyway, it must've been a strange hour. It ended in a curious way. By now, Janine had moved in with me, in the flat I shared with Ivor. I was out when the doorbell rang. She answered, to see Ivor on the doorstep with my dad. My brother was still not talking. But my dad said to Janine, 'What's going on? Why is he like this?' And she tells me now she can't remember what she said – but does remember thinking, *Well, you tell me.*

Zulaka

As I say, this isn't a misery memoir. Despite that, I guess the question should be asked: what damage? I've used the word, but I'm not quantifying it. What actual psychological havoc was wreaked on me by this upbringing, with all its over-broadcast infidelity and terrifying bedroom noises and Olympian negligence and too much fucking *golf*?

It's hard to tell. I said earlier that I didn't consider it damage, as I am happy in my own skin. Susceptible at times to low-level depression, but what thinking Jew isn't? I am sometimes plagued by a sense life will go wrong in ways that can make me feel like God – in whom (as I have already said and added a book plug in a footnote) I do not believe – is laughing at me. I felt this very strongly only this morning when I cut myself trying to open a box of plasters.

But that assessment – and that joke – is probably a form of denial. It leaves out, for example, the fact that I spent most of my thirties in therapy. Despite those years, I'm still hard-pushed to say what it was about my childhood that directly led to whatever issues I have now. I can parse a few of them. I'm very un-angry. I almost never get angry about anything, and I think that's because my dad was so quick to anger that I have gone the opposite way. I am also obsessed, as you know, with truth, and again I think that's in reaction to my upbringing. (I don't believe the Freudian nursery slopes idea that one must always perpetuate or repeat the dysfunction of your childhood

– I think you're just as likely to push back against it.) I think my mother's self-dramatizing creation of herself as north London's Erotic Golf Empress has led me to a sometimes-stark commitment to the unvarnished truth of things. Which may be why I've ended up writing non-fiction.

Some other aspects of my personality, viewed as consequences of my early years, are harder to deconstruct. I am, or certainly have been for most of my life, obsessed with sex. Despite this I've never been promiscuous. During the whole period of the early nineties, when I was in *Newman and Baddiel*, and then later working with Frank Skinner, when, to be honest, sexual opportunities were not a diminishing resource, I was mainly monogamous. This was perhaps odd, given that the thing I most wanted at that point in time was a lot of mindless sex with many different people. But I had stayed with my first girlfriend, Janine, from the age of sixteen to twenty-seven – a long time for a first relationship – and I think that meant I didn't really know how to do promiscuity. I'd had no practice.

Because it's not that easy. I don't mean the sex. I mean the after-sex. Paradoxically, to do promiscuity properly, you have to be a bit of a wanker. You need to be able, that is, in the morning – or even halfway through the night – to say to someone who you've just been intimate with, who you may have professed interest in as a person, to whom you may even have inferred that there might be a future relationship, cheerio. Like, forever. And you need to be able to say that a lot: you need to be able to say it morning after morning after morning. I found this difficult. As can perhaps be garnered from the fact that my first relationship went on for eleven years, I've never been good at splitting up with people. I'm with George: Costanza, that is. In the seventh season of *Seinfeld* – a show in which most characters are flitting in and out of relationships, doing what Americans call dating, in that weightless sitcom way – George is supposed to marry someone called Susan. He doesn't want to – he hasn't wanted to for some time – but he's been avoiding the issue, and in the final episode he's distraught, because she's printed out the wedding invitations. Jerry asks him: 'Why don't you just break it off?' And George says: 'Because I can't face that scene! I would rather be unhappy my whole life than face something like that.'

I think this is high art. I think it points to a very deep truth about relationships, one that most human dramas haven't dealt with, which is that an awful lot of people end up together – and stay together, despite unhappiness – because they can't face that conversation, the one about not being together any more. It's certainly true about me. I did talk to my therapist about this, but I'm not sure the issue was ever resolved. After about four years in therapy, it became clear to me that I couldn't split up with my therapist.

I feel it worked out in the end. I am very happy with Morwenna. Plus, recently, I think I have got my own back. For many years, I was somewhat bitter about my failure to take sexual advantage of fame. For some time, I used to beat myself up about the fact that I did actually have a window, in my late twenties, when it wouldn't have been that creepy to have a lot of sex with strangers, and I didn't. For decades, I would be haunted by the spectre of Sir John Betjeman, on his deathbed, being asked about regret and saying, allegedly, 'Not enough sex.' And then #MeToo happened, and I realized that most of my comedian peers who had taken libidinous advantage of their fame were going to spend every night from then on waking up at 4 a.m., sweating and terrified, trying to remember whether they'd wanked off in front of someone in a hotel corridor twenty years earlier. Finally, some payback.

I think for the real test of how well I've survived my parents, you must look at my parenting (a modern word, implying that there is a right and wrong way to do that job); but I hadn't even begun parenting before my parents interceded. They are weird about names. Because my father was Welsh, my older brother is called Ivor. At one point, they were apparently going to call him Ben and use Ivor as a middle name – but changed their minds when they realized his initials would then spell BIB. They thought other kids would tease Ben mercilessly at school because his initials spelled . . . a useful household item. So they called him Ivor Ben Baddiel. And for many, many years, Ivor went through school with other kids calling him Ivor the Engine, Ivor Biggun and Ivor Got a Fucking Stupid Name.

More name madness took place after the birth of my first child, who is called Dolly. My parents – never country music fans – didn't like the name and my dad, at that time not showing symptoms of dementia, took me aside to tell me, in great seriousness, that Dolly was a very bad idea because other children would call her a dolly bird. I said, they won't. He said: how do you know? And I said, because it isn't 1953.

But still, they just weren't happy. They were totally convinced, despite the Ivor disaster, and the fact that Colin Brian was called Colin Brian, which as Morwenna once said is basically the same name twice, that they knew best when it came to naming. My mother, with all the tact and grace that you'll realize by now marked her out, went over to Dolly, gurgling in her crib, and said: 'Well, *I'm* still going to call her Ms Question

Mark!' She said this as my mother said many utterly infuriating things; that is, with a sense that it was completely adorable.*

So the night after Dolly was born, when Morwenna and I were in a hospital room, still reeling from the shock of being suddenly responsible for a whole new human being, a small envelope was sent up from reception. I opened it: on two bits of scrappy card were written some suggestions my mother and father had separately written down for names for our child that they felt were better than Dolly. At no point, by the way, did Frommet Fabian-Baddiel spot the irony of the fact that this was basically what was done to her parents by the Nazis.

Here's my mum's:

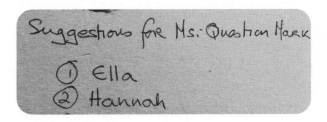

Suggestions for Ms. Question Mark
① Ella
② Hannah

---

* My mum also felt that the day of our second child, Ezra's birth was a good one to hand me this press cutting from the *Daily Mail*:

> A lot of people have wanted to tell pleasedwith-himself TV comic David Baddiel to go to hell. Happily, I can reveal, the broadcaster has taken his critics at their word.
>
> He and his pregnant other half, comedienne Morwenna Banks, who is expecting their second child, have just spent a weekend at the Hell Bay Hotel on the Isles of Scilly, last stop in Britain before Manhattan.

Who knows whether she'd read it first. I pointed out that it wasn't necessarily something I would have wanted to see, and she just looked blank. It was one of those times when I saw what my dad meant when he described my mother as 'like a blancmange'.

There you have, of course, the double-downing of the adorable phrase Ms Question Mark. Anyway. Ella. Hannah. Fine.
But it's not over:

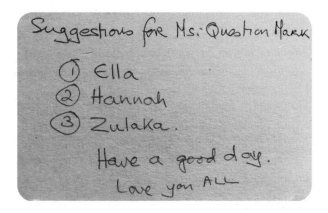

Zulaka. *Zulaka.* What even is that? Is it the Yiddish pronun-
ciation of Zoolander? Is it a meat Zulaka or a vegetable Zulaka?
I've googled it. It doesn't exist. It's not a real name. The nearest
is Zulaikha, which is an Islamic name. This is interesting, as I
think one reason why my mother didn't like the name Dolly
is that she didn't think it was very Jewish.* This was confirmed
at the birth of my second child, Ezra. When I told her his name,
she clapped her hands together, saying, 'Oh! It's an Old
Testament name!' Which it is, but I couldn't resist replying,
'Yes, but we've actually named him after the vicious antisemite
Ezra Pound.'†

---

* I don't know if it is or not. If you google 'Dolly Jewish', you get a story
about Dolly Parton doing some Jewish charity event, and that's it. Which
might suggest my mum was right. Except if I think about an old Jewish
lady called Auntie Dolly – if I hear those words said with a hefty Jewish
accent – it sounds fairly right to me.
† This seems a bit cruel to me now, although it was true. Pound was a
terrible antisemite – worse than his mentee, T.S. Eliot – but I have always
thought that Ezra Pound, just from a sonic point of view, is a very cool name.

Either way, I'm not convinced the name Zulaka would've cocooned my daughter from teasing and bullying at school. But my dad's suggestions were worse:

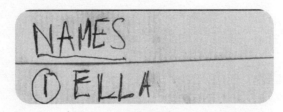

Ella. Again, fine. But please, don't rest easy.

No: no one's going to tease anyone at school for being called Shenandoah. Obviously. Plus, it's a man's name. Well, it's a river's name, but the river, in Virginia, is named after a man, an Oneida Iroquois chief. This is Shenandoah:

Who I agree looks like a dignified and inspiring character, but not redolent much, I would say, in the way of *these* vibes:

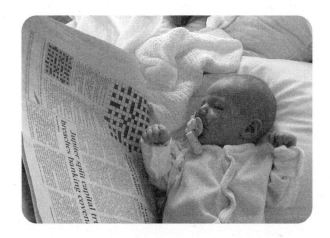

But better yet, in my dad's further thinking about 'names that no child could ever distort to a mocking version':

Titiana. TITIANA. It made me wonder if my parents had ever been to school. If they'd ever met *any other children*. They thought the bullies would have nothing – nothing – to get their teeth into with a name that to a child's ears just sounds like Booby Bumhole.

Dementia

As I say, at this point my father didn't have dementia, or at least, had not been diagnosed. He was sixty-seven when Dolly was born, a fact that causes me some anxiety, as the already-mentioned contraction of time as you get older means that I feel Dolly's birth (which at the time of writing was twenty-two years ago) to be something that happened yesterday. And I am fifty-nine. Which means that tomorrow, I will wake up and be eighty-one.

But even without my father's diagnosis, I had of course noticed a change in him: noticed, that is, that he was repeating himself, asking questions he had just asked, losing stuff. The Pick's disease part of it came later. The first symptoms were the first symptoms. The same as they always are.

He never once acknowledged it. It's clear to me from working with various organizations like the Alzheimer's Society what the good default is. I've seen it in the promotional, consciousness-raising films. It is a person who recognizes they have the disease and, alongside their loved ones, comes to terms with it, with some poignant background music. Trouble is, none of those people in these films look or feel like Colin Baddiel. A man who, after all, was in denial his whole life was never going to come to terms with this diagnosis. *It's so tiring living without an emotional life.* What my mother, in her moment of insight was pointing to there was that my father, a very intelligent man, did not have much in the way of what's called emotional intelligence, but would better be called emotional articulacy. In truth, for men, particularly of my father's generation, the inability to talk about emotions is really about fear, a fear of appearing unmanly. Because the first realization, before the window of awareness has closed, that you may have dementia is terrifying, and the first thing you need to do with fear, emotionally, is admit to it. My father's intelligence gave him no tools to negotiate that terror, and so he just shut down.

As I mentioned earlier, my mother didn't play the expected role either: she was never the default, good, dementia sufferer's spouse. She became a member of a local support group in Harrow, which was made up mainly of the wives of men living with dementia. She told me and Ivor most of the meetings consisted of these women declaring to the group how much they loved their husbands, and how much they were going to be there for them throughout the trials of dementia, no matter how bad it got. My mother meanwhile was keen to tell the group she was, in her words, 'fucking furious'. She told us she had stood up and said that one of her friends had a husband who was ninety and who was totally fine and played golf – yes, bloody golf – every day, and, not to put too fine a point on it, why couldn't she have one like that?

In truth, my mum was furious for much of her life that my dad was my dad, and not David White, so she was never going to be that patient about becoming his carer. It didn't help that his particular form of dementia meant he became *more* my dad, not less. But I admired her honesty, as she told it. I admired her crashing through the support group virtue signallers and telling her truth, especially as, in other parts of her life, she'd never quite known what this truth was.

· · ·

One of the things about having a parent with dementia is it makes you more hypervigilant – and not in a good way – about your own memory. The standard cognitive decline that comes with age (what a depressing opening to a sentence) becomes constantly measured in the (declining) mind against whatever slippage you've set yourself that would mean 'Oh Christ, this *isn't* standard cognitive decline.' I have several regularly moving goalposts here. For example: older people reading this book – OK, don't laugh, there might be some younger ones – will know that the first thing to go is names. As a result, I have a bank of names – included in them are such diverse characters as Melanie Blatt, Gil Scott-Heron and Colin Farrell* – who I use as a kind of memory checklist against which non-dementia-ness can be judged. No doubt the day will come when I will not be able to remember the name of the person who wrote and performed 'The Revolution Will Not Be Televised'. Let alone who the bloke in *Ballykissangel* was. But for now, they remain etched into the increasingly sloping cliff of my mind, to which I can fasten my 'I'm still OK' crampons.

Then again, dementia isn't just about memory. Any confusion, particularly around your normal routine, can make you feel your cognitive quota has started to expire. For example, every night, usually, before I go to bed, I put my clothes in the laundry basket. Which means, I go over to the laundry basket, holding my dirty clothes under one arm, I lift the lid on the laundry basket and I throw my clothes in there. But recently, before I put my clothes in the laundry basket, I went to the toilet first, holding my dirty clothes. I lifted the toilet seat and threw my clothes down the toilet.

---

* Had some trouble remembering Colin. But didn't google. Phew.

This made me so depressed and convinced I already had dementia that for a while I stood there just thinking, Fuck it, I'm going to flush.

Similarly, about a year ago, I was on a plane and wanted to watch a movie, but I couldn't find the headphones that had been given out at the start of the journey. I knew the flight attendants had handed me a pair, but they were nowhere to be seen. I'd dropped them under the seat or something – I just couldn't find them anywhere. Then I noticed the bloke next to me had fallen asleep with his headphones on his lap. I considered what to do. He was fast asleep. It seemed a shame for them to be lying there, unused. The child within me – always so near the surface – felt a sense of unfairness about the situation. So, gingerly, I reached over to his head-phones – I was only intending to borrow them – and, almost as soon as my fingers touched them, he woke up. Somewhat shocked, he said: 'What are you doing?' I lied – which as we know never works out for me – and said, 'Sorry, I thought these were *my* headphones.' And he said, 'Your headphones are on your head.'

These are obviously what are called, with sometimes irritating reassurance, senior moments. But as time goes on, it's harder to spot the moments becoming hours, becoming days. I'm wary of speaking about this too much. This might seem to contradict my commitment to self-declaration but there is a bit of a smudge on all that, which is to do with fame. I've said already that fame distorts who you are. But it also distorts what you say. When I first started doing interviews with journalists, I would speak as I do naturally; that is, without filter. But then I realized my own lack of filtration didn't extend to the presentation, and indeed reception, of my answers.

You learn many things the hard way through being in the public eye, and one of them is that illness is a scoop. In 2015, I was doing an interview with the *Daily Mirror* about a new kids' book I had written. I'd done a few warm-ups of *My Family: Not the Sitcom,* and talked a little about my father's illness in public. The journalist asked me a lot of questions about it. I was hesitant. I said: 'I think if I talk about my father's dementia, you'll take it out of context and highlight it in the wrong way and besides, this is an interview for a book I've written in which some twins discover a magic video game controller, so I'm not sure banging on about my dad's dementia is very on-message.' But she kept asking. Eventually, as a mollification, I said something I thought was very bland. I said, 'Well, one thing I can tell you is, because of my dad, every time I forget something now, I get a stab of fear, thinking, *Uh-oh, early onset.*'

It's not truly a very original thought: everyone I know whose parents have dementia monitors their own forgetfulness. The interview ended and I thought no more about it, until that weekend when the *Mirror* piece on my new children's book, about how it's really a jolly romp for nine- to twelve-year-olds, came out:

David Baddiel reveals he fears he has dementia aged 51 as dad battles condition

21:45, 9 OCT 2015 | UPDATED 09:50, 10 OCT 2015 | BY CLEMMIE MOODIE

The TV star, who is dealing with the recent loss of his mother to pneumonia as well as his dad's illness, talks about loss, laddishness and parenthood

SHARES | COMMENTS

Enter your e-mail for our celebs newsletter | Subscribe

Rex

I'm sure my publishers, HarperCollins, could do some market research to find out how many copies of *The Person Controller* sold off the back of this piece. Possibly none. Possibly some were even returned.

This article came out on a Saturday morning. By Saturday evening . . . well, I'll show you:

The Telegraph

Home   Video   News   World   Sport   Finance   Comment   Culture   Travel   Life   Women
Politics   Investigations   Obits   Education   Science   Earth   Weather   Health   Royal   Celeb

HOME » NEWS » HEALTH » HEALTH NEWS

David Baddiel: 'I fear I have dementia at the age of 51'

David Baddiel is worried he may have already begun to show symptoms of Pick's disease - the rare form of dementia which afflicts his father

497   0   22   519   Email

Belfast Telegraph

David Baddiel reveals dementia fears after watching his father suffer

PUBLISHED
10/10/2015 | 16:36

David Baddiel says he is already forgetting names

Comedian David Baddiel has spoken of his fears that he is developing dementia after watching his father suffer from an

By the time we get to the *Express,* I've started to forget names. It's getting worse:

EXPRESS

'I've started to forget names' David Baddiel, 51, fears he has dementia like his father

DAVID BADDIEL is convinced he has already started suffering from dementia at the age of 51.

By JESSICA EARNSHAW
PUBLISHED: 16:14, Sat, Oct 10, 2015 | UPDATED: 16:41, Sat, Oct 10, 2015

SHARE f TWEET y 8+ ✉ ◁ 269   11 💬

GETTY · TWITTER

By the time we get to the *Mail,* I'm in agony:

Mail Online

David Baddiel's agony amid fears he is contracting dementia - the condition that is slowly claiming the comedian's father

- The 51-year-old's father suffers from Pick's disease - rare form of dementia
- Symptoms affect behaviour, typically inappropriately sexual or swearing
- Baddiel says he's started to forget important things and had anxiety attack
- Writer also revealed that he's battled depression on and off for 10 years

By GEMMA MULLIN FOR MAILONLINE
PUBLISHED: 10:42, 10 October 2015 | UPDATED: 17:42, 10 October 2015

      163
shares

David Baddiel has revealed that he fears he is contracting dementia - the condition that is slowly claiming his father.

It was everywhere.

I immediately started getting concerned phone calls, including from my dad's friends. Some of whom I had in fact spotted signs of dementia in, so I wanted to say, 'No, I haven't got dementia, *you've* fucking got dementia . . .'

One particular tabloid headline that took my notice ran in the *Star*:

'I've started already to forget names' David Baddiel in dementia scare

COMEDIAN David Baddiel is pretty sure he has inherited dementia from his dad.

This seems an odd sentence construction. Surely it should be: I've already started to forget names. Perhaps the *Star* was trying to imply that as my brain atrophies I become more Jewish. In which case the headline should really have been 'I've started to forget names already'.

Note, by the way, the photoshoot a lot of them have used. I don't remember this photoshoot – obviously: I've got dementia – but clearly the picture editors at the various newspapers have chosen it because in it I look old. And mad.

The next day, I wrote a piece in the *Guardian* about how I didn't have dementia. Which was designed to put the record straight. Here is the headline:

The Guardian

David Baddiel: rumours about my dementia are greatly exaggerated

Great. Except they used this fucking photo:

Which is the worst one of the lot. What am I *doing* in that photo? That's what Jenni Murray, the former presenter of *Woman's Hour*, used to do in her photos:

To illustrate my article making it clear that I am in fact of sound mind, they've chosen a photo where I look like an insane cross between Jenni Murray and Alan Yentob.

Obviously, I also attempted to close this thing down on Twitter. As soon as I realized it was getting out of hand, I tweeted:

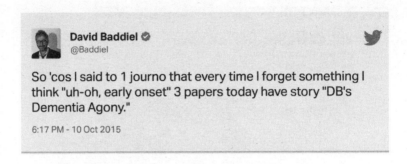

David Baddiel ✓
@Baddiel

So 'cos I said to 1 journo that every time I forget something I think "uh-oh, early onset" 3 papers today have story "DB's Dementia Agony."

6:17 PM - 10 Oct 2015

Which was asking for trouble, as someone called @DazBoot immediately responded:

daz boot
@FacileTalk

@Baddiel That's the third time you've tweeted that today.

6:18 PM - 10 Oct 2015

Not Me

While we're here, allow me to let you in a little on my life with the British tabloids. Round about the same time, I also appeared in the *Daily Mirror* with this headline:

Latest Celebrity Big Brother gossip >   WEBSITE OF THE YEAR   Our new FREE Mirror iOS app is here >

.ıl Most read ★ Top Videos   News ▾ Politics   Football   Sport ▾   Celebs ▾   TV & Film   Weird News

TRENDING   CALAIS MIGRANT CRISIS | REVENGE PORN | NEXT LABOUR LEADER | ISIS | UK WEATHER   Technology   Money   Travel   Fashion   Mums

▢ · News · UK News · Court case

Pervert policeman called David Baddiel found guilty of having 'extreme' pornography

14:09, 27 AUGUST 2015   BY ALEX WELLMAN

★ Recommended In News

Except as you may notice, I'm not a pervert policeman. Well. I'm not a policeman.

This was someone else called David Baddiel. I couldn't discover from the main news reports what form of extreme pornography he'd been found guilty of having. Eventually, I did find the info, in the *Jewish Chronicle*:

> A special constable was given a conditional discharge on Wednesday after being found guilty of having photos of women performing sex acts with a horse.
>
> David Baddiel, 33, from Hendon, who runs a tyre-fitting service, was convicted of . . .

If one was to consider the semiotics here, I'd say the reason the *JC* printed this information about the horse, and no other news outlet did, was because this David Baddiel is Jewish, natch, and so they were keen to make it clear the porn that this particular Jew was found in possession of was horse, rather than child. If we extend that analytical touch to the way this story was reported in general – indeed, to the fact of it being reported at all – I think we can ask the question: why would the *Daily Mirror* be mentioning the name of this particular pervert policeman in the headline? Assuming – which is unlikely – that a special constable possessing horse porn would in normal circumstances make the *Mirror*, the headline would simply be 'Pervert Policeman Found Guilty of Possessing Extreme Pornography'. The addition of 'Called David Baddiel' is there for one reason and one reason alone, which is to make people think it's me.

The *Mirror* are helped in their objective here by the idiosyncrasy of my name. There are other people called David Baddiel, but none of them are well known, and thus only one person is brought to mind. A sweeter – but still awkward – moment resulted from the same issue when I was taking Dolly for a walk when she was about three. At this point in her life, she called me Daddy, as you might expect, but had heard people call me David, which confused her a little, and occasionally she would call me that. On this day, we were in the park and suddenly she needed to go to the toilet. I managed to find one and did that awkward thing of holding her while weaving through the men standing in there towards the cubicle. I got her in, sat her on the seat, pulled her pants down – and that was the moment she chose to say, far too loudly, 'David Baddiel!'

And I could feel all the men outside stop pissing, and clearly think: *That's weird, I had assumed he was her father* . . .

But the base reason why I don't always sit well with fame is because I really have only one motto in life, and it is: the truth is always complex. And the truth about people – about who I am, about who you are – is the most complex of all. But fame doesn't allow for that. Fame allows only for a very narrow focus of personality. Because to be famous, you have to be narrativized – you have to be part of a story, and we don't have time for complex stories. It must be simplified, it must essentially be a panto, with villains, heroes, maidens and clowns. Which means fame is always going to be a type of mistaken identity.

With fame, you are mainly defined by however you are viewed at the beginning. In my novel *The Death of Eli Gold*, the titular character, who is a famous American writer, says at one point, 'Fame is like starlight . . .' By which he doesn't mean it's beautiful and glittering: he means that, like the light of stars, what you see when you look at a famous person tends to be from long ago – from when you first made up your mind about them. Or to quote a real great American writer, John Updike, 'Fame is a mask that eats into your face.' By which he means: fame has no plasticity – it cannot change and move with time and circumstance, like personality, like a real face, does. Whoever the culture has decided you are, that sets on you, like plaster of Paris, and whatever you say, to try and prove that you are someone else, just remains muffled beneath it.

In my case that mask was set early on: at its worst, somewhere in between a shouty lad and a racist stereotype of an arrogant Jew. Here is an example of fame making my face into that mask. In 2011, I went to see Peter Gabriel at the Hammersmith Apollo. It was orchestral arrangements of his songs, so you had to listen hard and stay quiet, which I did. But the next week this article appeared in *The Times* diary section:

theatre diary

Is Baddiel the rudest Gabriel fan ever?

The diary could have done with a real sledgehammer, rather than a mere song title, at Peter Gabriel's recent concert in Hammersmith. Not to attack the impassioned singer — no one should hurt PG, who performed a generous, crowd-pleasing meander through his back catalogue. No, we needed it to wallop the over-chatty comedian and big time Gabe fan David Baddiel, who talked so loudly throughout that you could barely hear the former Genesis frontman through Baddiel's self-absorbed North London drone. When asked to pipe down by those around him he declared that he had bought his ticket and could do what he damn well wanted with it. We can think of a good place for it.

Tiff guy: Baddiel got lippy when fellow fans asked him to be quiet

One thing to note here is the phrase 'self-absorbed North London drone'. This was before I wrote *Jews Don't Count,* but one of the things that may have led up to that book was noticing the creeping, insidious way the British press discreetly like to tell their readers that someone in the public eye is Jewish. The primary code for Jew in the press is probably this *North London,* particularly its application as an adjective. I first noticed it, I think, when Lord Levy was Tony Blair's envoy to the Middle East and would continually be referred to as 'North London businessman' Lord Levy or 'self-made North London millionaire' Lord Levy, or 'NW3 person good with money likes herring' Lord Levy.

Anyway, I read this bit in *The Times* diary section and was flabbergasted. I rang the guy I went to the concert with and said: 'What happened? Did I black out and forget all this?' And he said, 'No, you whispered about three things during the entire gig.' So I phoned *The Times* and they said, 'Definitely, it's true. In fact, we left stuff out to make it seem not so bad. You were completely drunk and when you were asked to be quiet by a woman, you told her to fuck off, three security men were called, *you offered them out for a fight* . . .' I mean, really, it's not sounding very me, is it? Although if you want to know how persuasive and assumed-to-be-true stuff in print is, Ivor told me he'd read it and thought it *was* true, until I told him what *The Times* had said about me offering out the security men – then he knew it wasn't.

The guy I went with, by the way – I have to tell you this for the story, it's not just name-dropping – was Richard Curtis. The man who set up Comic Relief, the most morally unques- tionable – least likely to lie – person in the world. That is important for you to know, because he wrote to *The Times* on my behalf. Actually, he went so far as to say: 'It's very unlikely David would have said "he'd bought his ticket and could do what he damn well liked with it" as he hadn't – I had.'

The Times weren't interested. They said, no, we have witnesses. You behaved like a terrible person. It was making me go mad. In desperation I emailed Peter Gabriel. It felt pathetic to email my teenage idol about something so absurd, but this is what fame – understood as a persona that apparently is you but that you don't recognize – can drive you to. And he said, 'I'm very surprised you were there watching a clapped-out old rock star, in fact.'

No, he didn't. That *is* a lie. It is what we in the trade refer to as a call-back. This is what he said:

From: Peter Gabriel
Date: 29 March 2011 18:27:09 BST
To: David Baddiel
Subject: Re: impersonation

Hi David

I think this is a case of mistaken identity.

I had heard a rumour that someone had complained to you to stop talking and that you had told them to fuck off - but this was definitely on Thursday.

I know you and Richard came on the Wednesday, so, end of story.

Caroline is our PR so i will ask her what she knows.

You need some quality control for your lookalikes

all the best

peter

Right. That's it, I thought. From the hero's mouth. I phoned *The Times* again and amazingly the diary editor *still* didn't believe me. He started saying, *Well, if it wasn't you, who was it?* And while I was on the phone, this second email, from Peter Gabriel's road manager, came through:

From: Mike Large
Date: 30 March 2011 10:21:26 GMT+01:00
To: Caroline Turner, Peter G

I believe the gentlemen in question was this young man:

IT WAS IAN BROUDIE! IAN BROUDIE, OF THE LIGHTNING SEEDS.

I mean, I'm not denying I look like him. That picture is cropped. Here's the original . . .

. . . and clearly the photographer has put me and him on either side of Frank for the sake of symmetry.

Ian, by the way, is from Liverpool. So that self-satisfied north London drone all the witnesses reported hearing – it's *very* north of London, isn't it? But then again, he is Jewish.

After all this, *The Times* finally admitted they got it wrong and printed an apology. This apology:

CORRECTION
On Monday we reported that the comedian and writer David Baddiel spoke noisily throughout a recent Peter Gabriel concert and refused to be quiet when asked to do so by fellow concert-goers. This was entirely incorrect. We accept that the disruption was caused not by Mr Baddiel, who is a longstanding Peter Gabriel fan and always an entirely conscientious audience member, but by a lookalike. It was a case of mistaken identity. We apologise profusely to Mr Baddiel.

'A longstanding Peter Gabriel fan and always an entirely conscientious audience member . . .' Hmm. *The Times* are taking the piss here, aren't they? I knew this, even though they ran

the wording of this apology past me first. They said, in a somewhat passive aggressive way, we've written it like this, because
we don't want to seem too serious about it. And I, wanting to
play along and not seem pompous, said, yes, OK. But I shouldn't
have done. I should have said, well, for a very long time, you
were *fucking* serious about not printing an apology, so print a
proper apology.

My point is: fame is a mask that eats into the face: the
person who fame has made of me, in this case it actually was
me – a loud-mouthed shouty lad/arrogant Jew – is not me. And
the person in *The Times*' diary column was actually not me.
But how hard was it to prove that it was not me.

By the way: after this happened, I phoned Ian – who is a
lovely man, extremely well-behaved and nice, most of the time
– and he said, 'Oh God, yes, on that night I got a bit out of it
and had a row with some people in front of me and yeah, it's
me.'

And then he said:

'Don't tell anyone.'

Sorry, Ian.

Colin

In the mid-1990s, my parents split up. Neither me nor my
brothers ever totally got to the bottom of why. Yes, I know you
the reader will say, 'Well, I can think of about a thousand
reasons and we're still only halfway through the book', but
what I mean is, we don't know what the catalyst was. We don't
know if, sometime in 1993, my dad burst in on her and David

White *inflagolftee*. Or alternatively, if she decided one day that it was simply too tiring living without an emotional life.

Anyway, split up they did. My mother went to live in Cambridge, where she had grown up. She managed to find, in one of the most beautiful towns in the UK, a fairly hideous bungalow on a fairly hideous street, and declared she had fallen in love with it. My father, meanwhile, stayed in the house in Dollis Hill and set about the business of becoming a homeless person, with a house.

To be clear: the house in Dollis Hill was never very clean. This again goes against the Jewish stereotype, which would be house proud, perhaps to the point of showy. Forty-three Kendal Road cannot be said to have fallen into that trap. My mates, in particular, would be amazed by the state of the kitchen, especially the grill. I should explain for any younger readers that grill in this context does not mean some sort of glitzy interior barbecue oven attachment. The grill in our house lived above the gas hobs, at about eye level, and you had to pull it out to put bacon rashers or sausages or indeed bread (we didn't have a toaster) into it. And because it was never cleaned, a thick layer of grease built up over time on, and especially in the valley beneath, its rusty rungs. This made lighting it incredibly hazardous.*

---

* This health and safety issue was not improved by my mother's attitude to cooking chips. She would do this in a chip pan that, once upon a time, had been blue, but over time, an extremely long time, had turned very black indeed. It was possible the oil in it had not been changed since it was blue. As far as I could make out, my mother saw no reason ever to change chip oil.

This is another way in which she didn't conform to the Jewish mother stereotype. Jewish mothers are supposed to be obsessively good with food. My mother's idea of cooking was to put an enormous vat of water on the stove for two or three days, occasionally throwing in some giblets and the odd claw: this she then scooped out into bowls and called chicken soup.

For a while we had a cleaning lady called Mrs Miles – I never knew her first name – I'm guessing Edna – but I don't remember her ever making much impact on the cleanliness of the house at any deep level. By the time my parents split up, she was long gone anyway (although I do remember her turning up in the front row of one of my stand-up shows and just looking upset by how dirty *that* was). My dad was not at all interested in keeping the house clean. I did offer to pay for a cleaner, but for my dad, of course, that was just *aggravation*. Cleanliness was aggravation.

I don't remember my mother doing much housework, but she must have because it was incredible how quickly after she left our childhood home that it turned into a dangerous slum. To illustrate this, I need to tell you a disgusting story. Sorry. It involves me being on the toilet. Sorry, again.

Our house had two toilets. The one on the ground floor was always a bit dodgy. It had a sliding door that never shut properly and was also next to the garage, which was used to store the endless surplus of stuff – of my dad's toys and my mum's golf memorabilia. If you went into the downstairs toilet, you ran the risk that they were going to be next door fussing with their things, on the other side of a very thin wall. I always preferred the upstairs one, which was next to my bedroom and, by the standards of our house, habitable.

I went round to see my father about two months after he and my mum parted ways. I had a sense that things were going downhill. Thus, when I realized I needed to use the toilet, I instinctively went for the upstairs one.

I – and I apologize again for the visual image – went and sat on the upstairs toilet. I had nothing to read – this was before the days of mobile phones – and I couldn't even do the emergency 'nothing to read in the toilet' strategy of reading the back of a toilet cleaner bottle, as, obviously, my dad hadn't bought any. Therefore, I just stared at the floor, at the lino, and its unchanged-since-I-was-a-kid white and black diamond pattern.

Suddenly, I felt a tap on my neck. And then another. And another. My first thought was: Oh Christ, the roof is leaking. That'll be something else to deal with. But then, I noticed, next to my feet, very close to my rolled-down trousers and pants, on its back with its legs twirling in the air, a black beetle. With another black beetle in the same position next to it. Soon, another appeared from above.

With a fair amount of fear – this is one of a few moments in my life that felt like being in an actual horror film – I looked up. The light fitting in that toilet was an oblong of frosted glass on the ceiling, open at the edges. Or maybe it was plastic. I don't know. What I do know is that it was teeming with beetles. I've never seen so many beetles. So many that the light fitting was trembling with the movement of them all. They were all . . . beetling around really fast – it's hard to know exactly what they were doing there – it seems an odd place for beetles to want to be, given that they aren't moths – and every few seconds, another one would fall off the edge. I must have woken them up by switching the light on.

Anyway. Having said it was a horror film moment, it's clearly to some extent a comedy horror we're talking about, as I am, let's face it, on the toilet. The horror and the comedy are perhaps encapsulated together by the fact that being in this position, with the threat of hundreds of beetles about to fall on me,* I

---

* In later years, it's possible the trace memory of this event is why I've always turned down *I'm a Celebrity . . . Get Me Out of Here!*

couldn't move that quickly. Without going into detail, there were ablutions to be done.

By now, a separate community of floor beetles – none of whom seemed to have been that bothered by their Icarus-like fall – were congregating around my feet, threatening to climb up my legs. I considered screaming but screaming on the toilet just feels . . . wrong. I – apologies *again* – rushed the last wipe, did my trousers up and ran out of the toilet.

I went downstairs to tell my dad, and we went into the upstairs toilet, which felt more than a little incongruous, standing together in the loo with my dad looking up at the festering light. And here's the thing. He wasn't bothered. He just shrugged. This may have been because he was depressed, having faced redundancy, infidelity, separation and, now, a toilet light full of beetles. At some level, though, it was because the toilet light full of beetles genuinely didn't bother him. And of course, cleaning them out would've been aggravation.

They got back together. Divorce papers were drawn up, but they never went through with it. This may be because, after #BeetlesInTheLightGate, my dad realized he couldn't survive, hygienically, without a wife. But more likely, as far as I can make out – none of this involved any conversation with me at the time; I'm piecing it all together from documents I've found since their deaths – they got back together because of money. A sale of 43 Kendal Road was mooted, and the divorce seems to have foundered there. My instinct is that my dad eventually decided he would rather forgive my mother her transgressions than split the proceeds of the house with her. Or at least, if he *was* going to have to split those proceeds, he may as well fucking live with her.

There is more to it, of course. I've said earlier that my mum never gave up on David White. But like many damaged people, she could divide herself in contradictory ways. So, although she held out some kind of candle for her golfing memorabilia lover her whole life, she accommodated within that desire the dysfunctional comfort of taking Colin back. I was keen on my parents separating. I think I was keen on them separating some years before it happened. It was obvious to me they weren't happy together and I was optimistic about the idea that there was still time for both to find that happiness elsewhere.

But I was wrong. I see now how unlikely that elsewhere-happiness was. They were both so singular, and so obsessive about the stuff that obsessed them, that it would have been too difficult for them to find other people to be with. In a bad way, they did fit together, like a jigsaw puzzle showing a picture of something comically bleak. I'm more surprised about my mother, who despite age and the facial ravages of Bell's palsy, continued, admirably, to consider herself a top sexual prize. But this didn't seem to filter down into her actually dating anyone in her late fifties, or early sixties, and so back to Sarah and Colin it was. They sold Dollis Hill and he moved into her fairly hideous bungalow in Cambridge.

It seems to me they were, in fact, reasonably happy for a few years there. Or at any rate tolerated each other, in a way they hadn't before. In the early 2000s, I guess to be closer to me and Ivor, although this was never actually stated, they moved to London, to a Brookside Close*-style house in North Harrow. My mum loved that house. And the tolerant, OK, low-level happiness might've continued, had my dad not at that point begun to show signs of dementia.

---

* Second reference: apologies to the occasional younger reader.

Sarah

When they were in North Harrow, my mother started working
for a local charity shop, for St Luke's Hospice. This is a nice
thing to do. But, as ever, my mum put a spin on it. When we,
and my brother, had kids, she would come round with toys.
Loads of toys, which she had helped herself to. From the
charity shop. We tended to refer to these, ungenerously, as
meningitis toys. Because we thought they would give our
children meningitis. My mother had a funny conception of
largesse. By which I mean, she'd endlessly, on birthdays, on
anniversaries, on Jewish High Holy Days, come bearing
gifts, often an absurd number. But I'm afraid they would be
tat. I know this sounds ungenerous and entitled. Sorry. I'm
a truth-teller. They would be tat. And possibly infested with
meningitis.

And also, it interests me as a way into her character.
Because, I think once more, my mother, in her own parallel
universe, the one without Hitler, would have been a person
of largesse, an aristocrat who'd arrive at her grandchildren's
houses with champagne and caviar and Fabergé eggs and I
don't know what else aristocrats arrive at their grandchildren's houses with. But that universe was denied to her, so
she came instead with light sabres that didn't light up, many-
coloured xylophones with missing keys and huge bags of

loose Lego that didn't fit together to build anything recognizable.*

I mean, this may be unfair. She may have paid for all these things. But I kind of doubt it. I doubt it because she sometimes cut out the middleman – under the auspices of the shop she'd go to help with house clearances but end up passing some of the goods on. She once offered my brother a dead man's TV (however it sounds, this is not gangster parlance for something else).

The job in St Luke's, as well as giving her access to cheap or possibly free gifting opportunities, also provided my mother with a way of getting out of the house, which after my dad's dementia began to take hold, she wanted to do a lot.

Since her death in 2014, I've been plagued by guilt that I didn't get carers in for my father earlier. I've suggested she had elements of Munchausen's but Munchausen syndrome implies hypochondria – faking illness in order to be the centre of attention – and my mother wasn't faking. She liked to be the centre of attention, and she also liked to be attended to by men who she thought of as high status, which would include doctors, but from mid-life on, she also, objectively, was not a well woman.

This wasn't helped by my dad's decline. As we know, caring for him did not come naturally to her. Plus the nature of his dementia meant he was an incredible handful. As well as the standard irritation that goes with having to live with someone who asks you the same question every ten minutes, the Pick's

---

* I asked my children for more examples of my mother's gifting tendencies. Dolly said, 'Teddy bears with yarmulkes on.' Ezra said, 'Expired credit cards.' These, of course, are not toys. But yes, I remember her giving them to my children anyway.

disease part of his condition meant she had to deal with even more insults than usual.

My mother projected an idea of us as a nice Jewish family; this was, of course, a fantasy. But she followed it through with regular get-togethers, on birthdays and other occasions, and latterly, these were simply exercises in Colin control. Especially if we went out to restaurants, where I would have a quiet word with the waitress first, explain the situation, hope the word disinhibition was comprehensible and apologize in advance.

The stress clearly took a toll on her. There are quite a few revelations in this book, aren't there, but here's another: my mother was, I think, by the end of her life, a drug addict. I'm not talking about street drugs – not really her thing: when a member of my family got addicted to meth, she would always refer to it as 'the meth crystal' – but prescription ones. She took, for example, OxyContin. And if I was to tell you why she died, early, really, at seventy-five, I would suggest it was probably of a drug overdose.

When I did *Desert Island Discs* in 2018, I included a lot of songs that only made sense in terms of my personal history. I know everyone is meant to do that. Some do and some don't. Some, politicians particularly, curate their choices to give no sense at all of who they actually are, only how they want to be perceived. I couldn't do this. I chose, for example, 'Three Lions', even though it's annoying when people go on *Desert Island Discs* and pick their own songs, but I took the conceit seriously enough to consider that if I was going to be on a desert island for the rest of my life, I'd like to be able to remind myself of one of the most amazing parts of my life.

More obscurely, I also chose a song called 'Love Will Find a

Way', which I wrote with Erran Baron Cohen for the musical version of *The Infidel*. It premiered at Stratford Theatre Royal in early October 2014. My mother died just before Christmas that same year. I put 'Love Will Find a Way' into *Desert Island Discs* (a somewhat rough demo version of it sung by Erran) because the premiere of *The Infidel* musical was the last time I ever saw my mum happy.

I've said before that she loved the showbiz part of my fame much more than the work itself, and she really loved that premiere. It was showbizzy – we'd managed, even though it took place at the less fashionable end of east London, to get Jonathan Ross and Sacha Baron Cohen and other luminaries to come along – and, of course, it was Jewish. Which two elements made it all very, from my mother's point of view, what's not to love?

On *Desert Island Discs*, Kirsty Young made me cry. She said she remembered seeing photos of my mum in the paper after the premiere and that she was 'shining'. That was the word Kirsty used, and it triggered tears in my eyes. She was. She wore her heartbreaking tiara; the one she'd worn as an extra in the film.

The next time I saw my mother she wasn't well. She sounded like she couldn't breathe very easily. We went to see a film with my kids in Harrow. It was the night of Chanukah. We'd lit the candles and sung the songs. My mother, for the children – she used to do them for me, Ivor and Dan when we were kids, too – crammed sweets onto a paper plate. These special plates were called Bunter Tellers, as they'd been called in Germany and then in England when she was a refugee, at least by her parents. I had a sense something was wrong, but she batted me away, saying it was a chest cough.

That was a Wednesday. On the Friday night, she was playing the Big Jewish *macher* again: she'd organized for the next day, the Saturday morning, a Kaddish for her parents. She seemed, in her old age, to do this all the time. They didn't always go right. Once, she had a cover made for the Kol Chai Sefer Torah – the scroll on which the Old Testament is written, which is brought out for the congregation to revere in every synagogue ceremony – with the names of her parents, Ernst and Otti, embroidered on it (Torah covers are normally made of fine silk and decorated exquisitely). Only when this particular Torah came out and was held aloft for worshippers to touch and kiss, clearly there'd been a drop-out in my mother's communications with the embroiderer, as the cover displayed, in beautiful silver thread, the words 'Ernst and Otto'. Which made my grandparents sound like some sort of Siegfried and Roy-style Vegas act.

Here it is, thankfully spelled correctly now.

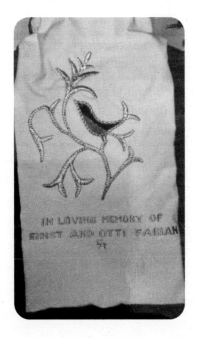

My brother Ivor, always the most responsible of the three sons, had said he would go to my mother's event that Saturday morning. He'd spoken to her the night before and her chest sounded worse, but she said – and this is why I think she died of a drug overdose – that she would dose up on pills overnight and was certain she'd be fine in the morning and was looking forward to seeing him there. I was driving to Cornwall with my family – my kids were twelve and ten at the time. We'd just got out of London onto the M4 when Ivor called. He'd arrived at Kol Chai and she wasn't there. This was already not good news: if my mother organized a synagogue event, she'd be there before everyone else, making sure the bridge rolls and the plastic cups of warm red wine were positioned correctly on the trestle table (note the singular: these would rarely be events of great plenitude).

Ivor drove to their house in Harrow, but when he got there no one was answering the door. He banged on it. Nothing. Eventually, he called an ambulance. The paramedics had to smash the door down. They ran upstairs to my parents' room. According to my brother – I feel sorry for him now writing this, knowing the trauma it must have caused him – my mother was out cold, half-out of the bed, foaming at the mouth. My dad, in bed, was already too far gone with dementia to understand the seriousness of the situation. But not too far gone not to swear and do a lot of V-signs at the paramedics as they tried to save his wife's life.

When I got the call, I didn't think my mother was dying. Ivor had tried to play it down. A desperate optimism kicks in at a time like this, that surely everything will be all right. Before either of your parents die, you live with the knowledge that it will, of course, happen someday but, like your own death, you don't really believe it. There'd even been talk of us driving on to Cornwall. But something cut through the confirmation bias and I turned the car around.

When we got to Northwick Park Hospital, the truth hit.

Popular culture, Hollywood and all that, trains you for certain idealized expectations around looks, relationships, happiness, money – we have been inculcated to expect that all these things can be optimized. But, also death. And similarly, as when looks, relationships, happiness and money turn out not to match up to the ideal, and reality can feel like a shocking drop-off, so it is with death. Somewhere in our heads, we have reserved an image of a white room with white curtains, a parent weak but smiling, a hand being held, perhaps some wise last words gifted down from that sad height, followed by an 'I love you', or similar, and then a nurse enters and discreetly draws a hand over their face, shutting your loved one's eyes.

What we do not have is: your mother semi-conscious on a trolley, in confusion and pain, raising her hand to her head trying to communicate something she cannot, perhaps because she is a drug addict who as well as dying is going through withdrawal. What we do not have is chaos; harassed medics running in and out, not knowing the name of the patient or what might be wrong with her. What we do not have is six hours of her floating in and out of consciousness, while your children sit in a tiny room nearby full of fear. We do not have, towards the end, awful attempts using defibrillators to revive her as she slips away, her body jerking upwards in terrible spasms as the electricity fails to jump-start her poor, exhausted heart.

And what we do not have, in the idealization, is a vision of ourselves, before it is over, walking away from the deathbed, because we can't take it any more. That is what happened. I still feel terrible about it. I still wake up breathless with guilt, an emotion not natural to me, about it. But as the minutes passed that day, I could sense the damage building inside me. It was like experiencing your mental scars forming in the moment. The enormous sense of helplessness didn't, well, help. It was hard to tell whether or not my mother knew we were there, and in the confusion, in the not-knowing-where-to-put-yourself-ness of it all, I ended up spending a lot of time in the hospital corridor or in the tiny room where my children were, checking back in to the emergency room every so often to see if there had been any change in her condition. I'm aware that 'I ended up' is doing a lot of heavy lifting here. It was an escape. There is another version of this day where I do not seek an escape; where I suck up all the trauma of staying in that room with her, for eight hours, whatever it takes, and maybe that is what I should've done.

I was there when she died, as the Hollywood ending demands, but again, it was not Hollywood. It was not lyrical, or poetic. It did not grant me any insight into the mystery of the universe. It was just more people in blue and green scrubs running around, more shouting, more defibrillating: more of a sense that the body is a husk and that there is no such thing as a soul, because it does not slip away in a reverent whoosh. Life is ejected from the body, like vomit.

Her body was brought into a small room connected to the visitors' room, the one where my children and my brother's children had been sitting the entire day. We took them away so they wouldn't see her body come through. And then, once she was laid out, and the door shut, they came back into the main room again. I went into the small room. It was dark. I could make out that they hadn't taken off any of her rings. My mother wore quite a lot of rings. Her fingers had swollen up. That was probably why. I don't know.

It's hard to write this part. Partly because it just is hard, and partly because it seems to me that I cannot but devolve into one particular cliché. Which is: beyond good or bad, beyond judgements, particularly judgements of appropriate parental behaviour, my mother was an enormous source of life. She was full to the brim of her small cup, the cup that circumstance and an angry husband and state-sanctioned antisemitism had left her with. She filled it with what she could – golf, Jewishness, sex – but principally with herself, and it always overflowed. And now, standing in that room, looking at her laid out, it was impossible to imagine that all that life could be contained only in this cold mould of flesh. It felt like so much energy must go somewhere. But I looked into the darkness of that tiny room helplessly for it.

A rabbi came. He said Kaddish. It was a different Kaddish than the one my mother had planned. I have never felt more of an atheist.

Colin

It was, as perhaps you've worked out, a difficult day, and it was about to get worse. I'm sorry this bit is bleak. But, as they say on *Love Island*, 'It is what it is.' Nothing, I think, is more what it is than death.

Part of the complexity of the day was that my dad hadn't come to the hospital. We wouldn't have been able to explain to him what was going on and, therefore, the necessity of coming. He was also physically very immovable. We would have had to drag him, bodily, to his wife's deathbed.

But of course, it was a worry that we had left him on his own in the house. A good person from the NHS did go and check on him, but he was there, alone, for most of the day. After my mother had died, and our children and wives had gone home, and we'd signed the requisite death forms and stood by the rabbi saying Kaddish over her dead body, Ivor and I went to my dad's house – it was by now the evening – and told him.

My parents, as is perhaps clear, didn't have a great marriage. Apart from all the sexual secrets my mother was not being very secretive about, they argued a lot. Well, argument implies an amount of back and forth, but it was mainly my dad being irritated with my mum and her deflecting this in ways that made him more irritated. When he described her as a 'blanc-mange', it wasn't a body-shaming remark about her size – which in fact was variable across their marriage, not least because at one point she was smoking about eighty menthol cigarettes a day – but was expressive of his frustration at the way his anger seemed to bounce off her. I remember crossing the Severn Bridge on the way back from one of our yearly holidays to Swansea, when the toll was a pound. After handing over the money, my mum asked, 'What are we paying that for?', and my dad went ballistic. In my memory, he was shouting angrily at her for her ignorance and stupidity all the way back to London. I can't remember her ever shouting back. It revealed, I guess, the truth that she was not an intellectual and this was always at some level eating away at him. Thing is, I *am* an intellectual* and *I* don't really know what that quid went to.

Anyway, my parents' was a very ragged version of love, if it was love at all. I remember as a young teenager during another row, listening from behind my bedroom wall to my dad for once not making animal sex noises but shouting sarcastically,

---

* I'm aware you're not supposed to say this.

'We're supposed to be in love!' Which, again, was not great parenting or, perhaps more accurately for Sarah and Colin Baddiel, not parenting that showed much awareness of the proximity of their children.

But couples who have been together a long time, even if it's an argumentative, difficult, not-corresponding-to-Hollywood-expectations-of-love time, that is still their life. That relationship, and its survival, will still be their principal story. I saw this very distinctly when my brother and I told my dad that his wife had died. He was sitting on the sofa in their living room in Harrow. He had adopted, on seeing us, and our grave expressions, a very Colin-ish attitude, smirking and calling us twats and saying, 'What is it, then? Get on with it!' His face continued to hold that man-shield as we started to speak. And then, as we said, 'The mother died', I saw it crumble. I saw a man whose default setting was *I don't give a fuck about anything* collapse into absolute vulnerability.

I'd never seen him look so scared. You have to remember, of course, that the dementia meant he wasn't aware my mother had been taken away that morning by paramedics: the news would have come to him out of a clear black sky. Perhaps, as well, the dementia creates something else, which is – not in words, not in actual understanding, but in animal instinct – a sense that without this person, your carer, the woman who looks after you, all is lost.

We are not a huggy family. I hug my kids a lot – more than they want – but that doesn't come from a 43 Kendal Road inheritance. My dad in particular – *I didn't know you cared?* – was not given to physical shows of affection with his children, or anyone else. But suddenly, my brother and I were around my father, on either side of him, holding him as best we could, telling him everything was going to be OK even though we had no idea whether it was going to be. I think I may have said I was sorry a lot. I was.

It was awful. It was everything that is bad and wrong about growing up. I felt blasted with sadness.

And about half an hour later, we had to tell him again.

The first time it happened came with a specific dread, an immediate realization that this was a very particular circle of hell that we were, for the foreseeable future, going to be looping around. We lived in that circle for maybe a year. The explaining and the consoling would go on for about half an hour, and then there would be an evanescent, hard-to-define point when the fear would go out of his eyes, even though he'd still be nodding and apparently engaged in the story of Sarah's passing . . . and he'd look up and say, 'So . . . where's the mother?' Or 'Where's Sarah?' And I, we, would take a deep breath and start again.

Eventually, we had to put a note up. It's interesting how over the different ages of your life, which come at you slowly, you can find yourself living an experience that before was just a story. By which I mean: an ex-girlfriend once told me that her new boyfriend's grandmother had dementia, and also a dog, Boris, who died. After his death, she'd go out every night looking for Boris and calling for him. Eventually, her family had to put up a large sign in her living room saying, THE DOG IS DEAD.

I always thought that was funny. I nicked the story and used a barely fictionalized version of it in my novel *Whatever Love Means*. I still think it's funny, even now, that my life has involved agreeing with a carer that a piece of paper with the words SARAH DIED on it should be laid on the table in front of my dad's chair. Admittedly, it is less funny when the sign refers to your mum, rather than a dog.

For weeks, telling my dad this old news, that was always new news to him, would elicit the same shock. And yet over time, while he'd still ask the question, and still look confused and vulnerable on getting the answer, it seemed to me the trauma receded. Perhaps some trace memory somewhere in the dementia-impacted brain* builds up over time, so that unconsciously the truth is actually known or, at least, less unfamiliar when it comes. Either way, eventually he wouldn't look so shocked. Rather, he'd act more in a kind of 'Oh yes, I knew that' way. He would even sometimes – this was a few months after the event – adopt a sort of interested, enquiring air, saying things like 'Heart attack, was it?' or 'Did she die in hospital?'

Given that my dad never at any point, not even when he was still mainly lucid, accepted he had dementia it's curious that in these moments he never considered it at all odd that he had forgotten the details of such a big thing as his wife's death, but the disease comes with its own weird raft of accommodations.

Anyway. Despite his memory not in any way improving, somehow imparting to my father the fact that my mother was dead gradually got easier. In fact, sometimes, after absorbing the information, he would surmise that, being a bachelor now, he ought to go out on the pull.

---

* I often, from my time around people with the disease, think this. It feels to me like the reason people with dementia sometimes ask the same question again and again is not only that they've forgotten that they've already asked it – although they have – but also that they retain some amorphous memory of the question they wanted to ask.

Dan and Colin and Dolly

With my mum's death came a whole new world – but not in a Disney way – of dealing with my dad. It became abruptly clear to Ivor and me that as Colin's children we were suddenly required to be our parent's parents. Which isn't an unusual situation for children in their forties and fifties to find themselves in, but that doesn't make it any less challenging. Not least when the type of dementia your parent has involves them calling you a cunt a lot.

My younger brother Dan took the initial burden. He came home from America for our mother's funeral and stayed for a few months, to look after my dad while we were trying to sort long-term care.

This wasn't easy. We tried at first with care homes, but when we met with their representatives, or rather, when we introduced them to Colin and he called *them* cunts, there were, to put it mildly, some issues. Most just said, 'No, he's too challenging, goodbye', or 'Well, as he's so aggressive, we'd need to put three or four of our staff on him all the time to make sure he doesn't upset the other residents and that'll be five grand a week.'

So he stayed at home with Dan. Who, after a few months, couldn't cope with it any more. This is hardly surprising. Dan filmed some of his interactions with my dad. In one of them, my dad is on the sofa, speaking to Dan, who is behind the camera, and it goes like this:

DAN: I'm a what?

COLIN: Ugly fucker. Fucking ugly fucker.

DAN: Runs in the family.

COLIN: Probably, but I was a genetic error.

DAN: You were a genetic error?

COLIN: Yes, cos I'm beautiful, and you're a fucking ugly
bugger.

This by the way is very unfair. My younger brother Dan is not
just *not* ugly: he lives in New York and has worked as a cab
driver there, and in a recent Manhattan Cab Drivers Charity
Calendar, he was Mr February. Really.

It's a strange photo, particularly, I think, because my brother's leg looks like an enormous turkey drumstick: like an animal's leg. Which makes him look like a mythological creature. The whole image looks to me like: The Kidnapping of Mr Tumnus Turned Out OK!

I don't want you to think this means my younger brother is not a serious person: here he is demonstrating, by himself, outside of Trump Tower.

Which is very impressive, although it was not, as you can see, a hunger strike.

Dan stayed for about three months, after which we decided to keep Colin at home but employ an agency to give him live-in care. Over the next seven years, this meant various carers – notably a Kentish man-lad called Clive Bowles and a small powerhouse of a woman from Sunderland called Sandra Wiseman – effectively became part of our family. And of course, they took a lot of stick from Colin as well. That's one of the paradoxes about Pick's disease – the person with it mainly ends up surrounded by people trying to look after them and be nice to them, and so they're the ones who mainly get called, sorry to say it again, cunts. Pick's brings into focus in a very sharp way the platitude that dementia can sometimes be worse for the people around the disease than it is for the person who has it.

To be fair to my father, his utterances didn't just become a torrent of straightforward abuse. Sometimes he could be pretty left-field. Often, I would be with him when he was visited by people from Harrow social services who were assessing the level of care he needed. These people would usually be trying to do their very best for Colin.

Sometime in 2015, I remember him being visited by a very nice Indian woman, who had to deal with being asked contin-ually by my father if she was a virgin – which did at least make her laugh a lot and say, 'You'll have to ask my husband!' She was wearing a sleeveless top. After a certain amount of talking to Colin, she turned away from him, shutting out his ribald attention for a minute, and started speaking seriously to me about the council's policy towards residents with dementia. I listened carefully to everything she said. Until my dad, who had not turned away from her, and was still looking at her quizzically, said, thoughtfully: 'Quite a fat arm.'

And she's still looking at me and still telling me all this important stuff, and God help me, I can't stop laughing. I'm like a kid who's heard a fart noise while being told something very important by a teacher. It's not fair – it's not fair to her, at all (luckily, she didn't seem to notice) – but y'know: quite a fat arm . . . it's the specificity of it, the flat statement of it. It's the word 'quite'. It's the fact that my dad has made a considered judgement about the fatness of this lady's arm. And then said it out loud.

Sidebar: the information that the woman from Harrow Council was Indian may seem irrelevant, but I've included it because one thing that I am proud (I think the word is proud, although it's a hard one to call) of as regards my father and his dementia is it revealed him to be remarkably unracist. By which I mean: there was a point when the Pick's had eaten away so completely at my dad's frontal lobe that he was operating at a completely unfiltered level. During this time he came into contact with many different health workers, all of whom he liked to insult as much as he could. Some of these were people of colour and I never once heard him say anything racist to any of them. Sexist, yes. I mean, really a lot of sexism, quite a fat arm being just the tip of the things-you-shouldn't-be-saying-to-women iceberg. This seems to prove that at his core, given that at this time his core was continually on show, racism was not part of Colin Baddiel's being.

It was hard, in these situations, not to feel like I was at some level enjoying my dad's dementia. Because in these situations, I was. Moments like these represent a tiny element of it, in truth, compared to everything else – the despair and the sadness and the grim administration of it. But they fade in the memory quicker than the disinhibition. As I say, my dad was never a man to hold back for any form of standard politeness, but once Pick's took hold and added its frontal lobe release to his basic personality template, he was perhaps for a brief period the most disinhibited man in the world. That level of disinhibition is bracing – it's liberating – to be around.

You don't, of course, just get it from the elderly. When my daughter Dolly was three, I took her to see a matinee of *Joseph and His Amazing Technicolor Dreamcoat* in the West End, starring H from Steps. Dolly was on my knee for most of the show and seemed to be enjoying it. However, there comes a moment – you'll know it, of course – when the mood changes in *Joseph and His Amazing Technicolor Dreamcoat*, the lights go down, and Joseph, from his imprisonment, sings, 'Close Every Door to Me'. H from Steps, in this particular production, gave that moment everything. He sank to the floor in a white spotlight, looked up in pain and yearning, and began:

Close every door to me
Hide all the world from me
Bar all the windows, and shut—

That's as far as H got before Dolly started saying, loudly:
'I don't like it. I don't like it. I don't like it any more!'

She kept on saying this, despite me saying shush. She got louder and louder, into something of a scream. I saw H's eyes – he carried on singing, of course, he's a trooper – flicker towards the audience, uncertainly. There was no other choice but to pick up my daughter and carry her out of the auditorium. At no point did she stop shouting.

'I don't like it! I don't like it any more!'
And at no point did I stop laughing.

I have an editorial note here from a reader saying that this bit may come across as unkind, not to H, but to Dolly, who was three, and frightened by the darkening change of mood in the musical at this point (all credit to H and the gang for so landing that gear change). But I wasn't seeing her here as a frightened child – even though obviously that's what she was – but as a (hilarious) heckler. At some level this would be true of my dad at the same time. His disinhibition was a symptom of the degeneration of his frontal lobe, and so should be, for his son, mainly a cause for concern. But many times, however, that disinhibition was funny – and also seemed like (even when we were not, which we never were with him, in a theatre) heckling – and laughter has a tendency to smash through what you're supposed to feel.

It's been said many times that dementia – that old age in general – returns us to childhood, but it's always said in a melancholic way, associated as it is, obviously, with decay and with loss of control and independence. Those things are melancholic, but there is another aspect of the return to childhood, which is this sense of liberation. Because that's what disinhibition does, whether it be in a child or in someone with Pick's disease. It breaks you free of social constraint and makes you say the thing that is in the front of your head. The thing you are not meant to say. The disinhibited follow the mantra on TV's *Catchphrase* to say what they see – *I don't like it any more* or *quite a fat arm* – and it's often hilarious. There is a sadness, of course, in this happening unwittingly to a person who perhaps in the past was deeply serious and possessed only of self-control and dignity (this would not be my father), but to be honest, none of that makes it, in the moment, less funny.

Or to put it another way: the way my life went, it's good I was a fan of *Derek and Clive*.

Being around someone this disinhibited is a bit like being in Ricky Gervais' film *The Invention of Lying*, in which everyone feels compelled to tell the truth about each other all the time, and the result is just a very extreme default level of rudeness. Because I have a notion of myself as being possessed by a truth urge, it is astonishing to suddenly be around someone who speaks the truth as they see it all the time. Obviously, by the truth here I do not mean larger truths, about life or politics, or humanity. I mean micro-truths like quite a fat arm. However, there is a pushback to this, which is that, as the relative of the person with Pick's, you do a lot of apologizing. You say a lot: I'm so sorry, he's got dementia; he's got Pick's disease.

The trouble with that, in the case of Colin Baddiel, is that I, big fat Mr Truth-Teller, always felt like I was lying. Not about his diagnosis but about the idea the diagnosis was somehow an excuse. For example: my dad had a hip operation in 2015.* I was with him as he was being wheeled on a gurney into the operating theatre. I had scrubs on. He was surrounded by

---

* Which itself involved some lying. Because my dad, despite being in obvious pain every time he took a step, refused to accept that he needed a hip operation, and so we had to lie and tell him he was going into hospital just for a check-up. I'm using the continuous past there because we had to tell him it over and over again, particularly when he was in hospital and pissed off about it. Thank Christ, really, that he couldn't walk more than a few steps without being in pain, as otherwise he would've left the hospital in his gown.

several very caring, very reassuring male and female nurses who were all saying that everything was going to be fine. And meanwhile, he was lying on his back, flicking V-signs at them.

All the way into theatre. He'd sometimes focus on a particular nurse, normally one who was most earnestly saying, 'Don't worry, Mr Baddiel', and plant his two arthritically stiff but-still-very-able-to-form-a-V fingers as close to their face as possible. Even the bloke pushing the trolley from behind – my dad was meticulous about sticking two V-signs at him. I was by the side of the gurney, looking at each of them and saying, plaintively, as they looked more and more depressed and dismayed, 'Sorry, so sorry, it's the Pick's disease'; but another part of me was thinking, No – this is *exactly* who he is.

Colin

I have spoken already about how doing *My Family: Not the Sitcom* was, in terms of my mother, an act of retrieval, a way of fishing out the real her from death's net of bland memorialization. The same would be true of my dad and dementia. Dementia, like death, seems to erase the person. This erasure can happen as much, or more perhaps, around the person as inside their head. Before the dementia sufferer is actually bereft of life, they end up secreted away in shame and talked about in whispers.

Because my dad's version of dementia didn't involve an erasure but a kind of magnification of self, talking about it felt to me a way of combating the process. And because I'm a comedian, my weapon of choice for this combat was comedy

(I'm aware this is a slightly Alan Partridge turn of phrase, but I like it).* Which is a long-winded way of saying I thought it was fine to do jokes about my father's dementia and to relate stories of funny things he's said and done because of having Pick's.

To some extent, a lot of the comedy revolves around my dad refusing the dignity of age. The dignity of age, as we know, is not a real thing – we become less dignified with age, and Western society reflexively humiliates and ignores old people – but we still imagine it to be a thing. You can see it in its contravention, in the completely overdone trope in comedy of old lady characters who swear or twerk or whatever, in the notion that such behaviour is incongruous. But my dad was a real pro, a one-man subverting of the dignity-of-age factory.

One supreme example of this can be seen in a film he appeared in for Jewish Care, which is a charity that does what it says on the tin: it provides care for Jews, old ones, mainly. It's very respectable and proper and obviously its films, which are promotional two-minuters hoping to raise money, portray these old Jews in a very sensitive way. At the time my dad was going, regularly, to a day care place in Harrow called the Leonard Sainer Centre, run by the charity. They asked us if he might be one of the subjects of a short film, which they were planning to show to some of their donors at some big dinner, and we said yes. Here's a still from the film:

---

* I've noticed this is my fourth reference to Alan Partridge. This may betray a subconscious anxiety that writing a book like this, which I would say is cross-generic, but one of those genres could be considered to be celebrity memoir, overlaps with many books written by Alan. The other possibility is that I just really like, and have a tendency to watch and rewatch, the entire Partridge canon.

It includes him being led in, laughing, with a lovely nurse; playing Connect 4 with Dan; Ivor talking about how great the Leonard Sainer is, and so on. They made him look like a sweet old man.

Which I genuinely hope was great for fundraising. It isn't true. As I said earlier, the good default, the people with dementia shown in such films, were not Colin Baddiel, even though he appears in this one. Which perhaps can be demonstrated by the fact that, soon after this film was shot, Jewish Care *banned* my dad from the day care centre. They banned him for *getting into a fight*. With another eighty-year-old man with dementia. He told that man he had a big nose – which he probably did; it was after all a Jewish day care centre* – and the big-nosed man, not completely grasping that my dad was only saying such things because he had dementia – possibly because *he* had dementia – punched him. My dad punched him back and after they were separated, Colin was the one shown the door.

· · ·

---

* This is another joke I am allowed to make.

Here's the best, and simultaneously the worst, story. It is the most challenging story of my father's disinhibition, but I can't miss it out, I think, because it does bring together all the key things about this book. It brings together, that is, my father, my mother, sex, dementia, Jewishness and death. OK, not golf, but you can't have everything.

After my mum died, we sat shiva. This is a Jewish wake. You have open house in the home of the deceased and as many people who want to from the local community can come and pay their respects. There are prayers and food – bridge rolls – and everyone is invited to tell stories and share memories of the person who has gone.

It's supposed to go on for seven days. Ours didn't. We did three days. The first was the fullest turnout: about forty people in my parents' small living room. As part of the shiva, the close family members sit in the middle of the room on a row of low chairs, to indicate humility. The guests line up, bend down and shake the hands of those mourners, and say, as they do at funerals, 'I wish you long life.'

We sat there, on the tiny chairs, Dan, Ivor, me and my father. People filed by, bent down and said, 'I wish you long life.' I recognized more of them than at the funeral. There wasn't in general that sense of alienation, of feeling that none of these people actually knew my mother.

But then someone appeared who I didn't know, a very nice-looking woman in her early sixties, her face full of concern, bending down and doing the thing. She shook Dan's hand, and said: 'I wish you long life.' And Dan said thank you. She shook Ivor's hand, and said: 'I wish you long life' and he said thank you. She shook my hand, and said: 'I wish you long life' and I said thank you., Lastly, she shook my dad's hand, and said:

'I wish you long life.' And my dad said, 'I wish you would stay behind after everyone else has gone so I can rape you.'

Some of you will think, and you may be right, that I should not include this story, because it's meant to be funny and no reference to rape is ever funny. But, with apologies, I'll take that risk. As what is funny about it is nothing to do with that reference. Rather it is the sheer extremity of the moment; of a man saying this while he's supposed to be mourning his wife. The funny lies here. It lies in the way in which all the little niceties and politesse that we surround death with get totally stripped away by my dad's punk dementia.

In the terrible silence, I looked up at the woman. She looked visibly shocked and upset. And I said: 'I'm so sorry, he's got dementia, he's got Pick's disease', while inside thinking, No, this is exactly who he is.

Sarah

One of the positives about both my parents being hoarders is that, if you are going to do a show or a book about them after their deaths, you will find, in their house, a lot of mat-erial. I discovered many things while clearing out their stuff. Normally, at this point in a memoir, when talk comes to discovery, of things found in drawers

and attics, it's time for a twist, a surprise, a secret revealed. This didn't happen with my mother. Everything I found only confirmed who I already knew her to be. Like, for example, this suitcase, which sadly neither me nor Ivor could find room for, so we took to the local recycling plant (OK, let's call it the dump).*

But some of what I found confirmed her so deeply, it turned the corner into surprising. Some of it was so her, it surprised even my sense of her.

For example, you couldn't tell my mother anything. No matter how much we asked her not to bring our children meningitis toys – to maybe bring them fewer toys, not huge boxes obviously siphoned from St Luke's Hospice shop, perhaps even to buy them single nice items from a proper shop – she never did. Similarly, a corner of her collection, away from the golf memorabilia was, unfortunately, those offensive toys called – I'm going to avoid the full offensive term – gollies. She used to have loads of these up on shelves in the living room. Ivor and I often begged her to destroy them, particularly given that one of her granddaughters, Dan's daughter Dionna, is dual heritage, but she wouldn't listen; she just thought they were 'great fun'. I said, 'No, a bouncy castle is great fun, these are icons of race hate . . .', but it made no difference. Once, I played the nuclear option. To try and make her understand, to feel what those dolls truly represent, I searched on the internet to see if I could show her a toy that

---

* I tried for a while to convince the publishers that this photo, which I took just before I left Harrow Recycling Centre, should be the front cover of this book. For me it symbolises everything about the comedy and tragedy and defiance and randomness of my mother's journey. Particularly the idea that the thing that will raise her from the rubbish is golf. They disagreed.

might be equivalently antisemitic. Unfortunately, the only thing I could find were these:

Orthoducks Jews. Which she thought were great fun.

Late in the day, about a year before she died, the racist toys did vanish from the shelves. We thought that she'd finally thrown them out, but one of the first things I found while beginning the long and challenging process of going through her things was a drawer containing two of the bastards. Even death couldn't shift my mum's opinion.

It ramped up, the finding-things-after-death challenge. I have talked about my mother anticipating social media, mainly in her psychology, but it turns out also in the arena of the sexy selfie. I found a number of these not-very-well-secreted in her drawer. The question, of course, has to be asked: who took them? I find it hard to believe she was particularly good with a camera timer. It could have been my father.

You might be thinking at this point, Well, please, David, don't show us these. And perhaps I shouldn't. Perhaps I should just stick to the head shot.

I should be clear, however, the rest of the photo shows nothing more graphic than anything you might see today on Instagram. And there is another reason why it's hard to leave the full picture out of this book. As sometimes happens with a sexy selfie,

there's a prop involved, to help the sexiness along. I wonder if you can guess what it is.

Which revelation I think would also lead us to conclude that it was not my dad but another regular male visitor to our house who took this photograph.

Yet even the sexy selfies were not the most challenging item I found buried in the vast amounts of Sarah Baddielia in my parents' house after her death. That would be this, found at the bottom of a drawer in her desk:

It seems just like a note book, perhaps a school book, or something she used for bookkeeping the ins and outs of business at Golfiana. But no. It's a book of poetry. It's called *Feelings*.

I suspect it's named after the Morris Albert song from 1974, but I can't prove this. It is dedicated 'For My MDW', which would be Mr David White. And actually, it isn't 'Feelings, For MDW'. If you look closely you'll see it's 'Feelings', 'For My MDW from SB'. We shall come back to this punctuation.

As with many examples in this book, you may feel uncomfortable with me including these apparently private poems for public perusal, but I am also fairly sure, given that, as you can see, she wrote the word 'Copyright' on it, and editorial notes throughout, such as 'Page 29 as 1?' – and because there are typed-up copies of some of the poems elsewhere – that my mother would like to have published *Feelings*. I have to say I am glad that, at least when I was younger and less comically distanced from all this, she never managed to do that. Because it is a book of erotic poetry. At times, very erotic poetry. Dedicated to her lover. Which would have been a complicated thing for the fourteen-year-old me to see on the shelves in Foyles.

It was, in truth, not an uncomplicated artefact to find in 2015. I read it. There are many poems. Here's the first one, which is straightforwardly romantic:

2nd May. 1977.

Life has taken on a new meaning.
Someone wants me – I think.
I want him too.
Is this so wrong? No!
I enjoy him in all senses.

She ticks this poem, at the bottom, in pencil. Which I love – the idea that my mum was proofreading these and thought: That one definitely makes the cut. Actually, from a quick flick through, all of them seem to have ticks. Anyway. Here's the second one . . . a kind of haiku:

> I am a loner
> You are a loner
> But together . . . . .
> We love.

Which frankly, I think is pretty good. Or at least, certainly as good as anything you'll see written on a fridge magnet. Tick.

The poems clear up a number of issues. If anyone isn't certain that the DW referred to is David White of Golfiana (the original one), for example, this one, which begins . . .

> May I write to you – you ask
> That was a gift to me alone, my DW.

. . . kind of clears up any ambiguity on that issue by the end:

> I would occasionally.
> Like to spend an evening with you.
> How little I know about the game
>   of golf.

Personally, I think my mum is doing herself down a bit here. I feel, given her transformation into Golf Queen happened rapidly after meeting DW, that she already knew quite a lot about the game of golf by the time this poem came into being. Most of the poems, I notice, are written on the emotional back foot and give a sense that DW is not being particularly forthcoming, with his presence, time and/or love.

So it may well be that this is my mother trying to appeal to DW in the best way she knows how. The way to a man's heart – well, *this* man's heart – is through the offer of a long evening impressionably listening to his expertise on bunkers and flop shots.

Sometimes, he does show up, and my mum is absurdly grateful:

> An extra special day
> Because you asked me
> To join you for lunch
> When I thought you would
> Be miles away in Turnberry.

Although the writer in me has a need to query whether, because this is a poem, it shouldn't be:

When I thought you would be

Miles away in Turnberry.

But then again, that might be conventional of me.

The poems are sad. They are full of desperate and lost yearning. This is one of many that, without having the literary qualities of 'Dulce et Decorum Est' or Ben Jonson's 'On My First Son', is still heartbreaking in a way:

> Another day dawns
> I see no sun.
> For my sun is many miles away
> No special words
> No coming together.
> Life has no meaning.
> What is the point of my life?

Sarah

There is something noticeable about these poems for me, which is: there is no sign of any solace at all coming from my mother's home life. She just aches for David White, hungers and thirsts for him. Not only does she find no comfort in her children, we don't even get a mention. So much so that reading this one, I found myself thinking (even though the spelling makes it plain she is referring to the bright star in the sky that warms the earth), *Well, your son wasn't actually many miles away, he was in the next room.* He was in the next room, listening to you while you, as this one makes clear . . .

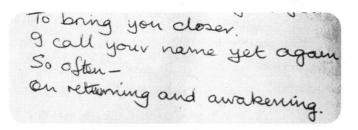

> To bring you closer.
> I call your name yet again
> So often –
> On returning and awakening.

. . . are shouting his namesake.

So obviously, the poems bring up some 'feelings'. But as ever, there is comedy to hand. Which is particularly useful when the poems become more, um, candid.

I referred earlier to my mum's tendency to overuse inverted commas as a sort of mum-ish thing to do. This tendency crops up a fair amount in *Feelings*. Here it is, in fact, around the word 'Feelings':

> Thank you for a lovely evening.
> "Feelings" of you are penetrating me
> That I cannot sleep.

Now, interestingly that is arguably a correct use of inverted commas. Insofar as obviously, feelings here is meant to have a double-meaning, made clear – a bit too clear – by the use of the words 'penetrating me'.

But in other poems, her usage isn't quite so on track. Another contains these reasonably standard erotic lines, again playing on the suggestion of sex:

> a painful but exquisite experience
> That is so beautiful
> Especially when we unite together

But it continues in a way that is not so standard. And indeed not so suggestive.

> a painful but exquisite experience
> That is so beautiful
> Especially when we unite together
> And you "talk" yourself through "coming"

OK. So. Let's just go back again to my grammatical points about the use of inverted commas and my mother's misunderstanding of them. *You use inverted commas when you want to indicate that you mean something other than what the word normally means.* But when she says 'talk' here – she means *talk*, doesn't she? She means words are emerging from David White's mouth. And 'coming' – well, we know what she means. She means that David White is speaking while orgasming.

Sarah

It's a very sexual sentence, but there is no double entendre involved, no double meaning. But clearly my mother was concerned her meaning might be ambiguous, because in the next line, she . . . clarifies:

> a painful but exquisite experience
> That is so beautiful
> Especially when we unite together
> And you "talk" yourself through "coming"
> I always hear you say "Oh! Oh! I'm coming"

And then to put the tin lid on it:

> a painful but exquisite experience
> That is so beautiful
> Especially when we unite together
> And you "talk" yourself through "coming"
> I always hear you say "Oh! Oh! I'm coming"
> and watch you 'play' your pipe

And pipe, please note, is *not* in inverted commas. Which is extraordinary. Because that's the word that *should* be. Because I assume by pipe, she *doesn't* mean his actual tobacco-filled meerschaum – or whatever the fuck pipe it was. I assume David

White wasn't actually *smoking his fucking pipe while he was fucking her.* I assume she means – this sort of pipe:*

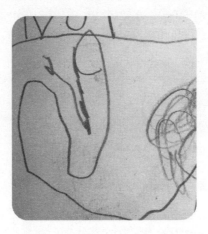

There's much, much more. Fasten your seat belts for this next poem.

Somehow the evening was too good
To 'grope' for release under the cloak of the car

Again, there is a basic misuse of inverted commas here. 'Grope' simply does mean *grope* here. If she was going to put inverted commas around a word in this line it should be 'cloak', as cars don't have cloaks. Unless the car in question – David White's or hers (a Citroën DS 21, if the dates are what I think they are) – had an all-weather cover.

---

* Although who knows? DW's pipe does crop up a lot in my mother's letters, and often in an ambiguous way:

Keep sailing and hold your pipe in that special way for me.

Sincerely yours.

The Nun.

Sarah

The poem continues:

> Somehow the evening was too good
> To 'grope' for release under the cloak of the car
> And I look forward with joy
> To your "coming" today
> When we shall be utterly alone
> To be free to love all ways

Now 'coming' here is actually – hooray – the correct use of inverted commas. Because the word can of course mean, simply, arriving. But – wink, wink – it can *also* mean spunking up through your pipe. So therefore, in this usage, we have a double meaning – coming is an innuendo, a euphemism.

But then straight away follows what I think of as the *pièce de résistance* of my mother getting inverted commas wrong.

> Somehow the evening was too good
> To 'grope' for release under the cloak of the car
> And I look forward with joy
> To your "coming" today
> When we shall be utterly alone
> To be free to love all ways
> And allow you to "nibble my clitoris" away
> As you devoured the spare ribs.

There is – I think this is perhaps an understatement – a lot to unpack there. I mean, just for starters – although I imagine it wasn't a starter – the sudden intrusion into the poem of spare ribs. To be fair, there has been mention in an earlier stanza of the joy of sharing 'excellent food, wine and company', but I think the reader may have assumed this to have been a private repast cooked at home,* not an all-you-can-eat blowout at TGI Fridays. Then there is the strange, floating – grammatically, and indeed visually, on the page – 'away'. I think my mother perhaps meant 'nibbling away at my clitoris' but felt that somehow the adverb didn't belong within the inverted commas – that it would disturb the purity of the phrase 'nibble my clitoris', and we certainly don't want to do that – so she moved it. But in so doing she creates an image that is frankly too troubling for me to express. And this is a book which, let's be honest, in most places, goes there.

Obviously, though, the money shot – as it were – is just the phrase itself. It's the use of the fantastically twee word 'nibble' juxtaposed with the frankly less twee word 'clitoris'. But for me, it's primarily about the extraordinary misuse of inverted commas. 'Nibble my clitoris' is my mother's greatest work in that regard, elevating, in my opinion, the misusing of inverted commas to the status of art.

Because, let's face it, 'nibble my clitoris' is not a euphemism. It's the opposite of a euphemism. Thank God my mother didn't write the previously mentioned *Carry On* films. No, Sid, 'Let's not call it *Carry On Dick*, let's call it *Here's My "Erect Penis"*. That's much clearer.'

---

* Possibly our home, although I think if anyone had tried to cook spare ribs using our grill, the whole kitchen would've gone up like a box of fire-crackers.

Sarah

There is much more poetry. I didn't realize how much. When my mother died and I found *Feelings*,* I thought this was her one foray into erotic verse. But the real uncovering-of-the-archive of my mum's affair happened after my father's death. This is a thing that happens to everyone who has two parents, but it only became obvious to me in January 2022, when my dad died. We – meaning my brother Ivor and I – had effectively deferred the process of properly sorting through my mother's things after she died, because while Colin Baddiel, however psychologically detached he became from the world, was still physically in it, so was his house, and we could just leave most of her effects there.

When he died, the scale of the task became apparent. Both my parents, as I've said, were hoarders. They hardly threw anything away. But because my mum was much more emotion-ally involved in life, and much more obsessive, she had more stuff: more letters, more clippings, more trinkets, more golf memorabilia, obviously, and more – many more – keepsakes. This was the point at which the magnitude of her obsession with David White became clear. She had kept every letter, every envelope, every cheque stub he ever sent her. She had copies of every letter, every envelope, every cheque stub she ever sent

---

* The poetry book, in case anyone is confused. I don't mean I found inner feelings I hadn't had before. Although I did that too.

him. She had endless photographs of him, some compiled into actual albums. She had every relevant golfing document that pertained to him and Golfiana. And it turned out that golf wasn't the only element of David White's personality she'd fetishized. Or at least I assume that's why she had a copy of this:

She also wrote, as I say, hundreds more poems, plus certain documents that are kind of poems, like these, which are lists of fictional book titles that she is pretending to be on the look-out for, for David White:

Adventures at Golf.

After Dinner Golf.

All About Golf.

At Random through the Green.

Before Dinner Golf is Best.

Comeback.

Dormie One.

Enchanted Golf Clubs.

Eighteen Holes Always in my Head.

Few Rambling Remarks.

Fresh Fairways.

Friendly Fairways.

Fun in the Rough.

Girl on the Green ... Waiting.

Golf and be Damned, My Man!

Golf at Pease Pottage.

Golf Craze.

Golf for Southpaws – Only.

Golf Girl.

Golf in a Secret Nutshall.

Golf in the Year 2000 – Still.

Golf is a Friendly Game.

Golf's Sweet Memories.

Golf on our Pillow.

Golf's Secret.

Golfers Dreams.

Golfers Treasures.

Green Memories Are Precious.

Half Hours with a Very Young Golfer.

I Love Golf.

I'll Never Be Cured...

Intimate Golf Talks.

It Ain't Necessarily So.

Joy of Golf.

Ladies in the Rough.

Live Hands.

Love on the Fairway.

Mixed Twosomes.

My King of the Kinks.

Never say Never.....

On and Off the Links.

On Many Greens.

Only on Everyday.

Par for Us.

Science of Golf.

Slice of Fun.

Some Friendly Fairways.

Songs of the Links 1904.

Side Bright Lights on Golf.

Super Golf.

Solving the Golf Problems.

Through the Green – Always.

Twosome at Rye.

Uncle David's Golf Match.

Velvet Touch.

Why Us.

Winning Shot.

Winning Touch.

World of a Golf Dustwrapper.

World of a Special Golf Book.

You've Got Me in a Hole.

Xrays to the Master.

It's hard to pin down a favourite of these titles, although *Golf in the Year 2000 – Still, My King of the Kinks* and *Uncle*

David's Golf Match are all up there. There is a later version of the same idea, which, although it begins as comically brilliantly as ever – with *Are Golfers Human?* and *Doctor Golf* (it's possible that the word golf has never, in recorded history, been repeated so much on two pages) – becomes, as it continues, and breaks down, genuinely sad.

BOOKS REQUIRED URGENTLY.

Addict to a Dustwrapper.	I wonder why?
Adventures Lost at Golf.	Have I lost you?
Are Golfers Human?	Some maybe.
Box of matches.	Very inflammable!
Burning Tree Club .	Absolutely sizzling.
Doctor Golf.	Is Dr. White on call?
Fun in the Rough.	With a certain person only.
Gol Golfing.	Alone?
Golf IS a Friendly Game.	Most of the time.
Golf on OUR Pillow!	
Golf with many Tears.	
Green Memories.	Is that all now?
I am a Golf Widow.	
I'll go where you hit me!	Far away?
I'll never be Cured of you.	
Intimate Golf Talks.	
It was Excellent whilst it Lasted.	
Lady in the Deep.Rough.	
Love on the Fairway.	
Lure of the White Links.	
Never say Never.	Please.
North Again.	But always alone?
Quiet on the Tee.	Did you call?
So What have I to Do?	Tell me, guide me.
Velvet Touch.	I miss so much.
Won over at the Last Hole.	
You're Got me in a Hole.	To keep, as always.

I find the titles, as they get progressively more pleading, and lonely, upsetting. I find the gaps in between the titles almost more so.

It is tempting to include it all, as many of the new finds are, in my opinion, as great as anything my mother ever wrote. This one – perhaps pointing forward to the medical years – is surely a masterpiece:

> I know I do not have an over active thyroid
>
> Only an over active love for you.
> Is that so wrong?
> I feel not.

And there is, as I say, much more poetry. The poems are mostly written neatly on folded pieces of A4, although there are scribblings on envelopes and note pads and match boxes. One is written on the back of two pieces of paper detailing what was available from Birds Eye Foods Ltd at the time:

> Not so long ago
> I was but rags and sawdust
> But you have waxed me
> Into a new person
> And now I cannot go back
> To what I was before.
> When first you noticed me.
> I want to give to you
> For you take
> But Don't "use" me.
> But love me.

CODE	PRODUCT	
MB	H. P. PEAS	2½lb
AK	" "	24oz
AT	" "	16oz
AU	" "	8oz
BY	" "	4oz
GF	H.P. MINT PEAS	16oz
GJ	" " "	6oz
CU	" " "	4oz
O5	H.P. S.G. BEANS	2½lb
MM	" " "	24oz
C5	" " "	16oz
8T	" " "	12oz
GM	" " "	8oz
GN	" " "	4oz
8F	CUT BEANS	8oz
8G	" "	4oz
GP	B. SPROUTS	12oz
FF	" "	8oz
F4	" "	4oz
ET	MIXED VEG.	8oz
	" "	4oz

(BIRDS EYE FOODS LTD.) BATCH/ INTERMEDIATE
/E unless otherwise stated

In these poems, we see more of the fabulous play of passionate yearning and golf that defined my mother's relationship with DW. For example:

> You have made me
> What I am today.
> "Not unique"
> But a woman
> Who has learnt
> (The joy and happiness
> Through pain
> Of being loved by
> You
> a truelly, unparrallel man
> Who is unique
> And will always be – privately
> Be In the "fore"
> Of my life for ever.

It takes a while to get there with that one, but it's worth it for the 'fore'. Or:

Alone I sit,
I could be elsewhere
But I choose to stay home
To "talk" to you.
But can you hear me?

The days slowly pass
An auction viewed
a golf book amongst a lot.
I must have it for you.

I try to "put you down"
But unknownly golf always crops up.
a dinner with friends last night
The Dunlop golf man there!

This one – let's ignore the inverted commas, I reckon we've covered that – demonstrates how much my mum wasn't bothered, in a brilliant way, with the boundaries between poetry and . . . just stuff that was happening in her life. Poetry, in general, relies on an intensity of experience – 'the spontaneous overflow of powerful feelings', as Wordsworth has it. To be fair, there's a lot that is overflowing, powerfully felt in my mother's verse, but what there also is, which is less conventionally poetic, is . . . well, as I say, just stuff happening in her life.

This is perhaps clearer if instead of showing her writings in her own hand on pieces of paper from the 1970s, we look at her poems set out like proper poetry, in a proper book:

My Family

The days slowly pass
An auction viewed
A golf book amongst a lot.
I must have it for you.

I try to 'put you down'.
But unknowingly golf always comes up.
A dinner with friends last night.
The Dunlop golf man there!

An appointment next Thursday
But not till 11 am at the BBC
In case you might wish to call me
Will you be in London already?

I mean – who's to say that isn't a radically new type of poetry, a Dollis Hill golf-inflected version of William Carlos Williams' 'I have eaten the plums'? Well, me, as I don't think my mum was bothered about redefining poetic content so as to encompass mundane reality. I think more that her reality was very mundane, and the intrusion of David White and golf into it was, in her mind, poetic. And that she lived life constantly in a too-much way, constantly trying to make of her life an epic poetic romance, and everything was included.

The poems are all pleas of yearning to David White. It wasn't initially clear to me whether she had ever actually shown any of them to him. And indeed, if she had, what feelings *Feelings* would've induced in him, given that he may have been uncertain about how she chose to express some of the revelations included there. He may, for example, have quibbled with the word nibble.

But after a while I realized that she did actually send most of these poems as letters to David White. I know this because of this poem:

My feelings for you.
Of your urgent call
"I want you
I am being selfish"
Happily, I came to you
For you had answered my inner calling.

You wanted to watch my expressions
of ecstasy and pleasure
That flow from you
Into me
To make me feel wonderful
and I hope my feelings
Will engulf you
And ~~keep~~ you happy
Until we may meet again.

Which is standard, Sarah Baddiel-esque erotic verse.

The rest is yearning and love and not-very-suppressed sexual reference, as ever. But there is, at the bottom of the page, a coda:

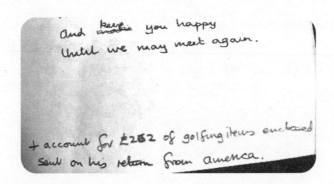

And keep you happy
Until we may meet again.

+ account for £262 of golfing items enclosed
Sent on his return from America.

Which is not so poetic or indeed erotic. 'Plus account for £262 of golfing items enclosed, sent on his return from America.' I love this. I love this so much. I love that even in the throes of passion recollected, even as she was trying to write out her deepest yearning, my mother did a bit of golf memorabilia bookkeeping.

Another example, at the bottom of the poem in which she says that DW will always be at the 'fore' of her life forever:

a smelly, unparralled man
Who is unique
and will always be – privately.
Be In the "fore"
Of my life for ever.

Snoopy "fore" enclosed

Quite hard to read, but I think it says 'Snoopy "fore" enclosed'. Which will have been something like this:

It also says:

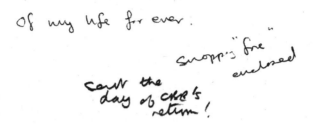

'Sent the day of CBB's return!' Which is a tad darker than 'Snoopy "fore" enclosed', given CBB is Colin Brian Baddiel. But the poems are a treasure trove of how my mother's affair worked.

More information lies at the bottom of this one:

'Read to him over the telephone at 9.00 am instead of sending.' That photo shows only the last bit of this poem. There are three and a half other pages. Which means we're talking about a twelve-minute reading. Before breakfast.

This might seem to be trying her lover's patience a little, but the reason why my mother performed this piece to him, rather just sending it like she did all the others, is revealed in a previous stanza, where she says:

> I had to tell you
> 'Talk to you'
> As to why
> You happened to find me
> Upon your doorstep last night.

When I discovered these letters, all of this was new to me. I had no idea she would actually turn up at David White's – a married man's – house, unannounced. I thought I knew all about her affair, because she was so flagrant with the basic information, but my mother was not a woman for detail at the best of times. The ways in which she would show off were in broad strokes, with the occasional bit of, normally golf-related, minutiae. It's apparent to me that however much she liked to flood the plain of her life with the fact that she was having an affair, the actual reality of it is still something I'm only just understanding.

By the way, you may have spotted something. If she sent these poems to David White, how come they were found among her things?

Because these are copies. She makes that clear on many, including the classic 'I Sit Alone (at the Cambridge Book Fair)':

> I sit alone (at the Cambridge Book fair)
> Feeling lost and lonely.
> No special you here
> To tide me over.
> I will not plan a travelling schedule yet
> Why?
>
> Copy.

My mother couldn't bear the idea of not having these poems any more, so she wrote them out again. But also, I think she did it because the person who was watching her do this, have this affair, write this love poetry, was herself. I'm making fun of how much the poetry details her mundane life, but of course what she was trying to do was something poignant: she was trying to make her mundane life poetic. She was trying to poeticize her unpoetic life. There's a desperate beauty in that, a desperate beauty that perhaps *requires* knowing nothing about poetry: about the things the culture considers worthy of poetry, that is.

Colin, Peter Alliss

Something I have wondered about, and people have asked me, is: do you think your dad had an affair?

I think this is to misunderstand the life I'm trying to describe here. It wasn't, obviously, a Puritanical uptight post-war no-sex-please-we're-British place – I refer you to the copy of *Club International* on the breakfast table – but conversely, my mum having an affair didn't mean our house was a 1970s hotbed of wife-swapping and bohemian marital code-breaking. That would have been far too glamorous.

My father, as is manifest, was different from my mother. Where she was incontinent, he was constipated (I'm talking emotionally here). Not with all emotions – not anger, certainly – but if my dad had been having an affair, he would have kept shtum about it. He would not have been doing it because of a desire to broadcast to the world that his life was exciting. It would be because he wanted to have sex with a woman who was not his wife.

Interestingly, my mother would disagree – about my dad having an affair, that is. She often hinted darkly that he was a terrible Lothario, which is borne out by The Answerphone Tapes. I have mentioned these before, but I think they now deserve capitalization. My mother did something – I suspect just by pressing record, because answerphones at the time were basically cassette machines – which meant she recorded all, or certainly a large proportion, of her conversations with David White. I always knew this, but it was only in my second dive into my parents' archive that I went so far as to buy an old cassette recorder to play them. The conversations with David White are . . . well, I'll come to those. Not least because I remain uncertain of the legality of quoting him when – I assume – he didn't know he was being recorded. I think it's unlikely my dead mother can be retrospectively sued for phone hacking her lover but I assume I can be, for publishing their conversations.

One of the things about The Answerphone Tapes is that they aren't just conversations with David White. It's clear my mother pressed the record button a lot when he phoned. What she then didn't do was press 'off'. Which meant many of her conversations were recorded: ones with me, my brothers, friends, business acquaintances. It's evocative to listen to, something of an audio time machine. I've just listened to one in which Peter Alliss – for anyone who doesn't know, probably the most famous BBC golf commentator of all time – phones her and asks if she has a copy of his autobiography from 1981. He says (I think I can quote him, because he's dead, and also because this is definitely not libellous), 'If you do, I have some friends staying and they'd like one.'

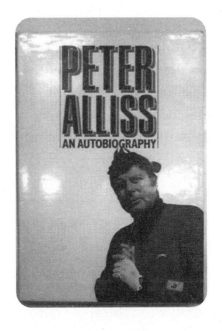

She says she's not sure but will check in the shop – by which she means her Golfiana stall at Grays Antique Market – and call him back. I find it odd that Peter Alliss didn't have a fair number of copies of his autobiography knocking about or couldn't get one from a bookshop, rather than from my mother. He was, as I say, a famous commentator, not J.R. Hartley (for anyone who doesn't know who *that* is, never mind). But it's a joy to hear.

Less of a joy to hear is a conversation she had with a lawyer, around when she and Colin were meant to be getting divorced. She talks about buying my dad out of the house, but then says he'll be getting a new place anyway. The lawyer asks why, and she says, 'Oh, I think it'll be easier for him to take all his women there rather than bring them back to the old family house . . .'

I don't believe this. Not because I'm in denial. I don't need – as is perhaps obvious – to defend a saintly version of my parents. I don't judge my mother for having an affair, so it's very unlikely – particularly given the issue of, well, balance – that I would think my father a bad man for having one. But I just don't have any evidence of it. What I do have evidence of is my mum constantly playing out a constructed, dramatized version of her life, and her husband being a shagger fits into that. It fits into that more glamorous, more bohemian sense of what her life should have been that she was always chasing. Also, this was a point in time when divorce was very much about fault, and so she may have been keen to suggest she wasn't the only one to blame in the infidelity stakes.

I did find something in my parents' archive that spoke so completely to me of my dad's relationship with other women I feel I should include it. It was a card. This one:

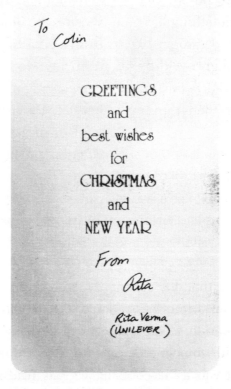

Again, context is everything. It's the fact that I found this card buried in a basket of letters and cards and poems written by my mother to David White – all of which are overflowing with extreme idiosyncratic eroticism – that delights me. I think it's possible its placement there is because she wanted to think of this as something she'd found that confirmed my dad was indeed the Lothario he needed to be to fit into her model of her life.

Except it so isn't. It's not just the lack of passionate words. It's the lack of words. Almost all the words, beyond 'To Colin', are expended on one thing, which is identifying who sent this card. You can, I think, sometimes read Sarah Baddiel's love letters to David White and wonder if he really ever gave her much thought, but if Rita Verma was Colin Baddiel's lover, then really, something has gone awry in the You Were Always on My Mind paradigm. Because plainly, when writing this card, Rita thought: Will he know who I am? She got to 'Rita' and thought: I'd better put my surname. And then thought: Still not sure. Better put where I work. With him. That'll probably do.

If it's a love letter, it's either a fabulous double-bluff, designed to thwart discovery (although my mother obviously thought: Aha!), or there was very little actual love in this love affair. If it is a piece of erotica, it is, as the great Sean Lock phrase has it, a challenging wank.

Having said all that, my dad did have an affair. To be clear: it wasn't really an affair. Well after the glory days of Golfiana, during their period of separation in the mid-nineties, he had a dalliance with someone he called a Macedonian. That's all I know. Well, it was a Macedonian woman. And she worked at Grays Antique Market. Selling what, I don't know. Almost definitely not Dinky Toys, or my dad would have been too furious about the competition to get involved with her. Either way, when I asked him about her, I just got back that she was *aggravation.*

This seems a little unfair, as it would have been during the beetles-teeming-out-of-the-upstairs-toilet-light years, so anyone willing to go anywhere near Colin Baddiel at this point was, at the very least, open-minded. It also sounds slightly troubling echoes in my mind with Jimmy Savile describing relationships with women in general as 'brain damage'. However, as we know, almost everything to my dad was aggravation, so maybe the Macedonian can just be slotted into the quite large Venn Diagram of Everything.

Colin

My father's dementia, as it remained until mid-to-late 2017, was dominated by Pick's disease. But as time went on, I have no doubt he also had vascular, Alzheimer's, aphasia – a whole dark rainbow of dementias.

Colin

And so, things changed. In *My Family: Not the Sitcom*, I chronicled his dementia mainly in terms of Pick's, which was lucky, from a storytelling point of view, as that's where most of the comedy was.* But there was something else. I came to understand how much of a mono-view we have of dementia, one repeated often in films and TV, which is based on the people who have turned their faces to the wall – the ancient man or woman staring comatose into space while care home workers change their blankets. Pick's creates a wildly different state, almost the opposite, from that image, a mad, antic condition, whirling and crazed and disinhibited, in which those with it take their clothes off in public and shout obscenities and try to have sex with people who are not their husbands or wives.

---

* People responded to this in a very liberated way. Dementia is a terrible condition but because it involves a shifted reality it also leads to many types of absurdity and it seemed as if in that show I was giving permission to the audience, many of whom were in the same situation, to laugh about it. I heard many stories afterwards from members of those audiences, keen to share. One man told me his mother had dementia and had recently had a fall. Despite it not being a life-threatening one, the care home had phoned him up and told him. He had said: 'Well, of course, she's recently had her leg amputated.' They said: 'Yes. She forgot that.' Meanwhile a woman told me her mum had said to her that her late father had suddenly appeared on the doorstep. She continued: 'I said what are you doing here, you're meant to be in heaven?' He said: 'Yeah, it's not all it's cracked up to be.' And my favourite, about a mother-in-law being given a cognitive assessment by a GP, who asked the usual type of questions: 'Who is the prime minister?', 'Who is the reigning monarch?', 'What year is it?', 'What city are we in?', and when she failed to answer any of them, the GP said, 'Perhaps you can tell us what kind of care home you'd like us to find for you . . .?' And she said, 'I'd really like to go somewhere where they put on a lot of quizzes.'

I wrote about this in a *Sunday Times* piece at the time:

For some, of course, this is entirely distressing. For the relatives of the many who have lived their lives in unfailing politeness and propriety, to see them suddenly acting like sex-crazed hooligans is upsetting in the extreme. To be embarrassed by the behaviour of someone you love is just a terrible add-on to their memory loss.

But not, quite, for me. And in this I am my father's son: I am a comedian, and one reason I am a comedian is that from a very early age, I was taught that there is very little that cannot be said, that swearing is perfectly normal, and that saying extreme things to shock may be gratuitous but can also be very funny. So that's why I have chosen not to be silent about my dad's dementia. Why I have chosen, in a strange way, in this new show, to celebrate it. It's a nightmare, obviously, and painful, obviously, and pitiful, obviously – and does indeed create massive awkwardness and anxiety and social embarrassment on any occasion my dad meets anyone – but it is, at least, life, of a sort. It is at least, him: this behaviour is very . . . the word me and my brothers use is *Colin-ish*. At my mother's funeral, two weeks after she died, my dad asked seven different women, all of whom were coming up to shake hands and comfort him with the kindly Jewish expression 'I wish you long life', to have sex with him ('fancy a shag?' is his preferred way of asking this). This is awful; it is hurtful; it is of course inappropriate in a thousand ways; but it is also, I would contend, funny, in the blackest way (virtually the dictionary definition of Nabokov's idea of 'laughter in the dark'). And: it is better than the alternative.

Colin

By which I don't mean death – that thing that people chucklingly say about growing old, 'It's better than the alternative.' I mean the living death, the present absence, the men and women who sit and sit and sit among the ruins: the gone girls and boys who indeed are no longer inside themselves. I would rather my dad is asking women to shag him at my mother's funeral than that.

Because, sadly – and I mean, with real aching sadness – I can see that happening. He is not quite as sweary and shouty and abusive as he used to be: not quite as Colin-ish. He is becoming quieter and more withdrawn and less manic. His face, I think, is turning to the wall.

It was. This was charted in a documentary for Channel 4, entitled *The Trouble with Dad*. It may surprise you, given that I had already started doing an extremely revealing one-man show about him and my mother, that I wasn't certain about this project when Ivor first suggested it. The difference being that I was totally in control of the one-man show and knew that whatever other interpretations could be made of it by audiences and critics, it was in intention an act of love. I also knew the portrait I was going to paint of my father was going to be true. Television, especially emotive television, is often not very interested in truth.

In the end, I agreed. While we're here, it's worth bringing up the issue of consent. My dad could not in any real way consent to this programme. But of course, by now my father could not really consent to most things that happened to him. He didn't want to have that hip operation I referred to earlier, for example.

But you – that is, the people around the person with dementia, sometimes the children of that person, who may in their deep self still feel this is the person who makes decisions for *them* – must decide for him. There are many ways in which people try to put a positive spin on dementia, and one of those is that people with the disease are *living*, according to the modern mantra, *in the moment*. Well, yes, in a sense. They have no choice, as all that exists for them is the moment. They live in the extreme present. How much this is a positive is debatable – the sense I get is that living in the moment is a dizzying, anxious and confusing place once it is not bounded by memories of past or an intimation of future moments – but it has a practical advantage for those entrusted with keeping some of a person with dementia's quality of life going.

That advantage is that if the person with dementia is exhibiting clear signs of enjoying themselves, maybe just go with it. It's hard to make decisions for someone who lacks decision-making capability, but if they are smiling and joking and having a laugh, well, you may as well accept that the decision you've made on their behalf is OK (even if you harbour misgivings that the same person, before dementia, may have had a completely different response). And my dad loved *The Trouble with Dad*. By which I mean he loved being filmed, he loved the opportunity to take the piss out of my brothers and me on camera, he loved the attention: he loved, for want of a better word, being a star.

Actually, that is the best word. My dad is the star of that film. Not just in the sense that it is centred on him, but because, in most of the scenes he's in, he dominates the room. He's funny and sparky and wild; putting everyone else down and winding everyone up, and the viewer, I would suggest, just wants to see more of him. I don't know if he fits the old

Hollywood male formula of 'women want to sleep with him, men want to be him' – probably not quite – but he is the star.

Watching it now, I notice I begin the documentary by asking his consent. At my first meeting with Colin– after I shout, 'Hello, how are you?' from the porch and hear him say, 'I'm dead' – I tell him who the director is and that we're making a film he's going to be in and is he all right with that, and he says: 'I don't give a rusty damn.' I realize that this does not constitute informed consent. It may not constitute consent at all, as it isn't the word 'yes'. But it demonstrates from the word go who my father is, and frankly – to go a bit Rhett Butler with it – I believe he indeed didn't give a rusty damn.

Within the first few minutes he's called me a fucking idiot, a total tit, a pain in the arse, a big shit and a lump of turd. I say I'd like to have some proper emotional connection with him before he dies, and he burps and laughs. I talk lyrically, much as I have in this book, about how the abusive way he expresses himself might be difficult to take but it proves he's still my dad. He says, 'What are you going on about? Keep babbling.'

Which means he's not the empty object of pity that documentaries and movies about people with dementia can sometimes make them out to be. He's not just sitting in a wheelchair covered in a tartan blanket staring into space. He's not *only* vulnerable. Just the opposite, for much of the time. He's dictating everything, making the conversation entirely about him and his bantz. He is what people schooled in improvisation technically call *high status*. He is anarchically powerful: a whirling dervish, a bull in the china shop of our usual politeness.

At least, for about two-thirds of the film he is. Then he gets a UTI.

• • •

UTIs were a recurrent problem for my dad. He, like all old men, had prostate problems – probably cancer, although it was never diagnosed – and being of an age when sorting it out wasn't viable, in his eighties he was fitted with a catheter. I won't describe in detail the terrible business of its regular changes – not that I, I should be clear, ever did that, but many nurses did, for which I continue to be ever thankful to the NHS – but it meant that latterly the most precarious element of caring for Colin Baddiel was that his catheter would get blocked, an infection would build up, and he would get kidney failure and/or a UTI. He would then be rushed to Northwick Park Hospital, the place where he remained unaware that his wife had died.

The peculiar thing about UTIs is you imagine them to be what they sound: a urinary tract infection. It doesn't sound nice, obviously, but it sounds, to the uninitiated, like not a big deal – like something you take some antibiotics for and it clears up with no lasting effects. But that isn't the case when you're old, or you have dementia. This became apparent during the filming of *The Trouble with Dad*, and so we have a record of how much it's not just a slight case of cock flu. Despite the infection being self-evidently an issue affecting him downstairs, the main impact seemed to be upstairs. Although before this, my dad was already, objectively, confused – in that he didn't, for example, know where he lived or how old he was, or that his wife was dead – he didn't *act* confused. He acted confidently and, as ever given his default personality plus Pick's, like *you* were the twat who had no idea of anything.

But suddenly he didn't. Suddenly, he was shaky and fragile and withdrawn and small. Weirdly, it felt like the UTI had given him self-awareness – awareness, that is, of his condition and how terrifying it was. I'm sure that is neurologically incorrect, but it felt like that.

However, the truth, as we know, is always complex. The story of my father's dementia would be a simpler, if not a particularly inspiring one, if it were just two chapters – 'Pick's and How It Made Colin Baddiel Even More Colin Baddiel-ish Than Ever', followed by 'The Decline of Colin Into the Sad Quiet Personality-Removing Dementia That Most People Have'. It was more like a constant oscillation between the two. It is true that after the first UTI, my dad was never quite the same again, at least in terms of constantly being out there and crazy. It was like that part of him got buried under the other. But it was buried alive. And it resurfaced often, like Carrie's hand.

In the film, *The Trouble with Dad*, even the latter half, when he is undoubtedly quieter, there are many examples of this. I find watching them now makes me cry and makes me laugh. What is particularly funny is how much the film, in its portrayal of us, the three brothers, around Colin, strains towards something nice, something serene, something that offers closure – like you might see in most films about dementia – and how he just shoots whatever attempt it is to do that down in curmudgeonly flames. We bring Lionel – previously mentioned as my dad's best friend, who he didn't speak to for years – down from Wales to see him. My father doesn't recognize him: when Lionel introduces himself, Colin says, 'You don't look like him', and Lionel, brilliantly, replies, 'I really do – I really do look like him.' And then Lionel, who has brought his clarinet, plays 'Stranger on the Shore'. He's a very good horn player and in any other documentary about dementia, particularly about a man meeting his best friend after not seeing him for years this would perhaps be the closing sequence, as music brings him back to his long-term home-town memories, connecting him for the course of the song to his old friend. But because the end of the clarinet is a bit too close to my dad's ear, he just tuts a lot and looks very pissed off and raises his eyes to heaven, again and again.*

Similarly, for my father's birthday – his eighty-second – since he loves cars, we rent a Rolls-Royce, something he once said he always fancied having a ride in. When it arrives, Ivor explains what we've done. My dad says, 'So?' In the car, Ivor asks what he thinks. He says, 'I don't think it's any different from anything else.' I say, 'It's your birthday treat – are you glad you came for the drive?' 'Yes,' he says, flatly. 'I'm not really feeling that,' I reply. Since we begin to think, during the ride, that he may have forgotten where he is, we repeat the fact of it a few times. 'Do you know what car you're in?' Ivor says. 'Does it matter?' says Colin. Ivor and I both agree that it does matter. But it turns out, only to us.

The most important moment – and the one that actually *is* a moment of closure, while still being my dad totally rejecting

---

* Sadly, Lionel died during the writing of this memoir. Ivor and I went to his funeral in Wales. While there, one of his children told a story about my parents' honeymoon stay with Lionel and his wife Mim, in their house in Thornbury. There's a reason of course why most people don't honeymoon in other people's houses. During the night, my mother and father were having sex so loudly that eventually Mim said to Lionel: 'Go and ask them to fucking keep it down.' Lionel did.

What most amazes me about this story is obviously not that my parents were loudly having sex in someone else's house on their wedding night. It's that they were apparently quieter after that. Because the one thing I would say that defined both my mother and father is they were not people who toned themselves down for the sake of others.

the niceties of all that – comes near the end. Sitting in my dad's living room, the director, who is looking for these emotional beats, asks Ivor and me – in front of Colin – if our father has ever told us he loves us. 'No,' I say. 'Of course not.' 'Why not?' 'I think because . . .' I reply, 'he didn't?' This is a joke. Of sorts. But the director runs with it, turning the camera on my dad and saying, 'Colin, your son is saying you never loved them.' And my dad says, 'That's a load of bollocks.'

This affects me deeply – you can see it in the film – but I have since come to see it as an extraordinary moment. Because, of course, it was true that Colin Baddiel had never told me or Ivor or Dan that he loved us. I tell my children I love them *all the fucking time.* They are no doubt bored of it, or perhaps find it cringey. This is maybe because I'm making up for the lack of that statement in my childhood, but more likely because I come from a generation of parents for whom parenting is more of a defining thing in their lives, and make a point of expressing that to their children, a lot, through the words 'I love you'. I'm not sure, in truth, that my generation's parenting style is necessarily better than our parents' was. I think it's possible that as well as social media, the reason for the epidemic of mental health problems in teenagers and young people now may be something to do with how difficult we as parents have made it – with our over-closeness to them, our insistence on *always, suffocatingly*, being there for them – for children to separate from their parents.

But meanwhile, for my generation, hearing I love you from your parents was and is a big deal. Especially from your father, especially for sons. It's another cliché, but certainly in my case true, that many of us were not raised by men in touch with their feelings, indeed, by men who saw being overtly in touch with one's feelings, and therefore freely able to express affection, as suspect. *I didn't know you cared.*

Which is why my father saying 'That's a load of bollocks' in this moment has this effect. It is the closest I will ever get – certainly now – to my dad telling me he loves me. And I'm not saying that, as some might, to prove that he was an emotionally stunted man. I'm saying it's, at least in terms of everything I've said in this book, *better* than him saying I love you. Because truer. Because that is who my dad was: someone who did love me, and my brothers, but could only express that as himself, because he was so deeply himself, and to do that he had to do it argumentatively, aggressively and with a swearword. He had to say that the idea that he didn't love me was a load of bollocks.

Colin Baddiel's bantz never completely stopped. It became harder and harder for him to find words, but he would still make faces, or blow raspberries. His attitude outlasted language and remained defiantly puerile, shot through with *fuck you* and *I-don't-want-your-pity*. In the final scene of *The Trouble with Dad*, we take him to the pub. We were not a regular pub-going family – not even my dad's Welshness and fondness for a drink could break through our basic Jewishness in that respect – yet something genuine happens.

My brother and I were cueing him. We were cueing him, that is, to do one of his catchphrases. We used to do this a lot. The catchphrases were the last frontier, the nuggets of Colinishness that we relied on to be locked deep inside the Fort Knox of his dementia, and we often tried to draw them out with prompts. Catchphrases, after all, frequently have a call and answer structure, and we, at least, could remember all the calls.

You don't see this in the film but in the pub on that night, we tried quite a few. We tried 'hobble dee hi?' to which the answer is 'de hum di grum'; we tried the old stalwart 'I'm off!' but got no 'you've been off for years'. He was blank. And then, finally, I tried an old one. 'Have you got a match?' I said. 'No,' he said. 'No,' I said, more heavily, more, to be honest, desperately, *'Have you got a match?'* Something in him stirred – some deep-set cognitive machinery, rustily starting to turn – and he said: 'Yes.' I looked at him, my face pleading with *And?*

And he said: 'Your face and my arse.'

I say, with joy, 'He's still in there!' I was euphoric that we got that. That film, as much as anything else, was a keepsake, a way to chronicle my dad while he was indeed still in there. It was a holding-on. It speaks of something important therefore that my dad saying a phrase so low-brow and uncultured and unlyrical filled me with such joy. It speaks of the intense significance of context. Because undeniably 'Yes, your face and my arse' is no great shakes in the words of wisdom department. But in the context of my father, and the need for us to feel, to be shown, that he was still who he was, this was the best thing he could possibly have said. This is the store we put on selfhood.

Keats said, 'Beauty is truth.' A simplistic, no-doubt-not-what-the-poet-meant reading of that – that beauty and truth are aligned – would suggest it is wrong. The way we present physical beauty, for example, contains very little truth, contrived as it is with cosmetic trickery, lighting and all sorts of conventional pressures on both male and female gazes to attune ourselves to a fixed, oppressive to most people idea of what beauty is (little bit of politics there). But I would privilege Keats' next line, 'truth beauty'. Truth is beautiful even when it is ugly.

Truth, unlike beauty, is beautiful when it is *hard* to see, when it must be dug out, when it reveals itself despite everything. Which is why I'm happy my father did not, at that point, say something about silken flanks with garlands drest, or even I love you, but *your face and my arse.*

David White

Something that you may have been thinking at various points in this story, or at least the part of it about my mother's infidelity, is: What about David White? What did he think? Was he in love with Sarah Fabian-Baddiel? Where is *his* erotic poetry?

Well, there are issues there. David White, who at the time of writing may still be alive, is obviously in this story but the story I'm telling is about my parents. I don't own his story. I do own, or anyway believe I have the right to tell, my mother's story. I have the right, therefore, to portray him as he appears as a leading character – a leading man, in some ways – in that story (and my father's). But not to try and give his side.

All I can do is report back from my mother's archive. And within the teeming horde of letters and poetry to him from my mum, I couldn't find very much back *from* him. There are a few letters: legal ones. Most of these date from around the time of their big row about the dodgy golf memorabilia, the framed laser-printed forgeries. At one point, brilliantly, my mum suggests that to sort it out, David White should come round. They should talk it through; they should conflict resolve; and the arbiter between them should be: my dad.

I wish that, for the re-telling of this drama, that had indeed happened. It could have been a climactic scene, binding together so many elements of the whole story. The main characters, all in one room, in our house, like the final scene of a whodunnit; the sexual tension between my mother and David White that would have underpinned the row; my dad still assumed – which the suggestion that he should be the ref surely bears out – as not knowing what was going on between them and of course, crowning it all, the fact that it would've been about fucking golf memorabilia.

As it is, David White turned down the idea. Here he is turning it down:

> Sarah, for I have no business and no job. I would feel distinctly uncomfortable in the good Doctor's presence, for despite my attempts to be pleasant he goes out of his way to be both rude & boorish to me, often to the point of being insulting. I can hardly see him as representing an impartial listener and this surely you must understand.

'I would feel distinctly uncomfortable in the good Doctor's presence.' Well, David – maybe there's a good reason for that: you are fucking his wife. But, as we know, whether it was through denial or ignorance, the assumption of everyone involved seems to be that my dad didn't know about the affair. The tone of David White's letter confirms this. It appears to have been written by someone objecting, fairly pompously, that for no apparent reason, Colin Baddiel doesn't like him. Which means that that someone assumes Colin Baddiel doesn't have – or isn't aware of – any very apparent reason not to like him.

Which leaves us with two possibilities. Either my dad *did* know, perhaps unconsciously, and that's what my mother's lover was picking up on. Or more likely, my dad's default position to everyone was rude, boorish and insulting, and he was simply being no more rude, boorish and insulting to David White than to anyone else. So we are left with the strange conclusion that the person complaining about my father's character in print here is the one person who my dad had *every* reason to be rude, boorish and insulting to.

But this gets us no further with the question of David White's feelings for my mother. I have The Answerphone Tapes. On these, there are endless conversations between my mum and David White. As I clunkily switch on the old cassette recorder I bought from a Cost Collectors, I know, without having to wait for the words of the other speaker, when she's talking to him, because she puts on a special voice. My mother – this is a very 1970s thing – had a special phone voice anyway, posher and more self-consciously poised as she said 'Hello, Sarah Baddiel speaking?' than she was in normal speech. But when she's speaking to David White – as soon as she recognizes *his* voice – her voice goes soft and playful and flirtatious and stays soft and playful and flirtatious even when, as they always do, they end up discussing golf memorabilia prices.

There is, though, a lot of standard affair administration. Discussions of places to meet that they won't be too seen in; endless diary checking, often with David White letting my mother's expectations down as to when and for how long he'd promised to meet up with her; my mother providing as much information as she can as to exactly when her husband will be absent and away. There is flirtatiousness, reminiscences of stolen afternoons together (again: mainly referenced by my mum) and an awful lot of terrible jokes. An awful lot: he does loads of funny – by which I mean unfunny – voices, and says things like – will I get sued for this quote? – 'This is the Beast calling!' If the sexual contest – which never actually seemed to be in play, as my dad wasn't aware it was a contest – as to which of my mum's bedmates were funnier, my dad would have won hands down. Unfortunately, this relies on my mother's sense of humour, which was never her strongest point. She laughed a lot, but mainly at things that weren't funny.

But the overriding sense I get from The Answerphone Tapes is that David White is holding my mother at arm's length. He prizes contact with her for several reasons – some sexual, some to do with the thrill of secrecy, but mostly financial – and often he seems to be scolding her, either for failing to achieve the correct price for a piece of golf memorabilia he has passed on or for being too flagrant about their liaison. I have a sense, with that last issue, that he didn't know the half of it.

There is also one moment when he speaks to my father. It's enhanced, with hindsight, because my dad says, 'Oh, hello, David, she's in bed.' There's then a long, excruciating section as he decides to take the phone upstairs to see if she's awake and they talk mainly about this absurd new-fangled idea, a telephone you can carry around with you in your house. (David White plaintively says he doesn't have one and has to sit in his hallway on the landline.) When my dad gets to the top of the stairs, he calls out to my mother but she doesn't reply, sleeping through this outlandish scene. Two things occurred to me listening to it. First, that she would probably have been deeply annoyed to miss a call from her lover of twenty years, and frustrated with her husband for not making more of an effort to wake her. Second, and this is sad, that perhaps this was after her operation for acoustic neuroma, when she began taking a lot of pharmaceuticals, including sleeping pills.

But overall, in this emotional archaeology, not much comes from David White in the way of professions of love. The only thing I've really unearthed lies in an email exchange I read soon after my mother died. Because of the suddenness of her death, there was an autopsy, and, as happens in that situation, doctors asked for any supplementary medical information we might lay our hands on. I was checking through her emails to see if I could find out what her prescriptions had been just prior to her death when I stumbled upon one, written only a few months earlier, entitled:

Begin forwarded message:

From: David White
Subject: **Re: Golf and other stuff**
Date: 2 March 2014 at 13:42:15 BST
To: SFB

Which would be a response from him to an email from her, entitled 'Golf and other stuff'. In which David White wrote:

Begin forwarded message:

From: David White
Subject: **Re: Golf and other stuff**
Date: 2 March 2014 at 13:42:15 BST
To: SFB

It was the "stuff" I liked most xxx

So, obviously, the first thing to note here is: David White gets inverted commas *right*. By stuff, he doesn't mean stuff. He means sex. It's a double entendre. It's a textbook, bang-on use of the form. Finally. Maybe if he *had* written my mother more love letters in their time together, she'd have at last picked up on the correct usage herself.

But this is all I have in print back from David White that feels anything like a love letter, or at least, love recollected. Which may seem a little sad. And a little bleak. But not to my mother, who replied:

> Begin forwarded message:
>
> **From:** SFB
> **Subject:** **Re: Golf and other stuff**
> **Date:** 2 March 2014 at 13:45:17 BST
> **To:** David White
>
> ## MY CLITORIS IS ON FIRE !!!!!

There we have it. Amazing. My only worry is this date – the 2nd March – is actually my mum's birthday, and she was seventy-five years old, so if she had made herself one of her usual birthday cakes, her clitoris may actually have been on fire. This may just be an emailed cry for help. 'It's gone right up me dress, David, get a bucket of sand!'

Some of you may be thinking by now that there are one too many – obviously, for some, one will be too many – references in this book to my mother's clitoris. Well, all of this is real, and God love my mum, at seventy-five, for being open and unashamed about having one (a working one, clearly). She was not a political woman, but something political is happening here by chance. She crashed through boundaries like she wasn't aware – because, I think, she wasn't – they were even there. It never seemed to occur to her that copying her lover's interests and hobbies wholesale might be peculiar or provocative.

Similarly, when she says 'My clitoris is on fire!' it's as if she's failed to notice – brilliantly – that society in general abhors older women talking about their sexuality and, particularly, doing it graphically.

But more importantly, this book is a eulogy, one that is different from most eulogies, which in my opinion have the effect, in their sedate respect, only of burying the memory of the deceased along with their physical reality. And say what you like about seeing that your mum on her seventy-fifth birthday, the last one she would ever have, has written 'my clitoris is on fire!' to her ex-lover – it brings her back to life. It brings her back to fucking life.

Sarah

There are layers of memory. This seems a complex philosophical idea, but it isn't. What I mean is: this book draws on my memories of childhood, but they themselves draw on other artefacts, photographs, letters, phone recordings, that I encountered much more recently. My sense of my parents was sometimes confirmed, but sometimes shifted, as I encountered their relics. Finding the archive, looking through what's left behind, can colour in but also alter your memories.

It can also change what you decide to talk about. I'm aware there may be readers by now thinking, at least as regards the bits about my mother, *Is this what she would have wanted?*

The saying 'It's what he or she would have wanted' has always confused me, given that it implies 'if he or she were still alive', which is odd, as what he or she would have wanted if they were still alive is to be dug up. That repurposed old joke aside, beyond deep ethical musing on who owns the rights to tell the stories of the dead, beyond even my commitment to oppose post-mortem idealization, beyond all that: I do believe this is what my mother would have wanted. Not in every detail, perhaps. But she truly wanted her affair with David White to be known. I've detailed the myriad ways in which she would broadcast it, but it's also there in the enormous scrapbook she kept of her life, so many photographs of the two of them together, over many years, in which there is no getting away from how intensely happy she looks.

There are also an extraordinary number of photos just of David White by himself, or with other friends. They form a collage, the many moods of David White. Solitary, thoughtful David White: here, perhaps, thinking about writing a novel. About golf.

David White with his beloved sexy pipe, posing it seems for an album cover,

Perhaps one called . . .

David White playing golf of course, in some quite remarkable cunties.

David White, the life and soul of the party, having a right laugh.

Even, weirdly, some of David White, the charmer, flirting with other women. Somewhere, I can hear someone saying, *They're sex people, Lynn!*

And these pictures, too, cover the passing of time. My mother's love was nothing if not loyal.

But the stories we tell can't be judged, IMHO, by an idea of their effect on the dead. That's why that repurposed joke about 'what he/she would've wanted' has some value. There is some emotional point in asking what a deceased person would have wanted, but we tell stories of the dead not really for them, but to help the living.

And if there was one moment that led me to the decision to talk about this stuff publicly, it was this. A couple of days after my mum died, Ivor, Dan and I were at my parents' house starting the process of going through her things. Dan – who is a bit angrier than me about my mother's infidelity – suddenly handed me something, and said (angrily):

'I found *this* at the back of the cupboard. I was going to smash it . . . but you might want it.'

Which was an interesting intuition of Dan's, as I hadn't at that point decided I was going to do a show or write a book or anything about our mother, but he, at some level, knew better. Because it was this:

My late mother's lover . . . on a mug.
He's not just on one side, by the way. Oh no.

Sarah

I didn't smash it. It had only been seen by me and my younger brother. So, next time, when there was a need for a break in the drudgery and pain of the sorting process, without telling Ivor about this find, I offered to make the tea. And handed him his tea in that mug. And he pissed himself laughing. Which meant that for a moment at least, there was laughter in that house of death.

My mother's actual funeral was well attended but quick. This was partly because the slot at Golders Green Crematorium was short; it's a busy place, with a lot of bodies to burn, so we had only half an hour. That, allied to my mum dying so suddenly, and traumatically, meant that no one did a big speech. We were still in shock. I spoke for a few minutes and said that instead, later in the year, we would have a memorial service for her. We didn't do that. I'm not consumed with guilt about it. Instead I did a theatre show about her which I performed all over the country – all over the world, in fact, and now I've written a book. Well, it's about her and my dad, which would, I think, annoy her, as she'd much prefer a book to herself, but the dead can't have everything their own way.

I remain unsure about whether, at her actual funeral, these stories would have gone down that well. Also, I might have been tempted, since she was cremated, to do a joke about how in a minute, her clitoris actually will be on fire. Which I accept would've crossed some sort – maybe all sorts – of line. Instead, this – this book – is her anti-funeral speech funeral speech.

And I am fairly confident that, one or two anatomical references aside, my mother would've loved it. Or at least, she would've loved the fact in general that I'd written a book about her. Because my mother loved being in the spotlight. She wasn't interested in my fame, but she was very interested in how my fame reflected on her.

Here she is, at the aforementioned Infidel premiere, in the picture where Kirsty Young described her as 'shining':

And yes, she is shining. She is shining maybe because she is proud of me, after all. But more because she would've just loved the event, which was, like herself, glamorous and Jewish and mad. She would have felt herself where she needed to be, at the centre of things.

Sarah

When she died, seven years before my father, I posted about it on Twitter:

I've always loved this photo, of my mum young and beautiful, in the brief period of happiness after she'd escaped the Nazis and before she got married to my dad – which, of the two things, may have been worse. I think – I know – that she would have loved that Twitter took this to heart. She loved, as I said earlier, being in the picture. She'd particularly have enjoyed this . . .

. . . which is, in Old Twitter, Alan Sugar retweeting my mum's photo and wishing me long life. Obviously, it being Twitter, someone got it wrong and thought that Alan Sugar's mum had died:

For fuck's sake, Alan Sugar's mother must be two hundred years old, of course she hasn't just died – but meanwhile, in terms of my mother and the sort of things she liked, the idea of Alan Sugar putting her photo up there and wishing me long life for all the world to see – it's so slap bang in the centre of the wheelhouse of my mum's desires, I think it's possible that if you could ask her, she would have said it was worth dying for.

This story shows, perhaps, that in the end those people at her funeral were right – she was a wonderful person – but now I hope you understand exactly *how* my mother was wonderful. The Merriam-Webster Dictionary definition of the word is: *marvellous, astonishing, as in a sight wonderful to behold.* I know people normally mean a sunset or a newborn child, but for me that David White mug is right up there.

Also – in terms of correcting the record about my mother – it turns out, I discovered on checking a Yiddish-German dictionary, the mourners at her funeral weren't the only ones wrong about her. So were the Nazis. They, obviously, were wrong about a lot of stuff – we know that – but perhaps never more so than when they forced my grandparents to call my mad, wild, sex-and-golf-obsessed mother a name that means . . .

> ne became Frommet ("pious one") and developed into
> dish woman's name Fruma.

Pious One. 'PIOUS ONE' (inverted commas have never been more correct). I see my mum's whole life as a victory over that name.

Colin

As you'll have noticed, I bang on a lot about truth. This book is supposed to be an expression of my commitment to truth, to telling the truth about my parents. I'm fighting here against various ways in which memory is corrupted, either by posthumous idealization or by dementia. But the trouble is that truth is still reliant on memory: my memory. And memory plays tricks.

In 1993 the BBC made a documentary called *Newman and Baddiel: The Road to Wembley*, which was mainly footage of us trying out material in small venues, then honing it in bigger ones, until we got to the UK tour that ended up at Wembley Arena. I never watched this documentary when it went out, because Rob and I were falling apart at the time, as a double-act and as friends, and I knew he had said things on it that would upset me. But in the process of sorting through my mother's stuff after she died, I found that title scrawled on the side of one of her many VHS's in one of her many boxes. And I thought, Oh Christ, it's been twenty-two years, just watch it. So I did, in my parents' bedroom, where they still had a VHS player – in fact, one of those TVs with a VHS player built in. And the things Rob Newman said – mainly about how he couldn't understand why he was working with me at all – still upset me.

But not properly – not least because I was expecting him to say those things. It got under my skin enough to think about switching it off. But I didn't, and then, right at the end of the documentary, I saw something I wasn't expecting, had completely forgotten, and that properly upset me: it made me weep and weep. It's a bit of footage of me going back into my dressing room just after the Wembley gig, and my dad comes in with a bottle of champagne and says, 'You were absolutely superb.' We hug, and in a terrible mockney voice, I turn to camera and say, 'It's me dad.'

IT'S ME DAD.

And what made me weep was . . . it's my dad undemented, of course, and strong and healthy and vital, but most of all – it's him being *nice*. It's him being empathetic, and complimentary. Which made me think – perhaps his dementia has, after all, in a way, given me dementia. Perhaps his dementia so isolated and exaggerated the abusive, insulting part of him I forgot that he sometimes *was* nice. That he sometimes was a good dad. That he sometimes made me want to say, proudly, to camera: it's my dad.*

---

* As a postscript, something else about this bit of footage makes me cry now. Which is that as I walk into my dressing room, there's a little moment between me and the other comedian who was in that show, Sean Lock. It's a short exchange – he just pats me on the back and I say, 'Well done, Sean' – and then I go in to meet my dad. But it causes me a poignant stab of pain now to see him, so characteristically Sean-like with a fag on the go, now that's he gone so young from cancer.

Rob and I had both found Sean hilarious when he was just doing the circuit, and so asked him to play various characters we'd written for him in *Newman and Baddiel in Pieces*. He was great at it, and we asked him to come on tour with us. An urban myth has since appeared that Newman and Baddiel are not in fact the first British comedians to play Wembley Arena, as that would have been Sean, but I need to correct this, not just  because of my truth urge, or from a churlish need to confirm that it was us, but because Sean was not our support act. He didn't come on first. He was folded into the show and appeared throughout, always smashing it. He was more of a featured player than a support act. Indeed, at Wembley, at one point, as we were changing costumes, something went wrong and he was left onstage in front of twelve thousand people, and just had to ad lib. And, of course, did so hilariously.

Colin

My father died on the 18th of January 2022. I wasn't with him when it happened. By the time of his death, he'd been near-death so many times it was hard to do that thing of thinking, Oh *now's* the time. We humans put a lot of store on being beside someone at their deathbed but frankly, if someone is as out of it as my father was in the last few months of his life, short of moving in and sleeping on the floor by his bed, it's hard to guarantee you'll be there. He died on a Tuesday and I'd been to see him on the Sunday. His carer Clive called Ivor and Ivor called me and just said: 'He's gone.'

The flatness of that information is telling. My father had effectively been dying for a long time. But the death of a parent can be expected, prepared for, even a relief, and yet still shocking. It can still rent a tear in your life. The initial effect that comes with their death, before the long tail of grief, is disorientation. This is someone who will have been, for a very long time, very present in your life and now they are absent. That feels destabilizing. Even if dementia had eaten away at the presence of Colin Baddiel while he was alive, his physical actuality registered. When he is gone, there is actually a space. There, in that chair, where he used to sit all day. Or there, on the bed that we brought downstairs, where he was lying at the end.

I drove to the house in Harrow, to meet Ivor and to wait with him for the doctor to come and issue the death certificate.

Some readers will have experienced this, no doubt, but given my mother died in hospital, I hadn't. It's a very strange couple of hours. The two of us sat in Colin Baddiel's living room, with Colin Baddiel, as we had many times before, only this time he was a corpse. He was lying on his bed covered by a thin blanket, which I assumed Clive had put over him. Not completely covered: his bald head was peeping out from underneath it. I often see that bit of bald head in my dreams.

I can't remember what we talked about. Ivor and I have a running joke, which is whenever we're together, watching football or whatever, eventually one of us will say, 'So what else?' I'm pretty sure I got in first with it on this occasion.

The bed had just been installed with an electric mattress that tilted about continually to help – it didn't much – avoid pressure sores appearing on his body. When the doctor finally arrived, after the initial sad pleasantries, he approached the bed. At which point, some unknown foot button got pressed and the mattress started moving. We couldn't work out how to turn it off. The bed was going up and down and from side to side, with Colin sliding about on it, as if on a gently rolling wave, and we couldn't turn it off. At one point I crawled underneath it – underneath the bed with my dad's corpse *bodysurfing* above me – and still couldn't find the off switch. It felt like at any moment it was going to catapult him off like a fairground rodeo ride.

I couldn't even seem to switch it off at the mains, and meanwhile I could tell the doctor was getting irritated. At last he said: 'Look, it's very difficult to examine him. I'm sorry, I just don't think I can pronounce him dead while he's moving about.' And I wanted to say: 'You know what? I'm not a medical man, but, yes, I believe that is normally a *contraindication.*'

The black comedy didn't stop there. After we finally managed to get the deathbed to be still for long enough for the doctor officially to pronounce my father's mortal coil slipped off, this weird sub-Beckett play – *Waiting with Colin*, perhaps – wasn't over. We had to wait another couple of hours for the undertakers. By now, both small and big talk between Ivor and I was running dry. When they arrived, dressed in the customary black, they'd brought a stretcher. The senior undertaker looked at the narrow hallway and difficult turning circle out of the living room and said to me, 'This might be awkward – maybe you should wait upstairs? People often prefer not to see this bit.' So I did. I went upstairs and sat on my father's bed – the double one he used to sleep in with my mother – to avoid inflicting more parental-death-based damage on myself. But I still heard the two of them saying, 'OK, back up a bit . . . lift your end . . . go left . . . hold the door . . . look out!' with accompanied bumping and crashing.

Death has no dignity. But at least that means it provides laughs at the bleakest times. Besides, who gives a fuck about dignity? The real problem with death is that it has no life.

Colin Baddiel's funeral was held at the Jewish Joint Burial Society, which is a cemetery in north London – by which I mean *actual* north London, not some imaginary Jew land – near Waltham Abbey. A few people asked me why he had chosen this particular spot. Those people, imagining someone who had ruminated long and deep on where he might like to be buried, perhaps thinking of its beauty or of some personal connection, didn't really know my father. He would have chosen it because it was cheap – he'd been paying dues for some time at Kol Chai for the plot – and because it meant he didn't have to think about it. Because thinking about his death would've been aggravation.

Besides – sorry if you have loved ones there – the Jewish Joint Burial Society Cemetery in Waltham Abbey is not beautiful. Or anyway, it's as beautiful as a cemetery can be that is very, very close to the M25. A row of trees separates it from the motorway, which may shield the dead from the sight of the endless traffic but not from the sound. The one thing my dad will not be doing there is resting in peace. I see him swearing with rage as he is woken continually from his eternal sleep by yet another passing Eddie Stobart.

It was, though, a more authentic – truer, that is, to the spirit of the man – funeral than my mother's. One thing about the Jewish Joint Burial Society is: they are a no-frills outfit. The chapel – or whatever the Hebrew word for the building where the ollywollybolly happens is – is up in the fields above the cemetery and it's kind of a bandstand.

The day of my father's funeral, the weather was not like in the above photograph. It was freezing. The sky was the colour of concrete. Inside the chapel, there are no seats, only a bench around the interior. I wondered, as we waited, where the coffin – yet to appear – was going to be laid. A trestle table, bounded by flowers, perhaps?* Instead, wheeled in, with my dad's body box on top, was this:

I am still uncertain as to what type of vehicle it was: whether, that is, it's a specific coffin-carrying cart or something that's been customized – a soldered-together pair of Segways, perhaps

---

* Actually, it turns out that Jewish funerals and shivas discourage flowers as – I'm Mr Jew, I should know this stuff – flowers imply celebration, which would distract from mourning. So presumably the oft-heard funeral speech opening 'We are here to celebrate X's life, they would not want us to be sad' would be anathema to Talmudic rabbis.

– to do so. Excuse the blurriness, which fails to show, for example, just how muddy the wheels were.

Although all this added to the bleakness, it felt appropriate. Both my parents, and in particular my dad, were incapable of what we now call *having nice things*. They didn't really understand comfort and certainly not luxury. *This'll do*, said with irritation, would've been my dad's approach to almost any outing or gift or attempt to make our house in any way more well-appointed (which obviously never happened). I feel like anyone who might have queried the lack of opulence at his funeral would've been met with the same phrase.

My father, in his latter years, became a bit of a Twitter celebrity. I used to go and see him about once a week and I'd post photos and sometimes videos of him, and me, on there. This sort of thing:

 David Baddiel ✓
@Baddiel
   ···

My dad's usual response on being wished a Happy Father's Day. May he continue to do so for a few more yet.

10:03 AM · Jun 20, 2021

Twitter – I'm not going to call it X, obviously – is notorious for being a troll-infested cesspit. But, although trolls make a lot of noise, because they write in a way that comes close to shouting, there are many people on there being nice, in a quiet way. My posts about Colin would always provoke hundreds of poignant responses, often people telling me about their own passage through, as the comedian Janey Godley put it in one moving tweet, 'the hall of many emotional mirrors' that having a parent with dementia plunges you into.

When he died, I posted this:

David Baddiel ✓
@Baddiel
···

My dad Colin Baddiel died earlier tonight. Thank so much to all of you who sent unbelievably lovely messages about him in response to all my posts over the years. He leaves a huge hole in my sky.

9:39 PM · Jan 18, 2022

ılı View Tweet analytics

963 Retweets   **188** Quote Tweets   **134.1K** Likes

Which you may notice I haven't cropped, so that you can see how many likes it got. Although to be fair to me, that isn't, I think, purely narcissistic (despite the Like button on social media being the most pernicious panderer to human narcissism ever developed). It indicates, I hope, that stories of my dad and his condition – and my decision to broadcast them because I happen to have a platform – did speak to many people and maybe helped them feel less alone. Here are some of the hundreds of messages I received after my father died:

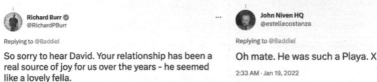

In a documentary I made for TV about social media, a thinker called Ayishat Akanbi said, of social media, 'We're living in an open-plan mansion with everyone we hate.' Which is a brilliant description of what's wrong with social media, but it does miss out the other possibility, only present in occasional moments like this, which is that it can showcase the kindness of strangers. I mean . . . someone I don't know did this:

David Baddiel ✔ @Baddiel · Jan 19, 2022 ···
On Instagram a woman called Hannah went to the trouble of cleaning up
that old photo I posted. It's one I've had for years with many marks on and
it's nice to see it sparkling. The kindness of strangers is quite something.

💬 155   ↻ 51   ♡ 8,200   ılıl   ⬆

Which to my old Photoshop-ignorant eyes looks amazing,
like a miracle of sorts. Even if it does make Dan's childhood
teeth a bit too prominent.

But my favourite consoling message came – how could it
not? – from Carol Decker of T'Pau. I have an interesting Twitter
relationship with Carol, based almost entirely on their great
late eighties hit 'China in Your Hand'. Carol tweets me a fair
bit about various things, but I always tweet back a joke, however

contrived, that gets that song title in somehow. For example, I bought a watch some time ago, on the internet, and posted it, to which Carol said:

David Baddiel ✓ · 17/10/2022 ···
Have bought a slightly ridiculous watch. My son said "it's like something Ben 10 would wear."

iⁱⁱ   ◯ 1,230   ⇄ 115   ♡ 5,806   ⬆

carol decker ✓ · 18/10/2022   ···
#wtf is that?
iⁱⁱ   ◯ 7   ⇄   ♥ 48   ⬆

And I replied:

carol decker ✓ · 18/10/2022   ···
#wtf is that?
iⁱⁱ   ◯ 7   ⇄   ♥ 48   ⬆

David Baddiel ✓
@Baddiel   ···

Replying to @caroldecker

It's something made in China on my hands.

So given that I have been, for some time, ever so gently, taking the piss, it was very good of Carol, on seeing that picture I posted announcing Colin's death, to send me a sympathetic message. This one:

And there's something very appropriate about that, because although as I have said in this book, through an ultra-male emotionally unexpressed prism, Colin Brian Baddiel was a father who did love his children, he was in the end a man dedicated mainly to himself, and I think quite a large part of him would indeed have preferred it to have been Ivor.

Cats

One upside of my dad's death was that we got a new cat, Zelda. Here she is over the page.

She is the daughter of Pip, the maternal cat who lives in my house with two of her children, Ron and Tiger. Zelda was given to my parents, by us, in around 2012. It's interesting that she's called Zelda, a name my mum chose. It's interesting because I

had a cat called Zelda in the
1980s. I think my mother liked
the name and just nicked it. A
bit like she did with Golfiana.
Only perhaps with slightly less
dysfunctional baggage.

I'm telling you this because
in my portrayal of my early
family life, in all its improba-
bility, and spiky edges, there
was one lodestar of niceness
and normality, which was cats.
I had a father who as we know,
in tune with the times, did not see much need to show love to
his children, or his wife, but an exception was made for cats.
Specifically, we had a cat, referred to already, called Phomphar.
This name was my father's idea, an onomatopoeic rendering
of the noise she made when she was happy, which most people
would call purring, but he Jewishly called phompharing (more
Jewishly still, he called one of the two kittens of Phomphar's
we kept Ben Phimphiling Phomph, which is a kind of Colin-ish
approximation of the Hebrew for 'Son of Phomphar'). This
indicates something, which is that if my father did have a softer
side, it was shown mainly to the cats. By softer side, what I
mean is he would pick them up and aggressively sniff their
heads and say, 'You're a great beast – what are you? A great
beast, yes you are!' But trust me, for Colin Baddiel, that was
effectively a love sonnet.

Cats therefore for me are a deep point of connection, with my childhood and with my now-gone parents. There was very little beauty in my childhood, but Phomphar was beautiful. Of course she was. She was a cat. Now, luckily, I have a lot more beauty in my life, and a lot more softness and a lot less gruff, blunt maleness, but one clear effect of my childhood is that I am still utterly in thrall to the beauty of cats. I am a funda-mental atheist, but when I look at one of my cats – I presently have four – curving like a Matisse in a shaft of sunlight, I believe in God.

I have never, since I was a child, not had at least one cat.

Even when I was at university and living in halls of residence, I smuggled in a stray and fed it regularly. I also had one when I shared a flat with Frank Skinner. Frank is not a cat man, but he is very committed to comedy, and the name of the tabby who lived with us, arrived at after a short brainstorming session (mainly driven by his extraordinary punning ability), was Chairman Meow. There are not many hills I am prepared to die on but that this is the best name ever for a cat is one. One proof is that it – the name, not the cat – was stolen soon after by the US sitcom *Will & Grace*. Another is that the first time I took her – Chairman was a her, which I know Zedong was not – to the vet and the receptionist asked for the cat's name, it got a massive laugh in the crowded waiting room. Obviously, I was very pleased about this, except I noticed the receptionist just wrote down, on her computer, 'Meow', as if it were her surname. Which meant that when I went through to the actual vet and saw him glance at the information on his computer about this new cat, I could tell, from a raised eyebrow, that he was thinking, Meow – what a shit name for a cat. *Supposed to be a writer and comedian and he goes that unoriginal on a cat name?* But it felt too late to explain.

Chairman Meow was haughty and decided, as haughty cats do, to find food elsewhere in our neighbourhood. One neighbour somewhat decided to take charge of her, and got her a collar, with my phone number on it. Only she – the neighbour – didn't put 'Chairman Meow' on it. She put my name on. She put 'David' and my phone number. Which meant that for years I was convinced that one day Morwenna would get a phone call from someone saying, 'I'm afraid David's been in a road accident . . . he's in a bin bag, shall I just hit him with a shovel? After all he did spend every day shitting in my garden.'

It isn't, however, between me and cats, just about beauty, because cats are not just beautiful. Because they don't pander to humans, they are thought of as inexpressive, but I've had a lot of them, and each one has been very different and absurdly idiosyncratic. Pip is often lazy and irritable, but will come over all kittenish and adorable if my wife sings her 'Only You' by Yazoo. Chairman Meow would stick her tongue out at you if you ran your fingers over a comb. Tiger will grab your attention by tapping you gently on the arm with his paw, which is not unusual in and of itself, but he sometimes becomes uncertain about the tap on the way to the tapping moment and so just stays with his paw poised in the air, staring at you in hope, which is so cute it makes me want to die. These are just the tips of the various icebergs of personality that a few of the cats I've owned display.

Cats are not selfish. They are selves, complete rounded rich and offbeat characters, but the idea that they have no empathy – a mistake humans make about animals in general, all part of human exceptionalism, which is what allows us to keep them as pets, but more importantly, eat them – is deeply mistaken. Monkey, a male cat who I gave to Morwenna when we first got together – I acknowledge this was presumptuous – I mean, a cat's not just for a one-night stand, he's for life or, at least, a long chapter within serial monogamy – was one of the nicest beings I've ever known. Once, he appeared upstairs in Morwenna's study, meowing and meowing. She assumed he just wanted food and was being annoying, but he wouldn't shoo away, so eventually she got up and he led her downstairs – to where Tiger had got his paw stuck under the door. Put that in your well-where-a-child-has-fallen-down and smoke it, Lassie.

Monkey (above) made it to the ripe old age of twenty. Obviously for a cat, this is a good innings (by the completely misconceived arithmetic of seven years for every one of ours, he was 140 and looked it). But still, putting him down was a very difficult decision. The longer an animal has been with you, the more of an actual member of the family they are: Dolly, who came with me to the vet – to help and support me, as well as to say goodbye to Monkey – said: 'But he's been there for every day of my life.'

Despite having had many cats in my time, for some blessed reason, I'd managed to swerve having to take any of them to be put down: it's always been someone else who's done that, or they've had the good grace to go away, as animals sometimes do, to die. But Monkey was never going to do that: he was a homeboy. Everything about the process – once I decided that his stumbling dizziness, his refusal to eat, his collapsing to the floor and his painful thinness had got too much – was awful. Even getting the cat box out of the cupboard was awful.

At the vet, she – a lovely woman – took one look and had one feel of his emaciated body, and said, yes, it's time. Would you like to spend a few minutes alone with him? she said, and left. This, I was not expecting. Me and my daughter stroked him and said we loved him and goodbye. Shatteringly, heart-breakingly, with a tiny, not-quite-able-to-do-it-any-more timbre, he began to purr. Even now, there was a sense of him being undemanding. Dolly cried; I was reduced to liquid form. The vet came back and put him, as we say, to sleep. Afterwards she said: Monkey's gone to heaven, and it felt, as well as an unwitting reference to the Pixies, a lovely untruth.

So the reason I've put it in this book, apart from my very strong feeling that cats are part of my family, is that I think I cried more at Monkey's death than at either of my parents'. But once I stopped crying about Monkey, a day or so later, I was fine. I was still sad he was gone, but soon, hey, we got Zelda. Which made me realize that crying is not the be-all and end-all of emotion. The amount of liquid you produce in moments of loss doesn't actually calibrate with the impact of the loss. I loved Monkey – I love all my cats – in a simple way. But I loved my parents in a complex way, and losing them is not simple. Losing them evokes not just sadness and not just tears, but all sorts of difficult-to-process and often contradictory sensations – despair, anger, relief, comedy, terror, confusion and many others. It is a profound dislocation of self, and tears don't cover it.

Zelda, being originally Pip's daughter, we took back to her

place of birth and re-introduced her to her family, which really didn't turn out like *Surprise, Surprise*. Unless I missed that episode where a mother growls and hisses at her long-lost daughter and then chases her under a cupboard.

Zelda, like all cats, has her own personality. She is neat, and complex, and eager for human company, so likes to visit us in our bedroom at night, and it turns out there's nothing more reassuring, when you wake in the night, perhaps tormented by the absence of your parents from this world, to feel the soft weight of their cat on you, and hear her comforting phompharing.*

---

* P.S. Alan Coren, I believe, once said that publishing lore has it that the books that sell best are the ones about Nazis, golf and cats.

Well: #waterfrontcovered

The Mother and the Father

My mother is not buried in the same place as my dad. As I said, topmost on my father's priorities would not have been spending eternity in the company of his wife. She, as I've also told you, via an unacceptable joke, was cremated, and her ashes lie buried near where we grew up, in Dollis Hill. Here is her grave:

Meanwhile, here is my father's:

It's a shame, in a way, that the graves don't face each other, as that would have continued the unexpected comedy of his stall at Grays Antique Market facing hers, emblazoned as it was with the word Golfiana; there seems no reason for death to stop reminding him of my mother's sudden obsession with that sport and its not-very-buried (no pun intended) motivations.

Children, traditionally, are very worried about their parents' estimation of them. Traditionally, even into adulthood, they are Toni Collette's character in *The Sixth Sense*. For anyone who doesn't know the film, Toni Collette plays a woman called Lynn, whose child, Cole, can speak to dead people, and – spoiler alert – at the end of the film he tells her he regularly speaks to his grandmother, her mother. Cole says his grandmother would like him to pass on a message to his mother, because when she, his mother, goes to visit her grave, every time she asks a question. The grandmother says the answer is: *Every day.* Cole asks his mother what the question is. Lynn answers – with difficulty, through tears – 'Do I make you proud?'

There are some issues here. Notably, why does the grandma not tell Cole what the question is? Surely he would've asked (to be clear for those who haven't seen it, ghosts in *The Sixth Sense* are pretty much like the living, and you can have extended chats with them)? There's no bridging information from Cole, along the lines of 'I asked Grandma what the question was but she said, "I think it's best you hear that from your mother, for some unexplained reason?"'

But the more pressing issue is why, when I first saw *The Sixth Sense*, and why now, when I just checked this scene on YouTube to make sure I was reporting it correctly, does it render my throat so tight with tears I cannot speak? Because if you asked me outright – is it important to you that your parents were proud of you? – I would say, no. I would say: I am not seven, my parents are dead, and my parents were never, in truth, that proud of me anyway – not because they hated what I did, but because they were so wrapped up in their own stuff that I'm not sure any of what I did really got through.

It is partly, perhaps, that I am sentimental. Cinema is the medium that has taught me this. When I was about twenty, I went, for a laugh, to see *E.T.* For a laugh, because my favourite film at the time was, from memory, Peter Greenaway's *The Draughtsman's Contract.* Yes. I was that much of a cunt. Anyway, by the end of *E.T.* – specifically the moment when the alien touches Elliott on the forehead and says, 'I'll be right here' – I was once again in pieces. Steven Spielberg had burst

a dam in my heart. Of course, if you examine these two bitter-
sweet scenes they are about similar things. They are about
memory, and death. They are about that most poignant of
human hopes, that you are still being thought about, still being
witnessed, somehow, after your witness has gone.

The truth is, I can't quite parse whether my parents' approval
counts – ever counted, still counts – or not. I don't quite believe
Julian Cope that my parents were always telling him about
their son David and their ambitions for him on the stage – I
think it's just his way of signalling, cheekily, the connection
with the name – but maybe they did. Maybe I am resistant to
that idea for reasons I don't quite understand.

After my dad died, and we finally cleared out the house, I
found among the rubble, a box of my mother's, containing
these:

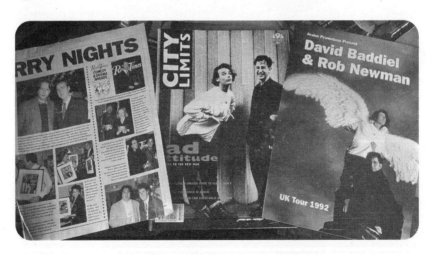

I was touched. I posted it on Twitter, and many people talked
movingly about finding mementos of themselves that they had
no idea their parents had stored away, after their death, and
how much it meant to them.

There was more, much more. The detritus of my appearances in the British press over thirty-five years was everywhere. Some of it was very much better forgotten.

Some evoked events that I have absolutely no memory of:

There I am at the Minerva Business Luncheon, whatever the Minerva that is. Some of it, much like the 'his critics will be pleased to hear that David Baddiel has gone to hell' cutting that she handed me on the day of Dolly's birth, was bad:

Which is a case in point. It meant a lot to me that my mother had cut out and kept all these things, and yet there was something very Sarah Baddiel about the way she had kept this stuff. It was hoarded, like so much else, in an almost indiscriminate way. I know some of you reading this will think that is harsh and over-critical but I'm not judging her for this: what I'm doing is refining the truth of it.

These are scrapbooks she made when she was a teenager, containing pictures of famous people cut out from the paper.

I don't think my mum was interested in any of these people. But having these scrapbooks would have made her feel in touch with glamour, with a version of her lost world. And also, I think that collecting for my mother was a boundary-less, brimming end in itself. She always had to have more and more of whatever it was that enabled her to feel identified as whatever version of herself was present in her mind at that moment. David White is kind of that too. David White defined who she was for a long time, and at some level her obsession with golf and with him was nothing to do with him, at least with whoever he really was as a person (about whom I still, from all this archive, know very little). It was just about having endless amounts of David White-iana, to bolster her primary identity, her sense of herself as David White's Lover.

I didn't find anything similar about me in my dad's stuff. He was a hoarder too, but not of his life, just of Dinky Toys. There was no archive of Colin's things to sort through. But while I was doing *My Family: Not the Sitcom* in the West End, I received this letter from a man called George Cox, who used to visit my dad's stall in Grays Antique Market on a regular basis. He told me some stories about my father, all gratefully received, if none of them surprising. At the end of the letter, he said:

one day this could all be yours?' " He liked that. Even if it merited an even more forceful 'F*ck off!' than usual.

You reflected in the show on whether he was proud of your achievements. I have no doubt about it. He'd never brag, quite the reverse, he'd express surprise and protest that he couldn't understand it. But he would always tell me what you were doing, and in all the time I knew him he only ever gave me one present. It was a hot-off-the-presses copy of your first novel.

He was proud alright.

Kindest regards,

George Cox

Which did also make me cry, and cry again. So maybe my parents' approval does matter, and maybe, like all children, I will continue to cry out for it and feel sad hope on discovering secret admissions like this one, even after they've gone, that every day, I did make them proud.

But the letter also made me laugh. Because I couldn't think of anything more Colin Baddiel than the fact that my dad had only ever given his friend one present, and that was something he got free. And which my mum had once described to my brother as 'shit'. The truth, as I say, is always complex.

Coda: Me

After my mother died, I wrote to David White. As we know, I had his email. I said:

Hello David
I hope you're well. I'm writing to let you know – in case you don't already – that my mother passed away, suddenly, on the 20th December last year. She was of course very much in love with you for much of her life, so I thought you should know,
  yours
  David Baddiel

He replied:

Dear David – Thank you for email; I really appreciate your thoughtfulness. Yes, I had heard the sad news about Sarah and shed many tears. Only rarely am I in London these days, as I live now in eastern Europe. I last saw her in London last July around the time of The Open Golf

Championship. At that time I was staging a golf art exhibition in a Museum Street art gallery and Sarah took the time to look in on me, albeit rather briefly. I could see then just how unwell she was, though she bravely dismissed any suggestion that it was anything to 'worry about'. Poor Sarah, she had a rough time health wise toward the latter years, though I do believe she lived her life to the full ...

My sincere condolences to you and the family

Sincerely yours – David W

I like this, in general. I think it shows, unlike the correspondence and the tapes I have in my possession, David White being considerate of my mum. When I sent it to my brothers, I said that I thought it was sweet but that he had not, of course, taken the bait. Meaning that despite my bald statement of the facts – that my mother had been in love with him for most of her life – he had not owned that or responded to it in any way.

Looking at it now, I realize I was wrong. Do you see it? That ellipsis. Those three dots after 'she lived her life to the full'. I hadn't spotted those before. I don't know David White, except through my mother's bizarre refraction, and yet that feels, from what I know about him, so *him*. I can hear him taking out his pipe and saying it, perhaps with a glint in his eye, and a wink.

I am a different generation to David White: he, in his own way, like my father, is not a man comfortable with emotions. As when my dad said, 'That's a load of bollocks' about not loving his sons, you must perhaps read between the lines of David's email. Or in this case – and let's not forget, he is the one who got inverted commas right – in the punctuation.

I am happy with this email. Unlike my younger brother, who

replied: 'Fuck David White.' Which is also of course what my mum would have wanted.

Early in this book, I discussed Erica Jong's mantra about how fame means that many people will have the wrong idea of who you are. But fame just multiplies a malaise that exists for all of us, because no one has the right idea of who you are. You don't have the right idea of who you are. There is a romantic hope that that's what love is, the feeling of being genuinely seen. But conversely, when we are in love, that's possibly when we most mistake the other, because we put so much hope into an idealized version of them. Point being, most of the time, we are all just getting everybody else wrong.

Fame makes it worse, however, and because everyone is kind of famous now, truth, at least the truth of personality, has become more and more unstable. Social media is a great constant oscillating exhibition of people getting each other wrong. At one end, people are putting out curated – therefore not true – versions of themselves; at the other, they are viciously attacking other people by creating versions of them so cartoonishly negative that they won't be true either.

The only way to combat untruth is with detail. To be more specific, with idiosyncratic detail. The more detailed and the more idiosyncratic the presentation of who you are can be, the more it works as evidence. As truth.

This is what I've been trying to do with this book, building my parents' identity with an accumulation of idiosyncratic detail, so that as near as possible – and it's still of course partial and contrived and mediated – you the reader have a concrete sense of who they were.

There is one joyful side effect of this approach, which is

when a version of me is presented to me that is wrong, I have a fair bank of idiosyncratic detail with which to refute it. Or to put it more simply: I can fuck up the assumptions of trolls with the weird specifics of my life story. For example, in 2017 Boris Johnson called Jeremy Corbyn a 'mutton-headed old mugwump'. I tweeted about this. At which point a man called Frank Watson, convinced he knew best, decided to take me to task:

David Baddiel ✔ @Baddiel · Apr 27, 2017
Nothing makes me want to vote for Corbyn more than Boris Johnson using - and thinking it's adorable - his stupid Billy Bunter language.

> In a deeply personal attack on Mr Corbyn, Mr Johnson said people did not realise the "threat" posed by the Labour leader.
>
> "They say to themselves 'He may be a mutton-headed old mugwump, but he is probably harmless'," he writes.

💬 169   ↻ 1.6K   ♡ 2.5K   ᵢₗᵢ   🔖 ↑

Frank Watson
@frankwatson58

You haven't read much Billy Bunter, have you @Baddiel ?

8:22 AM · Apr 27, 2017

You haven't read much Billy Bunter, have you Baddiel? Which allowed me to post:

Frank Watson @frankwatson58 · Apr 27, 2017
You haven't read much Billy Bunter, have you @Baddiel ?

💬 4   ↻ 7   ♡ 4   ᵢₗᵢ   🔖 ↑

David Baddiel ✔
@Baddiel

That is not correct.

And attach to the tweet, this photo:

David Baddiel
@Baddiel

That is not correct.

...as rear leg is pulled through.

ly Bunter fan David Baddiel with collection of old-time fictio

8:26 AM · Apr 27, 2017

Which is me in *The Young Observer* in 1975, with my collection – entirely provided by my mother, of course – of *Billy Bunter Holiday Annuals.*

'Ouch, yaroo you beasts'

DAVID BADDIEL goes to Haberdasher's School in Middlesex, but he would be equally at home at Greyfriars School. His bedroom bookcase is crammed with Billy Bunter books and he has carefully-conserved stacks of *Magnet* comic, with titles like 'Bunter the Punter' and 'Washing Day at Greyfriars'.

David goes to meetings of the Old Boys' Book Club where the fans of Greyfriars meet, and, at 11, he is by far the youngest member. He reads the fiction of boys long ago 'because it's well-written. Charles Hamilton – he wrote

Dandy, 'but they're not much good'. As for new comics: 'They're generally full of war. I don't mind that, but I wish they'd get their facts right. The Germans are the enemy in the comics and the British are always winning. It's not true, we were getting slashed too. And the Germans are always going round saying "*Achtung*".

Billy Bunter is, not surprisingly, his favourite character but he also likes Herbert Vernon-Smith 'who is a reformed blackguard. He breaks bounds and goes to pubs, but when it comes to the crunch, like saving peoples' lives, he's

Billy Bunter fan David Baddiel with collection of old-time fictio

he doesn't cherish dreams of going to a school like that. 'I'd rather go to a straightforward school where they aren't going

ing other books. He used to li the William books by Richm Crompton. 'But just now I rather captivated by Jam

Coda: Me

A response on Twitter that got 3.5k likes, and was described by the *Irish News* as:

THE IRISH NEWS

7 March, 2023

NEWS   OPINION   SPORT   BUSINESS   LIFE | MAGAZINE | ARTS

Science   Technology   All Entertainment   Movies   Music   TV   Soaps

David Baddiel with 'greatest Twitter own ever'

MORE I?

Mumf?
headli?

Blue P?

'Own', in case anyone doesn't know, means to put someone in their place – to win, basically. I am very against Twitter binaries, and particularly the way that nuance and debate on there has devolved into primitive crowing and shouting over who wins and who loses. Truth is not a matter of winning and losing. But fuck that. I'm very glad to think of this as the greatest Twitter own ever. I'm particularly glad that it was provided for me by something that symbolizes everything about my early life. Finally, my strange mad damaging childhood paid off. Thank you, Mother.

Acknowledgements

Many thanks in the creation of this book go to: Rozalind Dineen, Iain Hunt, Georgia Garrett, David Roth-Ey, Eliza Plowden, John Ainsworth, Molly Robinson, Patrick Hargadon, Jane Donovan, Jonathan Baker and Julian Humphries. Thanks also go to Jon Thoday, Julian Matthews, Mary-Grace Brunker and others at Avalon who worked on the original *My Family: Not the Sitcom* show. Thanks for help in the jogging of my memories for stories to Janine Kaufman, Ivor Baddiel, Dan Baddiel and Morwenna Banks. And, most obviously, and in absentia, thanks to my parents, Sarah and Colin Baddiel.